REEDS MARINA GUIDE 2014

Section 1

The Marinas and Services Section has been fully updated for the 2014 season. These useful pages provide chartlets and facility details for some 193 marinas around the shores of the UK and Ireland, including the Channel Islands, the perfect complement to any Reeds Nautical Almanac.

Section 2

The Marine Supplies & Services section lists more than 1000 services at coastal and other locations around the British Isles. It provides a quick and easy reference to manufacturers and retailers of equipment, services and supplies both nationally and locally together with emergency services.

Section 1

Marinas and Services Sect... 14

Section 2

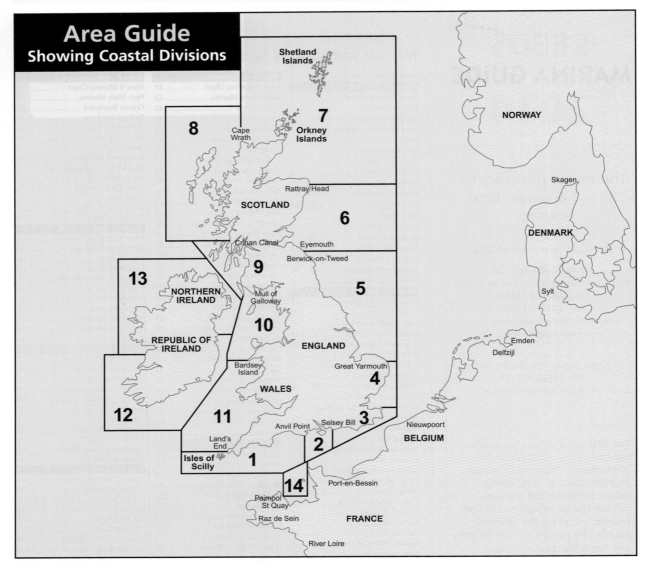

Area Guide
Showing Coastal Divisions

Shetland Islands	
7	Orkney Islands
8	Cape Wrath
NORWAY	
Skagen	
Rattray Head	
SCOTLAND	
6	
DENMARK	
Crinan Canal	Eyemouth
Berwick-on-Tweed	
Sylt	
13	9	Mull of Galloway
NORTHERN IRELAND	
5	
10	
REPUBLIC OF IRELAND	ENGLAND
Emden	
Delfzijl	
Bardsey Island	Great Yarmouth
4	
WALES	
12	11	Anvil Point	Selsey Bill	3
Nieuwpoort	
BELGIUM	
Land's End	2
Isles of Scilly	1
14	Port-en-Bessin
Paimpol St Quay	
Raz de Sein	FRANCE
River Loire	

Area 1 ..... **South West England** .... Isles of Scilly to Anvil Point

Area 2 ..... **Central Southern England** .... Anvil Point to Selsey Bill

Area 3 ..... **South East England** .... Selsey Bill to North Foreland

Area 4 ..... **East England** .... North Foreland to Great Yarmouth

Area 5 ..... **North East England** .... Great Yarmouth to Berwick-upon-Tweed

Area 6 ..... **South East Scotland** .... Eyemouth to Rattray Head

Area 7 ..... **North East Scotland** .... Rattray Head to Cape Wrath including Orkney & Shetland Is

Area 8 ..... **North West Scotland** .... Cape Wrath to Crinan Canal

Area 9 ..... **South West Scotland** .... Crinan Canal to Mull of Galloway

Area 10 ... **North West England** .... Isle of Man & N Wales, Mull of Galloway to Bardsey Is

Area 11 ... **South Wales & Bristol Channel** .... Bardsey Island to Land's End

Area 12 ... **South Ireland** .... Malahide, clockwise to Liscannor Bay

Area 13 ... **North Ireland** .... Liscannor Bay, clockwise to Lambay Island

Area 14 ... **Channel Islands** .... Guernsey and Jersey

SOUTH WEST ENGLAND – Isles of Scilly to Anvil Point

Key to Marina Plans symbols

🛢 Bottled gas		P Parking	
Chandler		Pub/Restaurant	
Disabled facilities		Pump out	
Electrical supply		Rigging service	
Electrical repairs		Sail repairs	
Engine repairs		Shipwright	
First Aid		Shop/Supermarket	
Fresh Water		Showers	
Fuel - Diesel		Slipway	
Fuel - Petrol		WC Toilets	
Hardstanding/boatyard		Telephone	
@ Internet Café		Trolleys	
Laundry facilities		V Visitors berths	
Lift-out facilities		Wi-Fi	

Area 1 - South West England

MARINAS
Telephone Numbers
VHF Channel
Access Times

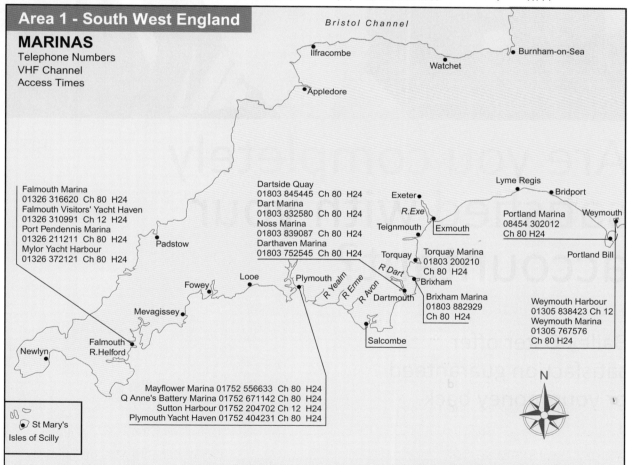

Bristol Channel

Ilfracombe
Watchet
Burnham-on-Sea
Appledore

Falmouth Marina
01326 316620 Ch 80 H24
Falmouth Visitors' Yacht Haven
01326 310991 Ch 12 H24
Port Pendennis Marina
01326 211211 Ch 80 H24
Mylor Yacht Harbour
01326 372121 Ch 80 H24

Dartside Quay
01803 845445 Ch 80 H24
Dart Marina
01803 832580 Ch 80 H24
Noss Marina
01803 839087 Ch 80 H24
Darthaven Marina
01803 752545 Ch 80 H24

Lyme Regis
Bridport
Exeter
R.Exe
Teignmouth
Exmouth
Portland Marina
08454 302012
Ch 80 H24
Weymouth
Portland Bill

Padstow

Torquay
Torquay Marina
01803 200210
Ch 80 H24
Brixham

Looe
Fowey
Plymouth
R Yealm
R Erme
R Avon
R Dart
Dartmouth
Brixham Marina
01803 882929
Ch 80 H24

Weymouth Harbour
01305 838423 Ch 12
Weymouth Marina
01305 767576
Ch 80 H24

Mevagissey
Salcombe

Newlyn
Falmouth
R.Helford

Mayflower Marina 01752 556633 Ch 80 H24
Q Anne's Battery Marina 01752 671142 Ch 80 H24
Sutton Harbour 01752 204702 Ch 12 H24
Plymouth Yacht Haven 01752 404231 Ch 80 H24

St Mary's
Isles of Scilly

N

Are you completely satisfied with your accountant?

Bailey Oster offer
satisfaction guaranteed
or your money back.

Call Ben Oster on **0161 358 1212** quoting 'Marina'

www.baileyoster.co.uk

FALMOUTH MARINA

Falmouth Marina
North Parade, Falmouth, Cornwall, TR11 2TD
Tel: 01326 316620 Fax: 01326 313939
Email: falmouth@premiermarinas.com
www.premiermarinas.com

⚓⚓⚓

VHF: Ch 80
ACCESS: H24

Falmouth Marina lies tucked away in sheltered waters at the southern end of the Fal Estuary. Welcoming to both visiting and residential yachts, its comprehensive facilities include a restaurant, convenience store and hairdresser, while just a 20-minute walk away is Falmouth's town centre where you will find no shortage of shops and eating places. Comprising more than 70 sq miles of navigable water, the Fal Estuary is an intriguing cruising area full of hidden creeks and inlets.

FACILITIES AT A GLANCE

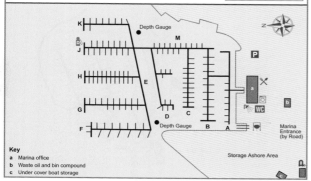

Key
a Marina office
b Waste oil and bin compound
c Under cover boat storage

FALMOUTH VISITORS' YACHT HAVEN

Falmouth Visitors Yacht Haven
44 Arwenack Street
Tel: 01326 310991 Fax: 01326 211352
Email: admin@falmouthport.co.uk

VHF: Ch 12
ACCESS: H24

Run by Falmouth Harbour Commissioners (FHC), Falmouth Visitors' Yacht Haven has become increasingly popular since its opening in 1982, enjoying close proximity to the amenities and entertainments of Falmouth town centre. Sheltered by a breakwater, the Haven caters for 100 boats and offers petrol and diesel supplies as well as good shower and laundry facilities.

Falmouth Harbour is considered by some to be the cruising capital of Cornwall and its deep water combined with easily navigable entrance – even in the severest conditions – makes it a favoured destination for visiting yachtsmen.

FACILITIES AT A GLANCE

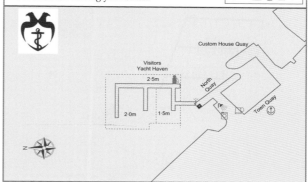

PORT PENDENNIS MARINA

Port Pendennis Marina
Challenger Quay, Falmouth, Cornwall, TR11 3YL
Tel: 01326 211211 Fax: 01326 311116
www.portpendennis.com

VHF	Ch 80
ACCESS	H24

Easily identified by the tower of the National Maritime Museum, Port Pendennis Marina is a convenient arrival or departure point for trans-Atlantic or Mediterranean voyages. Lying adjacent to the town centre, Port Pendennis is divided into an outer marina, with full tidal access, and inner marina, accessible three hours either side of HW. Among its impressive array of marine services is Pendennis Shipyard, one of Britain's most prestigious yacht builders, while other amenities on site include car hire, tennis courts and a yachtsman's lounge, from where you can send faxes or e-mails. Within walking distance of the marina are beautiful sandy beaches, an indoor swimming pool complex and castle.

FACILITIES AT A GLANCE

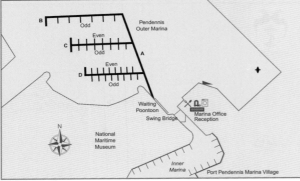

MYLOR YACHT HARBOUR

Mylor Yacht Harbour Marina
Mylor, Falmouth, Cornwall, TR11 5UF
Tel: 01326 372121 Fax: 01326 372120
Email: enquiries@mylor.com

VHF	Ch M, 80
ACCESS	H24

Situated on the western shore of Carrick Roads in the beautiful Fal Estuary, Mylor Yacht Harbour has been improved and expanded in recent years, now comprising two substantial breakwaters, three inner pontoons and approximately 250 moorings. With 24 hour access, good shelter and excellent facilities, it ranks among the most popular marinas on the SW Coast of England.

Formerly the Navy's smallest dockyard, established in 1805, Mylor is today a thriving yachting centre as well as home to the world's only remaining sailing oyster fishing fleet. With Falmouth just 10 mins away, local attractions include the Eden Project in St Austell and the National Maritime Museum in Falmouth.

FACILITIES AT A GLANCE

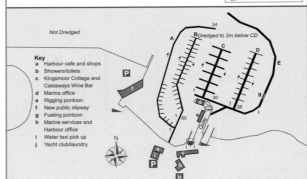

Key
a Harbour cafe and shops
b Showers/toilets
c Kingsmoor Cottage and Castaways Wine Bar
d Marina office
e Rigging pontoon
f New public slipway
g Fueling pontoon
h Marine services and Harbour office
i Water taxi pick up
j Yacht club/laundry

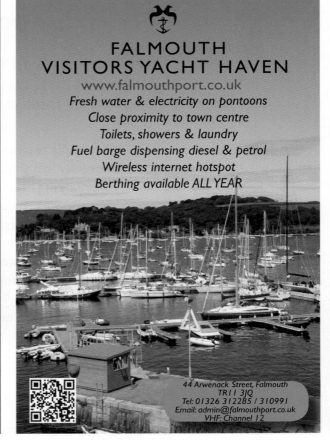

Hemisphere
Rigging Services

Standing & running rigging, deck gear & mast equipment for dinghies, cruising & racing yachts

Our services

- Mast & rigging inspections
- Winch servicing
- Furling kits & deckfittings
- Rig tuning
- Mast stepping
- Large stock rope at competitive prices
- Supply & Fit standing and running rigging
- Free estimates

2012/G4/e

Telephone : 07790 225511

Email: info@hemisphereriggingservices.com

Hemisphere Rigging Services Plymouth Yacht Haven

Shaw Way, Mount Batten   Plymouth PL9 9XH

MAYFLOWER MARINA

Mayflower International Marina
Ocean Quay, Richmond Walk, Plymouth, PL1 4LS
Tel: 01752 556633 Fax: 01752 606896
Email: info@mayflowermarina.co.uk

VHF Ch 80
ACCESS H24

Sitting on the famous Plymouth Hoe, with the Devon coast to the left and the Cornish coast to the right, Mayflower Marina is a friendly, well-run marina. Facilities include 24 hour access to fuel, gas and a launderette, full repair and maintenance services as well as an on site bar and brasserie. The marina is located only a short distance from Plymouth's town centre, where there are regular train services to and from several major towns and cities.

FACILITIES AT A GLANCE

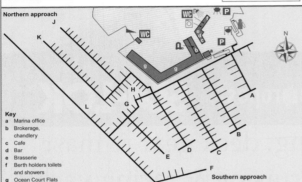

Key
a Marina office
b Brokerage, chandlery
c Cafe
d Bar
e Brasserie
f Berth holders toilets and showers
g Ocean Court Flats

Northern approach

Southern approach

QUEEN ANNE'S BATTERY

Queen Anne's Battery
Plymouth, Devon, PL4 0LP
Tel: 01752 671142 Fax: 01752 266297
www.marinas.co.uk Email: qab@mdlmarinas.co.uk

VHF Ch 80
ACCESS H24

At the centre of Plymouth lies Queen Anne's Battery, comprising 235 resident berths as well as a visitor's basin with alongside pontoon berthing. Located just south of Sutton Harbour, all berths are well protected by a breakwater and double wavescreen.

As Plymouth Sound frequently provides the starting point for many prestigious international yacht races, the marina is often crowded with racers during the height of the season and its vibrant atmosphere can at times resemble a mini 'Cowes'.

FACILITIES AT A GLANCE

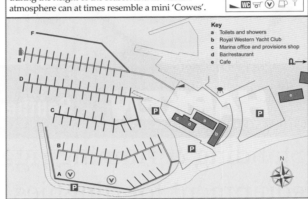

Key
a Toilets and showers
b Royal Western Yacht Club
c Marina office and provisions shop
d Bar/restaurant
e Cafe

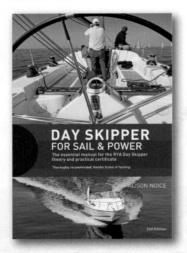
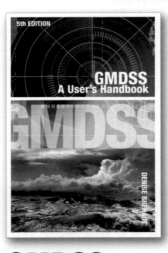

SUTTON HARBOUR

Sutton Harbour
The Jetty, Sutton Harbour, Plymouth, PL4 0DW
Tel: 01752 204702 Fax: 01752 204693
Email: marina@sutton-harbour.co.uk
www.suttonharbourmarina.com

VHF Ch 12
ACCESS H24

Sutton Harbour Marina located in the heart of Plymouth's historic Barbican area and a short stroll from the city centre offers 5-star facilities in a sheltered location surrounded by boutiques, waterfront bars and restaurants. Offering 490 pontoon berths with a minimum 3.5m depth, the harbour has 24-hr lock access on request with free flow approx 3hrs either side of high tide. The marina of choice for international yacht races such as The Transat and Fastnet. Visitors are invited to come and enjoy the unrivalled shelter, facilities, atmosphere and location that Sutton harbour offers.

FACILITIES AT A GLANCE

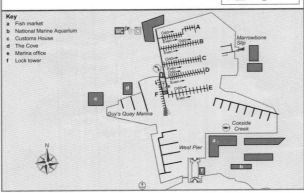

Key
a Fish market
b National Marine Aquarium
c Customs House
d The Cove
e Marina office
f Lock tower

PLYMOUTH YACHT HAVEN

Plymouth Yacht Haven Ltd
Shaw Way, Mount Batten, Plymouth, PL9 9XH
Tel: 01752 404231 Fax: 01752 484177
www.yachthavens.com Email: plymouth@yachthavens.com

VHF Ch 80
ACCESS H24

Situated at the mouth of the river Plym, Plymouth Yacht Haven offers good protection from the prevailing winds and is within close proximity of Plymouth Sound. This 450 berth marina can accommodate vessels up to 45m in length and 7m draught.
Members of staff are on site 24/7 to welcome you as a visitor and to serve diesel. 2008 saw the opening of The Bridge Bar and Restaurant at the heart of the marina. Within easy access are coastal walks, a golf course, and health centre with heated swimming pool. The city of Plymouth and historic Barbican are a short water-taxi ride away.
With a 75ton travel hoist, undercover storage, and extensive range of marine services onsite, Plymouth Yacht Haven has the perfect yard for any maintenance required.

FACILITIES AT A GLANCE

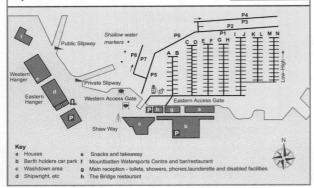

Key
a Houses
b Berth holders car park
c Washdown area
d Shipwright, etc
e Snacks and takeaway
f Mountbatten Watersports Centre and bar/restaurant
g Main reception - toilets, showers, phones, launderette and disabled facilities
h The Bridge restaurant

DARTHAVEN MARINA

Darthaven Marina
Brixham Road, Kingswear, Devon, TQ6 0SG
Tel: 01803 752242
Email: darthaven@darthaven.co.uk
www.darthaven.co.uk

| VHF | Ch 80 |
| ACCESS | H24 |

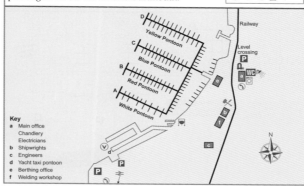

Darthaven Marina is a family run business situated in the village of Kingswear on the east side of the River Dart. Within half a mile from Start Bay and the mouth of the river, it is the first marina you come to from seaward and is accessible at all states of the tide. Darthaven prides itself on being more than just a marina, offering a high standard of marine services with both electronic and engineering experts plus wood and GRP repairs on site. A shop, post office and three pubs are within a walking distance of the marina, while a frequent ferry service takes passengers across the river to Dartmouth.

FACILITIES AT A GLANCE

Key
a Main office
  Chandlery
  Electricians
b Shipwrights
c Engineers
d Yacht taxi pontoon
e Berthing office
f Welding workshop

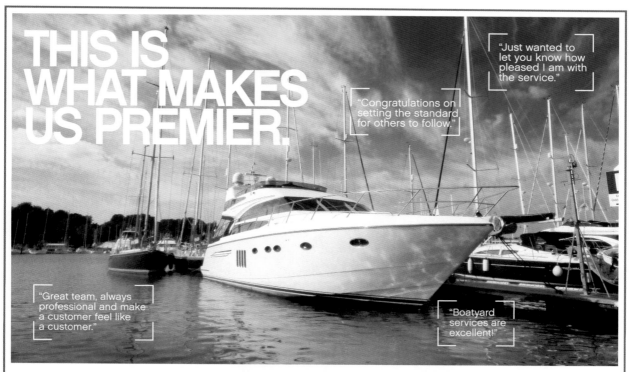

DART MARINA

Dart Marina
Sandquay Road, Dartmouth, Devon, TQ6 9PH
Tel: 01803 837161 Fax: 01803 835040
Email: yachtharbour@dartmarina.com
www.dartmarinayachtharbour.com

| VHF | Ch 80 |
| ACCESS | H24 |

Dart Marina Yacht Harbour, in one of the most stunning locations on the UK coastline, is a peaceful spot for simply sitting on deck relaxing and perfectly-positioned for day-sailing or more ambitious cruising. With visitor berths, 110 annual berths, all accessible at any tide, the Yacht Harbour is sought after for its intimate atmosphere and stylish setting.

Professional, knowledgeable and helpful, the marina team is on-site all year round and there are impeccable, stylish facilities including showers, bathrooms and laundry.

In Dartmouth, a short level stroll along the embankment, there are restaurants, bistros, cafes, delis, independent shops, galleries, a cinema, chandlers, antique and lifestyle shops in abundance.

FACILITIES AT A GLANCE

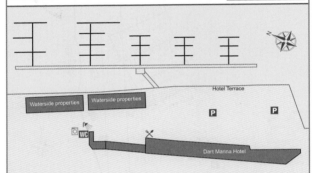

NOSS MARINA

Noss Marina
Bridge Road, Kingswear, Devon, TQ6 0EA
Tel: 01803 839087 Fax: 01803 835620
Email: info@nossmarina.co.uk
www.nossmarina.co.uk

| VHF | Ch 80 |
| ACCESS | H24 |

Upstream of Dartmouth on the east shore of the River Dart is Noss Marina. Enjoying a peaceful rural setting, this marina is well suited to those who prefer a quieter atmosphere. Besides 180 fully serviced berths, 50 fore-and-aft moorings in the middle reaches of the river are also run by the marina, with mooring holders entitled to use all the facilities available to berth holders. During summer, a passenger ferry service runs regularly between Noss-on-Dart and Dartmouth, while a grocery service to your boat can be provided on request.

FACILITIES AT A GLANCE

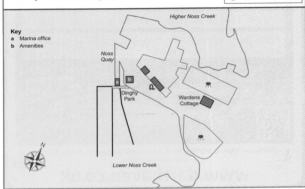

Key
a Marina office
b Amenities

Higher Noss Creek
Noss Quay
Dinghy Park
Wardens Cottage
Lower Noss Creek

DARTSIDE QUAY

Dartside Quay
Galmpton Creek, Brixham, Devon, TQ5 0EH
Tel: 01803 845445 Fax: 01803 843558
Email: dartsidequay@mdlmarinas.co.uk www.marinas.co.uk

VHF Ch 80
ACCESS H24

Located at the head of Galmpton Creek, Dartside Quay lies three miles up river from Dartmouth.

In a sheltered position and with beautiful views across to Dittisham, it offers extensive boatyard facilities. The 7-acre dry boat storage area has space for over 300 boats and is serviced by a 65-ton hoist operating from a purpose-built dock, a 16-ton trailer hoist and 13-ton crane.

There are also a number of summer mud moorings available and a well stocked chandlery, in fact if the item you want is not in stock we can order it in for you.

FACILITIES AT A GLANCE

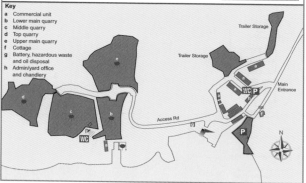

Key
a Commercial unit
b Lower main quarry
c Middle quarry
d Top quarry
e Upper main quarry
f Cottage
g Battery, hazardous waste and oil disposal
h Admin/yard office and chandlery

BRIXHAM MARINA

Brixham Marina
Berry Head Road, Brixham
Devon, TQ5 9BW
Tel: 01803 882929 Fax: 01803 882737
www.marinas.co.uk Email: brixham@mdlmarinas.co.uk

VHF Ch 80
ACCESS H24

Home to one of Britain's largest fishing fleets, Brixham Harbour is located on the southern shore of Tor Bay, which is well sheltered from westerly winds and where tidal streams are weak. Brixham Marina, housed in a separate basin to the work boats, provides easy access in all weather conditions and at all states of the tide. Established in 1989, it has become increasingly popular with locals and visitors alike, enjoying an idyllic setting right on the town's quayside.

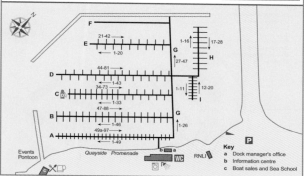

Local attractions include a walk out to Berry Head Nature Reserve and a visit to the replica of Sir Francis Drake's ship, the *Golden Hind*.

FACILITIES AT A GLANCE

Key
a Dock manager's office
b Information centre
c Boat sales and Sea School

ADLARD COLES NAUTICAL
The Best Sailing Books

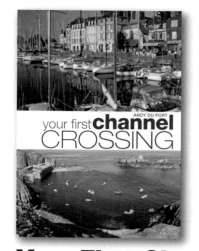

ANDY DU PORT
your first **channel**
CROSSING

Your First Channel Crossing

Andy Du Port

978 1 4081 0012 7

£16.99

Tel: 01256 302699
email: direct@macmillan.co.uk

TORQUAY MARINA

Torquay Marina
Torquay, Devon, TQ2 5EQ
Tel: 01803 200210 Fax: 01803 200225
Email: torquaymarina@mdlmarinas.co.uk www.marinas.co.uk

VHF Ch 80
ACCESS H24

Tucked away in the north east corner of Tor Bay, Torquay Marina is well sheltered from the prevailing SW'ly winds, providing safe entry in all conditions and at any state of the tide. Located in the centre of Torquay, the marina enjoys easy access to the town's numerous shops, bars and restaurants.

Torquay is ideally situated for either exploring Tor Bay itself, with its many delightful anchorages, or else for heading further west to experience several other scenic harbours such as Dartmouth and Salcombe. It also provides a good starting point for crossing to Brittany, Normandy or the Channel Islands.

FACILITIES AT A GLANCE

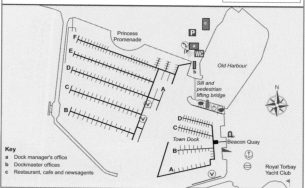

Key
a Dock manager's office
b Dockmaster offices
c Restaurant, cafe and newsagents

PORTLAND MARINA

Portland Marina
Osprey Quay, Portland, Dorset, DT5 1DX
Tel: 08454 302012 Fax: 08451 802012
www.deanreddyhoff.co.uk
Email: sales@portlandmarina.co.uk

⚓⚓⚓⚓

| VHF | Ch 80 |
| ACCESS | H24 |

New for 2009, Portland Marina is an ideal location for both annual berthing and weekend stopovers. The marina offers first class facilities including washrooms, on-site bar and restaurant, lift out and storage up to 320T, dry stacking up to 10m, 24-hour manned security, fuel berth, sewage pump out, extensive car parking and a full range of marine services including a chandlery.

The marina is within walking distance of local pubs and restaurants on Portland with Weymouth's bustling town centre and mainline railway station just a short bus or ferry ride away.

FACILITIES AT A GLANCE

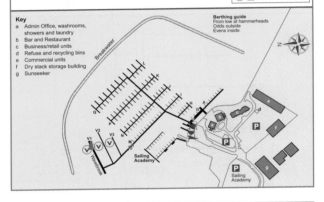

Key
a Admin Office, washrooms, showers and laundry
b Bar and Restaurant
c Business/retail units
d Refuse and recycling bins
e Commercial units
f Dry stack storage building
g Sunseeker

Berthing guide
From low at hammerheads
Odds outside
Evens inside

WEYMOUTH HARBOUR

Weymouth Harbour Master's Office
13 Custom House Quay, Weymouth, Dorset, DT4 8BG
Tel: 01305 838423 Fax: 01305 767927
Email: b.office3@westdorset-weymouth.gov.uk
www.harbour.weymouth.gov.uk

| VHF | Ch 12 |
| ACCESS | H24 |

Weymouth Harbour which lies to the NE of Portland in the protected waters of Weymouth Bay, benefits from deep water at all states of the tide. Located in the heart of Weymouth old town, the Georgian harbour offers plenty of places to berth overnight, please make sure to contact the berthing office on VHF Ch12 upon arrival. Vessels over 15m are advised to give prior notification of intended arrival. Pontoons on both quays benefit from free electricity and fresh water, as well as free showers and a coin-operated laundrette. Visiting yachtsmen are very welcome, both at the Royal Dorset Yacht Club and Weymouth Sailing Club, both situated directly on the quayside in the outer harbour.

FACILITIES AT A GLANCE

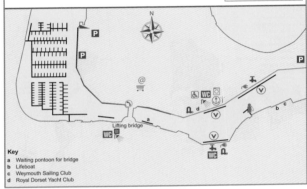

Key
a Waiting pontoon for bridge
b Lifeboat
c Weymouth Sailing Club
d Royal Dorset Yacht Club

WEYMOUTH MARINA

Weymouth Marina
70 Commercial Road, Dorset, DT4 8NA
Tel: 01305 767576 Fax: 01305 767575
www.weymouth-marina.co.uk
Email: sales@weymouth-marina.co.uk

| VHF | Ch 80 |
| ACCESS | H24 |

With more than 280 permanent and visitors' berths, Weymouth is a modern, purpose-built marina ideally situated for yachtsmen cruising between the West Country and the Solent. It is also conveniently placed for sailing to France or the Channel Islands. Accessed via the town's historic lifting bridge, which opens every even hour 0800–2000 (plus 2100 Jun–Aug), the marina is dredged to 2.5m below chart datum. It provides easy access to the town centre, with its abundance of shops, pubs and restaurants, as well as to the traditional seafront where an impressive sandy beach is overlooked by an esplanade of hotels.

FACILITIES AT A GLANCE

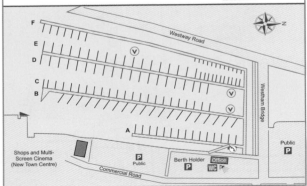

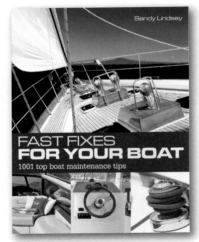

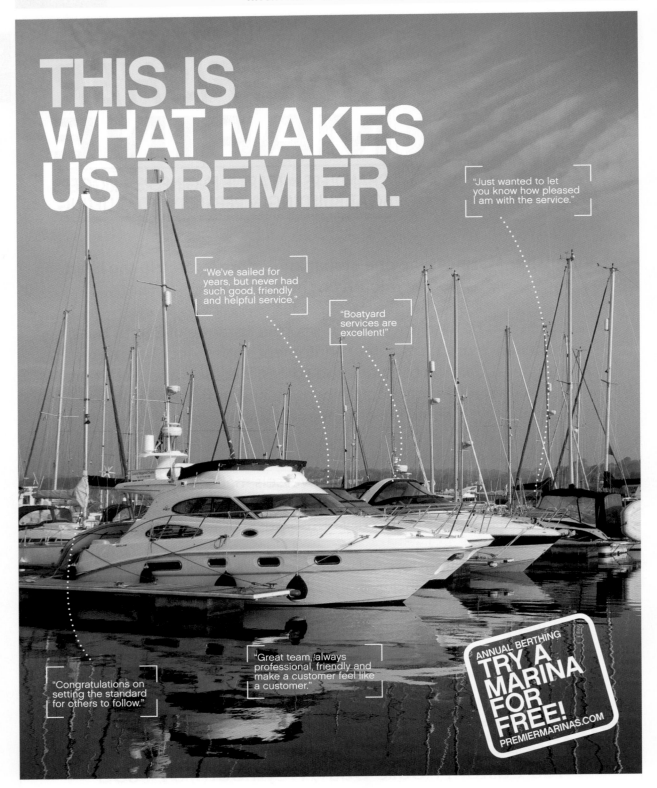

THIS IS WHAT MAKES US PREMIER.

"Just wanted to let you know how pleased I am with the service."

"We've sailed for years, but never had such good, friendly and helpful service."

"Boatyard services are excellent!"

"Great team, always professional, friendly and make a customer feel like a customer."

"Congratulations on setting the standard for others to follow."

ANNUAL BERTHING
TRY A MARINA FOR FREE!
PREMIERMARINAS.COM

YOU'LL LOVE OUR FIRST-CLASS MARINAS, OUR SUPERB FACILITIES AND OUR VALUE FOR MONEY PRICING, BUT BEST OF ALL, YOU'LL LOVE OUR PASSION FOR CUSTOMER SERVICE. FOR A 12-MONTH BERTHING QUOTE OR A 'FREE TRIAL NIGHT' GO ONLINE AT PREMIERMARINAS.COM OR CALL YOUR LOCAL PREMIER MARINA

EASTBOURNE 01323 470099   BRIGHTON 01273 819919   CHICHESTER 01243 512731
SOUTHSEA 023 9282 2719   PORT SOLENT 023 9221 0765   GOSPORT 023 9252 4811
SWANWICK 01489 884081   FALMOUTH 01326 316620

PREMIER
MARINAS

CENTRAL SOUTHERN ENGLAND – Anvil Point to Selsey Bill

Key to Marina Plans symbols

Bottled gas		P	Parking
Chandler			Pub / Restaurant
Disabled facilities			Pump out
Electrical supply			Rigging service
Electrical repairs			Sail repairs
Engine repairs			Shipwright
First Aid			Shop / Supermarket
Fresh Water			Showers
Fuel - Diesel			Slipway
Fuel - Petrol		WC	Toilets
Hardstanding/boatyard			Telephone
@ Internet Café			Trolleys
Laundry facilities		V	Visitors berths
Lift-out facilities			Wi-Fi

2

Area 2 - Central Southern England

MARINAS
Telephone Numbers
VHF Channel
Access Times

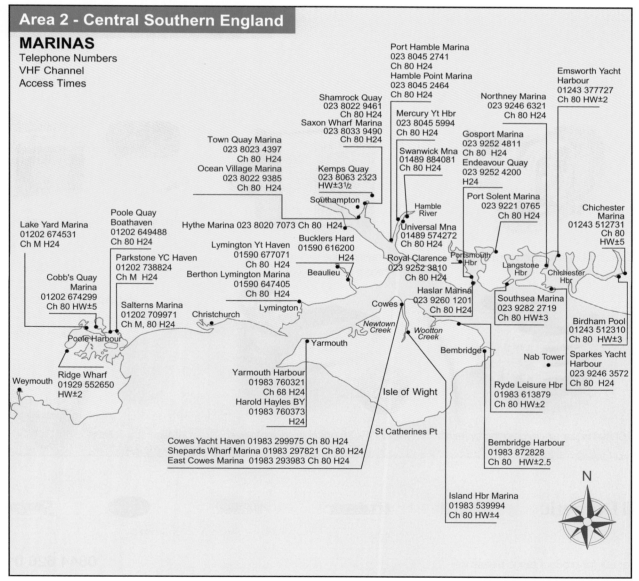

Port Hamble Marina 023 8045 2741 Ch 80 H24
Hamble Point Marina 023 8045 2464 Ch 80 H24
Emsworth Yacht Harbour 01243 377727 Ch 80 HW±2
Shamrock Quay 023 8022 9461 Ch 80 H24
Saxon Wharf Marina 023 8033 9490 Ch 80 H24
Northney Marina 023 9246 6321 Ch 80 H24
Mercury Yt Hbr 023 8045 5994 Ch 80 H24
Gosport Marina 023 9252 4811 Ch 80 H24
Town Quay Marina 023 8023 4397 Ch 80 H24
Swanwick Mna 01489 884081 Ch 80 H24
Endeavour Quay 023 9252 4200 H24
Ocean Village Marina 023 8022 9385 Ch 80 H24
Kemps Quay 023 8063 2323 HW±3½
Port Solent Marina 023 9221 0765 Ch 80 H24
Chichester Marina 01243 512731 Ch 80 HW±5
Southampton
Hamble River
Lake Yard Marina 01202 674531 Ch M H24
Poole Quay Boathaven 01202 649488 Ch 80 H24
Hythe Marina 023 8020 7073 Ch 80 H24
Bucklers Hard 01590 616200 H24
Universal Mna 01489 574272 Ch 80 H24
Lymington Yt Haven 01590 677071 Ch 80 H24
Parkstone YC Haven 01202 738824 Ch M H24
Berthon Lymington Marina 01590 647405 Ch 80 H24
Beaulieu
Royal Clarence 023 9252 3810 Ch 80 H24
Portsmouth Hbr
Langstone Hbr
Chichester Hbr
Cobb's Quay Marina 01202 674299 Ch 80 HW±5
Salterns Marina 01202 709971 Ch M, 80 H24
Christchurch
Lymington
Cowes
Haslar Marina 023 9260 1201 Ch 80 H24
Southsea Marina 023 9282 2719 Ch 80 HW±3
Poole Harbour
Newtown Creek
Wootton Creek
Birdham Pool 01243 512310 Ch 80 HW±3
Weymouth
Ridge Wharf 01929 552650 HW±2
Yarmouth
Bembridge
Nab Tower
Sparkes Yacht Harbour 023 9246 3572 Ch 80 H24
Yarmouth Harbour 01983 760321 Ch 68 H24
Harold Hayles BY 01983 760373 H24
Isle of Wight
Ryde Leisure Hbr 01983 613879 Ch 80 HW±2
St Catherines Pt
Cowes Yacht Haven 01983 299975 Ch 80 H24
Shepards Wharf Marina 01983 297821 Ch 80 H24
East Cowes Marina 01983 293983 Ch 80 H24
Bembridge Harbour 01983 872828 Ch 80 HW±2.5
Island Hbr Marina 01983 539994 Ch 80 HW±4
N

RIDGE WHARF YACHT CENTRE

Ridge Wharf Yacht Centre
Ridge, Wareham, Dorset, BH20 5BG
Tel: 01929 552650 Fax: 01929 554434
Email: office@ridgewharf.co.uk www.ridgewharf.co.uk

VHF
ACCESS HW±2

On the south bank of the River Frome, which acts as the boundary to the North of the Isle of Purbeck, is Ridge Wharf Yacht Centre. Access for a 1.5m draught is between one and two hours either side of HW, with berths drying out to soft mud. The Yacht Centre cannot be contacted on VHF, so it is best to phone up ahead of time to inquire about berthing availability.

A trip upstream to the ancient market town of Wareham is well worth while, although owners of deep-draughted yachts may prefer to go by dinghy. Tucked between the Rivers Frome and Trent, it is packed full of cafés, restaurants and shops.

FACILITIES AT A GLANCE

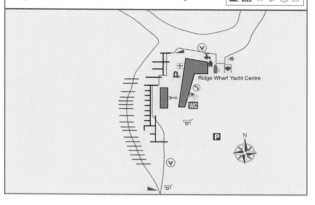

LAKE YARD MARINA

Lake Yard Marina
Lake Drive, Hamworthy, Poole, Dorset BH15 4DT
Tel: 01202 674531
Email: office@lakeyard.com www.lakeyard.com

VHF Ch M
ACCESS H24

Lake Yard is situated towards the NW end of Poole Harbour, just beyond the SHM No 73. The entrance can be easily identified by 2FR (vert) and 2FG (vert) lights. Enjoying 24 hour access, the marina has no designated visitors' berths, but will accommodate visiting yachtsmen if resident berth holders are away. Its on site facilities include full maintenance and repair services as well as hard standing and a 50 ton boat hoist, although for the nearest fuel go to Corralls (Tel 01202 674551), opposite the Town Quay. Lake Yard's Waterfront Club, offering spectacular views across the harbour, opens seven days a week for lunchtime and evening meals.

FACILITIES AT A GLANCE

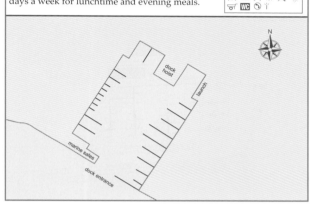

COBB'S QUAY MARINA

Cobb's Quay Marina
Hamworthy, Poole, Dorset, BH15 4EL
Tel: 01202 674299 Fax: 01202 665217
Email: cobbsquay@mdlmarinas.co.uk www.marinas.co.uk

VHF Ch 80
ACCESS HW±5

Lying on the west side of Holes Bay in Poole Harbour, Cobb's Quay is accessed via the lifting bridge at Poole Quay. With fully serviced pontoons for yachts up to 25m LOA, the marina can be entered five hours either side of high water and is normally able to accommodate visiting yachts. On site is the Boat House, which welcomes visitors to its bar and restaurant.

Cobb's Quay Marina also offers a convenient 240 berth Dry Stack system for motorboats up to 10 metres. Offering increased security and lower maintenance costs, the service includes unlimited launching on demand seven days a week. For location, Poole is one of the largest natural harbours in the world and is considered by many to be among the finest.

FACILITIES AT A GLANCE

Key
a Dock manager's office
b Information point
c Yacht club
d Convenience store

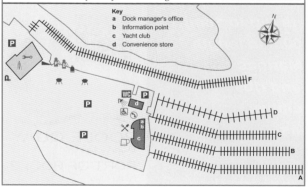

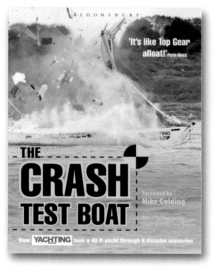

POOLE QUAY BOAT HAVEN

Poole Quay Boat Haven
Poole Town Quay, Poole, Dorset, BH15 1HJ
Tel: 01202 649488 Fax: 01202 785619
Email: info@poolequayboathaven.co.uk

VHF: Ch 80
ACCESS: H24

Once inside the Poole Harbour entrance small yachts heading for Poole Quay Boat Haven should use the Boat Channel running parallel south of the dredged Middle Ship Channel, which is primarily used by ferries sailing to and from the Hamworthy terminal. The marina can be accessed via the Little Channel and is easily identified by the large breakwater alongside the Quay. With deep water at all states of the tide the marina has berthing available for 125 yachts up to 35m, but due to its central location the marina can get busy so it is best to reserve a berth.

There is easy access to all of Poole Quay's facilities including restaurants, bars, Poole Pottery and the Waterfront Museum.

FACILITIES AT A GLANCE

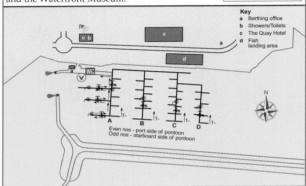

Key
a Berthing office
b Showers/Toilets
c The Quay Hotel
d Fish landing area

Even nos - port side of pontoon
Odd nos - starboard side of pontoon

PORT OF POOLE MARINA

Port of Poole Marina
Poole Town Quay, Poole, Dorset, BH15 1HJ
Tel: 01202 649488 Fax: 01202 785619
Email: info@poolequayboathaven.co.uk

VHF: Ch 80
ACCESS: H24

Beware of the chain ferry operating at the entrance to Poole harbour. Once inside small yachts heading for the marina should use the Boat Channel running parallel south of the Middle Ship Channel. The marina is to the east of the main ferry terminals and can be identified by a large floating breakwater at the entrance.

The marina has all tides deep water and berthing for 60 allocated permanent vessels with overflow from Town Quay berthing on the breakwater, wich is also suitable for super yachts.

A water taxi is available during daylight hours to access the quay for restaurants and shops, also accessible with a 10–15min walk round the quays.

FACILITIES AT A GLANCE

Even nos - port side of pontoon
Odd nos - starboard side of pontoon
Numbering starts at hammerheads

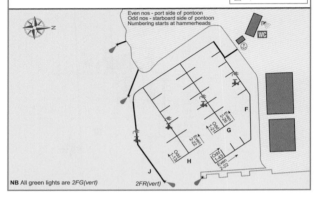

NB All green lights are 2FG(vert)   2FR(vert)

2

PARKSTONE YACHT HAVEN

Parkstone Yacht Club
Pearce Avenue, Parkstone, Poole, Dorset, BH14 8EH
Tel: 01202 738824 Fax: 01202 716394
Email: office@parkstoneyc.co.uk

VHF	Ch M
ACCESS	H24

Situated on the north side of Poole Harbour between Salterns Marina and Poole Quay Boat Haven, Parkstone Yacht Haven can be entered at all states of the tides. Its approach channel has been dredged to 2.0m and is clearly marked by buoys. Run by the Parkstone Yacht Club, the Haven provides 200 deep water berths for members and visitors' berths. Other services include a new office facility with laundry and WCs, bar, restaurant, shower/changing rooms and wi-fi. With a busy sailing programme for over 2,500 members, the Yacht Club plays host to a variety of events including Poole Week, which is held towards the end of August. Please phone for availability.

FACILITIES AT A GLANCE

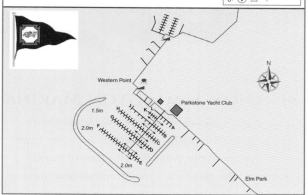

Western Point
Parkstone Yacht Club
1.5m
2.0m
2.0m
Elm Park
N

SALTERNS MARINA

Salterns Marina
40 Salterns Way, Lilliput, Poole
Dorset, BH14 8JR
Tel: 01202 709971 Fax: 01202 700398
Email: marina@salterns.co.uk www.salterns.co.uk

VHF	Ch M, 80
ACCESS	H24

Holding the Five Gold Anchor award, Salterns Marina provides a service which is second to none. Located off the North Channel, it is approached from the No 31 SHM and benefits from deep water at all states of the tide. Facilities include 220 alongside pontoon berths as well as 75 swinging moorings with a free launch service. However, with very few designated visitors' berths, it is best to contact the marina ahead of time for availability.

Fuel, diesel and gas can all be obtained 24/7 and the well-stocked chandlery, incorporating a coffee shop, stays open seven days a week.

FACILITIES AT A GLANCE

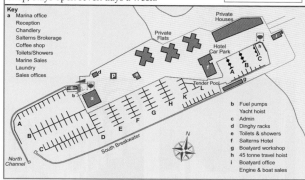

Key
a Marina office
   Reception
   Chandlery
   Salterns Brokerage
   Coffee shop
   Toilets/Showers
   Marine Sales
   Laundry
   Sales offices
b Fuel pumps
   Yacht hoist
c Admin
d Dinghy racks
e Toilets & showers
f Salterns Hotel
g Boatyard workshop
h 45 tonne travel hoist
i Boatyard office
   Engine & boat sales

Private Houses
Private Flats
Hotel Car Park
Tender Pool
South Breakwater
North Channel
N

YARMOUTH HBR/HAROLD HAYLES BY

Yarmouth Harbour
Yarmouth, Isle of Wight, PO41 0NT
Tel: 01983 760321 Fax: 01983 761192
info@yarmouth-harbour.co.uk
www.yarmouth-harbour.co.uk

VHF	Ch 68
ACCESS	H24

Harold Hayles Ltd
The Quay, Yarmouth, Isle of Wight, PO41 0RS
Tel: 01983 760373 Fax: 01983 760666
Email: info@haroldhayles.co.uk
www.haroldhayles.co.uk

VHF	
ACCESS	H24

The most western harbour on the Isle of Wight, Yarmouth is not only a convenient passage stopover but a very desirable destination in its own right, with virtually all weather and tidal access, although strong N to NE'ly winds can produce a considerable swell. The HM launch patrols the harbour entrance and will direct visiting yachtsmen to a walkashore or standalone pontoon berth or pile. The pretty harbour and town offer plenty of fine restaurants and amenities.

Walkashore pontoon moorings are available from both Yarmouth Harbour and Harold Hayles Boatyard in the SW corner of the harbour. Pre-booking is preferred for both individuals or rallies.

FACILITIES AT A GLANCE

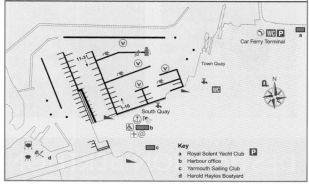

Car Ferry Terminal
Town Quay
11-3ft
1-10
South Quay
WC
N
Key
a Royal Solent Yacht Club
b Harbour office
c Yarmouth Sailing Club
d Harold Hayles Boatyard

DESTINATION

BERTHON LYMINGTON MARINA

Offering 280 deepwater, well-protected berths for yachts up to 45m (150ft) LOA in the Georgian town of Lymington on the West Solent close to Hurst Castle and the Needles. Lymington has long been a haven for mariners the world over as it benefits from double tides and a stunning approach up through the widely curving Solent.

- Everything you need for an overnight stay or a permanent base for your yacht
- Ample turning space and wide, stable pontoons
- 'State of the art' wifi providing excellent internet access
- Full range of valet, maintenance and repair services
- Short walk to Lymington high street where there are many restaurants, pubs, coffee shops, chandlers and a Saturday street market
- Easy access via land or water to Cowes, Hamble, Beaulieu, Newtown, Yarmouth, Hurst Castle and Alum Bay
- On the doorstep of the New Forest, 145 square miles of ancient woodland and heathland
- Easy access to the Salt Marsh nature reserve with a number of rare species of plant and a wide variety of migratory and breeding birds
- 40 minutes from Southampton International Airport, 90 minutes from Heathrow
- 12 hours sailing from the French coast
- Train access to London and the rest of the UK and Europe

2

LYMINGTON YACHT HAVEN

Lymington Yacht Haven
King's Saltern Road, Lymington, S041 3QD
Tel: 01590 677071 Fax: 01590 678186
Email: lymington@yachthavens.com www.yachthavens.com

⚓⚓⚓⚓

VHF Ch 80
ACCESS H24

The attractive old market town of Lymington lies at the western end of the Solent, just three miles from the Needles Channel. Despite the numerous ferries plying to and from the Isle of Wight, the river is well sheltered and navigable at all states of the tide, proving a popular destination with visiting yachtsmen. There is 24hr access to the fuel berth.

Lymington Yacht Haven is the first of the two marinas from seaward, situated on the port hand side. Offering easy access to the Solent, it is a 10-minute walk to the town centre and supermarkets.

FACILITIES AT A GLANCE

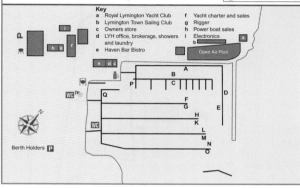

Key
a Royal Lymington Yacht Club
b Lymington Town Sailing Club
c Owners store
d LYH office, brokerage, showers and laundry
e Haven Bar Bistro
f Yacht charter and sales
g Rigger
h Power boat sales
i Electronics

BERTHON LYMINGTON MARINA

Berthon Lymington Marina Ltd
The Shipyard, Lymington, Hampshire, SO41 3YL
Tel: 01590 647405 Fax: 01590 647446
www.berthon.co.uk Email: marina@berthon.co.uk

VHF Ch 80
ACCESS H24

Situated approximately half a mile up river of Lymington Yacht Haven, on the port hand side, is Lymington Marina. Easily accessible at all states of the tide, it offers between 60 to 70 visitors' berths, with probably the best washrooms in the Solent. Its close proximity to the town centre and first rate services mean that booking is essential on busy weekends. Lymington Marina's parent, Berthon Boat Co, has state of the art facilities and a highly skilled work force of 100+ to deal with any repair, maintenance or refit.

Lymington benefits from having the New Forest on its doorstep and the Solent Way footpath provides an invigorating walk to and from Hurst Castle.

FACILITIES AT A GLANCE

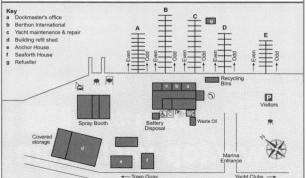

Key
a Dockmaster's office
b Berthon International
c Yacht maintenance & repair
d Building refit shed
e Anchor House
f Seaforth House
g Refueller

LYMINGTON HARBOUR

Lymington Harbour Commisioner
Bath Road, Lymington, S041 3SE
Tel: 01590 672014 Fax: 01590 671823
Email: harbouroffice@lymingtonharbour.co.uk

VHF Ch ??
ACCESS H24

Lymington Harbour Commission provides berths at Dan Bran Pontoon and Lymington Town Quay in addition to the river moorings.

Dan Bran is accessible at all states of the tide inside the wave screen. Power is available along its 650' length with use of the facilities at Lymington Town SC and walk ashore access to the town. It is sited between the marinas a short walk from Town Quay, and is an ideal for club rallies or events.

Town Quay provides shelter up river at the foot of the cobbles, which lead directly to the town centre. 25 boats (up to 2m draft) raft up to 5 deep on a walk ashore pontoon. 50 fore and aft moorings lie just off the quay.

FACILITIES AT A GLANCE

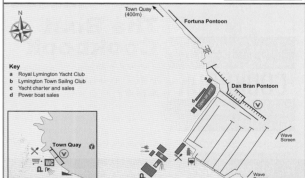

Key
a Royal Lymington Yacht Club
b Lymington Town Sailing Club
c Yacht charter and sales
d Power boat sales

BUCKLERS HARD MARINA

Bucklers Hard
Beaulieu, Brockenhurst, Hampshire, SO42 7XB
Tel: 01590 616200 Fax: 01590 616211
www.bucklershard.co.uk Email: river@beaulieu.co.uk

VHF
ACCESS H24

Meandering through the New Forest, the Beaulieu River is considered by many to be one of the most attractive harbours on the mainland side of the Solent. Two miles upstream from the mouth of the river lies Bucklers Hard, an historic 18th century village where shipwrights skilfully constructed warships for Nelson's fleet. The Maritime Museum, showing the history of boat-building in the village, is open throughout the year.

The marina is manned 24/7 and offers deep water to visitors at all states of the tide, although the bar at the river's entrance should be avoided two hours either side of LW.

FACILITIES AT A GLANCE

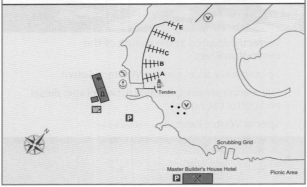

COWES YACHT HAVEN

Cowes Yacht Haven
Vectis Yard, Cowes, Isle of Wight, PO31 7BD
Tel: 01983 299975 Fax: 01983 200332
www.cowesyachthaven.com
Email: berthing@cowesyachthaven.com

VHF Ch 80
ACCESS H24

Situated virtually at the centre of the Solent, Cowes is best known as Britain's premier yachting centre and offers all types of facilities to yachtsmen. Cowes Yacht Haven, operating 24 hours a day, has very few permanent moorings and is dedicated to catering for visitors and events. At peak times it can become very crowded and for occasions such as Aberdeen Asset Management Cowes Week you need to book up in advance.

FACILITIES AT A GLANCE

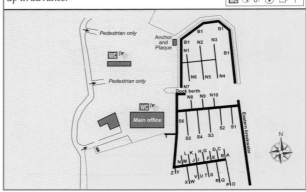

SHEPARDS WHARF MARINA

Shepards Wharf Boatyard
Medina Road, Cowes, Isle of Wight, PO31 7HT
Tel: 01983 297821 Fax: 01983 294814
www.shepards.co.uk

VHF	Ch 80
ACCESS	H24

Just south of Cowes Yacht Haven, still on the starboard side, is Shepards Wharf Marina and Dry Sailing Centre. Shepards operates on a first come first served basis except during Cowes Week and for organised rallies of six or more boats. All berths benefit from water and electricity with showers and Wi-Fi provided free of charge.

Onsite you will find the excellent Spanish restaurant Amabi, Solent Sail Company, Island Divers and Solent Yacht Brokers. For berthing availability, visiting yachtsmen should contact Shepards Wharf Marina on VHF Ch 80. Fuel can be obtained from Cowes Harbour Fuels located 100m south of the chain ferry (Tel 01983 200716).

Shepards Wharf is within easy walking distance of Cowes town centre (2min). Also worth visiting is the Sir Max Aitken Museum, Sir Max contributed enormously to ocean yacht racing and the museum is dedicated to his collection of nautical instruments, paintings and maritime artefacts.

FACILITIES AT A GLANCE

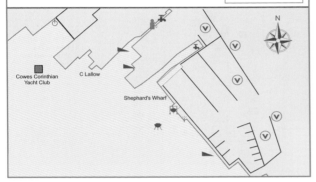

EAST COWES MARINA

East Cowes Marina
Britannia Way, East Cowes, Isle of Wight, PO32 6UB
Tel: 01983 293983 Fax: 01983 299276
www.eastcowesmarina.co.uk
Email: berths@eastcowesmarina.co.uk

VHF	Ch 80
ACCESS	H24

Accommodating around 235 residential yachts and 150 visiting boats at all states of the tide, East Cowes Marina is situated on the quiet and protected east bank of the Medina River, about a quarter mile above the chain ferry. A small convenience store is just five minutes walk away. The new centrally heated shower and toilet facilities ensure the visitor a warm welcome at any time of the year, as does the on-site pub and restaurant.

Several water taxis provide a return service to Cowes, ensuring a quick and easy way of getting to West Cowes.

FACILITIES AT A GLANCE

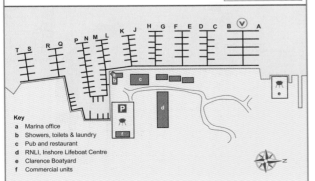

Key
a   Marina office
b   Showers, toilets & laundry
c   Pub and restaurant
d   RNLI, Inshore Lifeboat Centre
e   Clarence Boatyard
f   Commercial units

ISLAND HARBOUR MARINA

Island Harbour Marina
Mill Lane, Binfield, Newport, Isle of Wight, PO30 2LA
Tel: 01983 539994 Fax: 01983 523401
Email: info@island-harbour.co.uk

VHF	Ch 80
ACCESS	HW±4

Situated in beautiful rolling farmland about half a mile south of Folly Inn, Island Harbour Marina provides around 200 visitors' berths. Protected by a lock that is operated daily from 0800 – 2100 during the summer and from 0800 – 1730 during the winter, the marina is accessible for about three hours either side of HW for draughts of 1.5m.

Due to its secluded setting, the marina's on site chandlery also sells essential provisions and newspapers. A half hour walk along the river brings you to Newport, the capital and county town of the Isle of Wight.

FACILITIES AT A GLANCE

Key
a Control tower
b Bin store
c Chandlery
d Restaurant

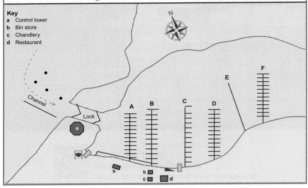

HYTHE MARINA VILLAGE

Hythe Marina Village
Shamrock Way, Hythe, Southampton, SO45 6DY
Tel: 023 8020 7073 Fax: 023 8084 2424
Email: hythe@mdlmarinas.co.uk www.marinas.co.uk

VHF	Ch 80
ACCESS	H24

Situated on the western shores of Southampton Water, Hythe Marina Village is approached by a dredged channel leading to a lock basin. The lock gates are controlled 24 hours a day throughout the year, with a waiting pontoon to the south of the approach basin.

Hythe Marina Village incorporates full marine services as well as an on-site restaurant and a selection of shops can be found in the town centre, a 5 minute walk away. Forming an integral part of the New Forest Waterside, Hythe is the perfect base from which to explore Hampshire's pretty inland villages and towns, or alternatively you can catch the ferry to Southampton's Town Quay.

FACILITIES AT A GLANCE

Key
a Restaurant and Bar
b Lock building
c Boat storage and
   Trailer park

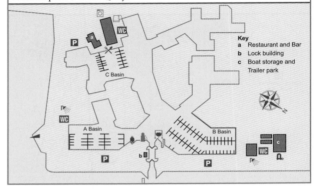

TOWN QUAY

Associated British Ports
Town Quay, Southampton, SO14 2AQ
Tel: 02380 234397 Mobile: 07764 293588
Email: info@townquay.com www.townquay.com

VHF	Ch 80
ACCESS	H24

Located on the eastern shores of Southampton Water, Town Quay offers unrivalled views of Southampton's busy maritime activity and direct access to the world famous cruising and racing waters of the Solent.

Town Quay Marina is the perfect base to explore the South Coast. Historic Portsmouth, the Isle of Wight, Beaulieu River and Poole Harbour are within easy cruising distance and for those wishing to venture further a field, Cherbourg, the Channel Islands and the Brittany coastline are less than a day away.

The marina is accessible at all states of the tide and the marina reception is open 24 hours a day.

FACILITIES AT A GLANCE

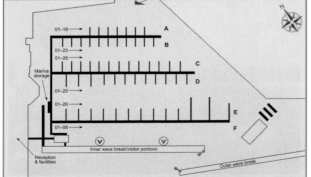

OCEAN VILLAGE MARINA

Ocean Village Marina
2 Channel Way, Southampton, SO14 3TG
Tel: 023 8022 9385 Fax: 023 8023 3515
Email: oceanvillage@mdlmarinas.co.uk www.marinas.co.uk

VHF	Ch 80
ACCESS	H24

The entrance to Ocean Village Marina lies on the port side of the River Itchen, just before the Itchen Bridge. With the capacity to accommodate large yachts and tall ships, the marina, accessible 24 hours a day, is a renowned home for international yacht races.

Situated at the heart of a waterside development incorporating shops, cinemas, restaurants and housing as well as The Royal Southampton Yacht Club, Ocean Village offers a vibrant atmosphere along with high quality service.

FACILITIES AT A GLANCE

Key
a Marina manager's office
b RSYC
c Dock office
d Harbour Lights Cinema
e Banana Wharf
f Pitcher and Piano

2

SHAMROCK QUAY

Shamrock Quay
William Street, Northam, Southampton, Hants, SO14 5QL
Tel: 023 8022 9461 Fax: 023 8021 3808
Email: shamrockquay@mdlmarinas.co.uk www.marinas.co.uk

VHF Ch 80
ACCESS H24

Shamrock Quay, lying upstream of the Itchen Bridge on the port hand side, offers excellent facilities to yachtsmen. It also benefits from being accessible and manned 24 hours a day. On-site there is a 75-ton travel hoist and a 47-ton boat mover, and for dining out there is a choice of restaurants and bars.

The city centre is about two miles away, where among the numerous attractions are the Maritime Museum at Town Quay, the Medieval Merchant's House in French Street and the Southampton City Art Gallery in the Civic Centre.

FACILITIES AT A GLANCE

Key
a Office, bar and restaurant
b Marina office
c Café

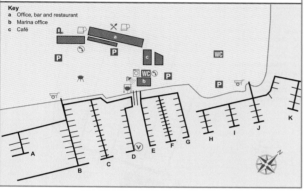

KEMPS QUAY

Kemp's Shipyard Ltd
Quayside Road, Southampton, SO18 1BZ
Tel: 023 8063 2323 Fax: 023 8022 6002
Email: enquiries@kempsquay.com

VHF Ch
ACCESS HW±3.5

At the head of the River Itchen on the starboard side is Kemps Quay, a family-run marina with a friendly, old-fashioned feel. Accessible only 3½ hrs either side of HW, it has a limited number of deep water berths, the rest being half tide, drying out to soft mud. Its restricted access is, however, reflected in the lower prices.

Although situated on the outskirts of Southampton, a short bus or taxi ride will soon get you to the city centre. Besides a nearby BP Garage selling bread and milk, the closest supermarkets can be found in Bitterne Shopping Centre, which is five minutes away by bus.

FACILITIES AT A GLANCE

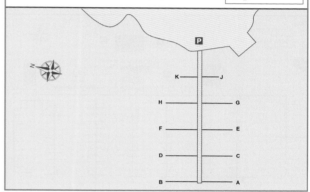

SAXON WHARF

Saxon Wharf
Lower York Street, Northam
Southampton, SO14 5QF
Tel: 023 8033 9490 Fax: 023 8033 5215
Email: saxonwharf@mdlmarinas.co.uk www.marinas.co.uk

VHF Ch 80
ACCESS H24

Placed on the River Itchen in Southampton, Saxon Wharf is a marine service centre specifically designed for the superyacht market. With a 200-tonne boat hoist and heavy duty pontoons, Saxon Wharf is the ideal location for large vessels in need of secure, quick turnaround lift-outs, repair work or even full-scale refits.

With a Dry Stack facility boasting the largest capacity forklift truck in the UK, Saxon Wharf can now dry stack boats of up to 13m LOA. There is also ample storage ashore and 24-hour security. Shamrock Quay, where there are bars and restaurants, is within 300 metres of this location.

FACILITIES AT A GLANCE

Key
a Office
b Security gate
c Southampton Yacht Services
d Offices

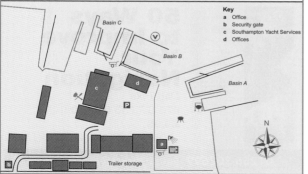

HAMBLE POINT MARINA

Hamble Point Marina
School Lane, Hamble, Southampton, SO31 4NB
Tel: 023 8045 2464 Fax: 023 8045 6440
Email: hamblepoint@mdlmarinas.co.uk www.marinas.co.uk

VHF Ch 80
ACCESS H24

Situated virtually opposite Warsash, this is the first marina you will come to on the western bank of the Hamble. Accommodating yachts and power boats up to 30m in length, it offers easy access to the Solent.

Boasting extensive facilities including 121 Dry Stack berths for motorboats up to 10 metres, the marina is within a 20-minute walk of Hamble Village, where services include a plethora of pubs and restaurants as well as a bank and a convenience store.

FACILITIES AT A GLANCE

Key
a Information
b First aid point
c Marina office
d Administration office
e Chandlery
f Sea Start
g Sailmakers

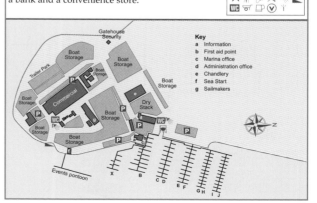

PORT HAMBLE MARINA

Port Hamble Marina
Satchell Lane, Hamble, Southampton, SO31 4QD
Tel: 023 8045 2741 Fax: 023 8045 5206
Email: porthamble@mdlmainas.co.uk www.marinas.co.uk

VHF Ch 80
ACCESS H24

Port Hamble Marina is situated on the River Hamble right in the heart o the South Coast's sailing scene. With thousands of visitors every year, this busy marina is popular with racing enthusiasts and cruising vessels looking for a vibrant atmosphere. The picturesque Hamble village, wit its inviting pubs and restaurants, is only a few minutes walk away.

On site, Port Hamble also offers excellent facilities including a bar and restaurant, which provides the perfect spot to meet, eat and drink by the water. Petrol and diesel is available seven days a week, as well as a range of oils. Locally there are a number of companies on hand who cater for every boating need with all the services a boat owner requires to maintain their vessel.

FACILITIES AT A GLANCE

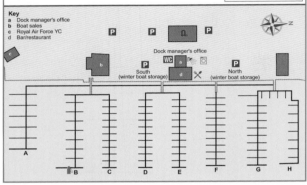

Key
a Dock manager's office
b Boat sales
c Royal Air Force YC
d Bar/restaurant

MERCURY YACHT HARBOUR

Mercury Yacht Harbour
Satchell Lane, Hamble, Southampton, SO31 4HQ
Tel: 023 8045 5994 Fax: 023 8045 7369
Email: mercury@mdlmarinas.co.uk www.marinas.co.uk

VHF Ch 80
ACCESS H24

Mercury Yacht Harbour is the third marina from seaward on the western bank of the River Hamble, tucked away in a picturesque, wooded site adjacent to Badnam Creek. Enjoying deep water at all states of the tide, it accommodates yachts up to 24m LOA and boasts an extensive array of facilities.

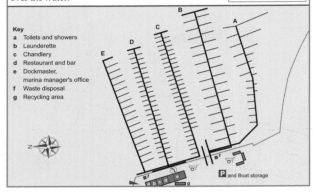

Hamble Village is a 20-minute walk away, although the on-site chandlery does stock a small amount of essential items, and for a good meal look no further than The Waters Edge Bar and Restaurant whose balcony offers striking views over the water.

FACILITIES AT A GLANCE

Key
a Toilets and showers
b Launderette
c Chandlery
d Restaurant and bar
e Dockmaster, marina manager's office
f Waste disposal
g Recycling area

UNIVERSAL MARINA

Universal Marina
Crableck Lane, Sarisbury Green, Southampton, SO31 7ZN
Tel: 01489 574272 Fax: 01489 574273
Email: info@universalmarina.co.uk

VHF Ch 80
ACCESS H24

Universal Marina is one of the few remaining independent marinas offering south coast moorings. Universal Marina's unique location is unbeatable, tucked in between the oak trees on the East Bank of the Hamble where 68 acres of natural wildlife and marshlands surrounds the busy and friendly marina. Positioned only minutes off the M27, it is one of the most accessible marinas on the south coast. The 250 berth complex, features all the latest facilities required by the modern day boat owner, recently upgraded pontoons, power, water and wifi available to each berth. Visitors are welcome & although there are no dedicated visitor berths these are available by prior arrangement.

FACILITIES AT A GLANCE

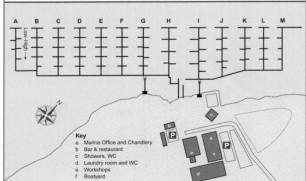

Key
a Marina Office and Chandlery
b Bar & restaurant
c Showers, WC
d Laundry room and WC
e Workshops
f Boatyard

SWANWICK MARINA

Swanwick Marina
Swanwick, Southampton, Hampshire, SO31 1ZL
Tel: 01489 884081 Fax: 01489 579073
Email: swanwick@premiermarinas.com
www.premiermarinas.com

VHF	Ch 80
ACCESS	H24

Situated on the east bank of the River Hamble next to Bursledon Bridge, Swanwick Marina is accessible at all states of the tide and can accommodate yachts up to 20m LOA.

The marina's fully-licensed bar and bistro, The Boat House, over-looking the river, is open for breakfast, lunch and dinner all year round. Alternatively, just a short row or walk away is the celebrated Jolly Sailor pub in Bursledon on the west bank, made famous for being the local watering hole in the British television series *Howard's Way*.

FACILITIES AT A GLANCE

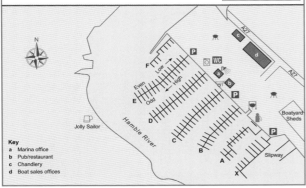

Key
a Marina office
b Pub/restaurant
c Chandlery
d Boat sales offices

RYDE LEISURE HARBOUR

Ryde Harbour
The Esplanade, Ryde, Isle of Wight, PO33 1JA
Tel: 01983 613879 Fax: 01983 613903
www.rydeharbour.com   Email: ryde.harbour@iow.gov.uk

VHF	Ch 80
ACCESS	HW±2

Known as the 'gateway to the Island', Ryde, with its elegant houses and abundant shops, is among the Isle of Wight's most popular resorts. Its well-protected harbour is conveniently close to the exceptional beaches as well as to the town's restaurants and amusements.

Drying to 2.5m and therefore only accessible to yachts that can take the ground, the harbour accommodates 90 resident boats as well as up to 75 visiting yachts. Fin keel yachts may dry out on the harbour wall.

Ideal for family cruising, Ryde offers a wealth of activities, ranging from ten pin bowling and ice skating to crazy golf and tennis.

FACILITIES AT A GLANCE

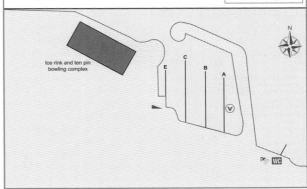

2

BEMBRIDGE HARBOUR

Bembridge Harbour
Harbour Office, The Duver, St Helens, Ryde
Isle of Wight, PO33 1YB
Tel: 01983 872828 Fax: 01983 872922
Email: chris@bembridgeharbour.co.uk
www.bembridgeharbour.co.uk

VHF	Ch 80
ACCESS	HW±2.5

Bembridge is a compact, pretty harbour whose entrance, although restricted by the tides (recommended entry for a 1.5m draught is 2½hrs before HW), is well sheltered in all but north north easterly gales. Offering excellent sailing clubs, beautiful beaches and fine restaurants, this Isle of Wight port is a first class haven with plenty of charm. With approximately 100 new visitors' berths on the Duver Marina pontoons, the marina at St Helen's Quay, at the western end of the harbour, is now allocated to annual berth holders only.

FACILITIES AT A GLANCE

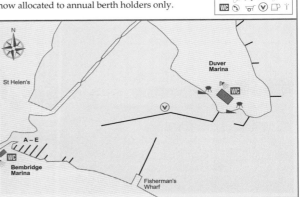

HASLAR MARINA

Haslar Marina
Haslar Road, Gosport, Hampshire, PO12 1NU
Tel: 023 9260 1201 Fax: 023 9260 2201
www.haslarmarina.co.uk Email: sales@haslarmarina.co.uk

VHF Ch 80
ACCESS H24

This modern, purpose-built marina lies to port on the western side of Portsmouth Harbour entrance and is easily recognised by its prominent lightship incorporating a bar and restaurant. Accessible at all states of the tide, Haslar's extensive facilities do not however include fuel, the nearest being at the Gosport Marina only a few cables north.

Within close proximity is the Royal Navy Submarine Museum and the Museum of Naval Firepower 'Explosion' both worth a visit.

FACILITIES AT A GLANCE

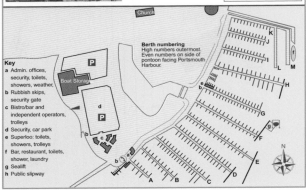

Key
a Admin. offices, security, toilets, showers, weather,
b Rubbish skips, security gate
c Bistro/bar and independent operators, trolleys
d Security, car park
e Superloo: toilets, showers, trolleys
f Bar, restaurant, toilets, shower, laundry
g Sealift
h Public slipway

GOSPORT MARINA

Premier Gosport Marina
Mumby Road, Gosport, Hampshire, PO12 1AH
Tel: 023 9252 4811 Fax: 023 9258 9541
Email: gosport@premiermarinas.com
www.premiermarinas.com

VHF Ch 80
ACCESS H24

A few cables north of Haslar Marina, again on the port hand side, lies Gosport Marina. Boasting 519 fully-serviced visitors' and 80 dry stack berths, its extensive range of facilities incorporates a fuel barge on its southern break-water as well as shower and laundry amenities. Numerous boatyard and engineering specialists are also located in and around the premises.

Within easy reach of the marina is Gosport town centre, offering a cosmopolitan selection of restaurants along with several supermarkets and shops.

FACILITIES AT A GLANCE

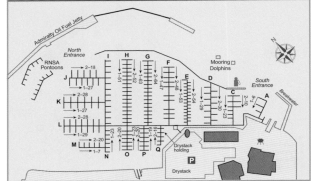

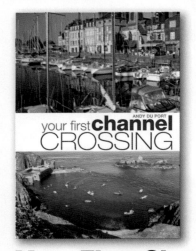

2

ENDEAVOUR QUAY

Endeavour Quay
Mumby Road, Gosport, Hampshire, PO12 1AH
Tel: 023 9258 4200 Email: enquiries@endeavourquay.co.uk
www.endeavourquay.co.uk

VHF
ACCESS H24

Endeavour Quay commands a prime
location in Portsmouth Harbour on the
Gosport waterfront with unrestricted
access to its modern facilities by deep
water. It is also a site of significant yacht
building heritage being the birthplace
of the famous yacht builders Camper &
Nicholsons.

Now modernised, the marina provides
a wide range of professional services from
boat lifting (180 tons max) craneage, deep
water berthing and outside/undercover
storage. The open yard policy and the wide
range of onsite marine related businesses makes
Endeavour Quay an ideal location for emergency
repairs to complex refit and specialist work for all
types of vessels.

FACILITIES AT A GLANCE

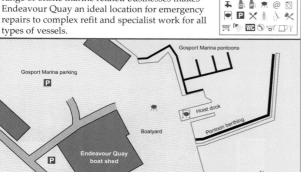

ROYAL CLARENCE MARINA

Royal Clarence Marina, Royal Clarence Yard
Weevil Lane, Gosport, Hampshire PO12 1AX
Tel: 02392 523523 Fax: 02392 523523
Email: info@royalclarencemarina.org
www.royalclarencemarina.org

VHF   Ch 80
ACCESS H24

Royal Clarence Marina benefits
from a unique setting within a
deep-water basin in front of the
Royal Navy's former victualling
yard. Only 10 minutes from
the entrance to Portsmouth
Harbour, it forms part of a
£100 million redevelopment
scheme which will incorporate
residential homes, waterfront

bars and restaurants as well as shopping outlets.
Among its facilities are fully serviced finger pontoon
berths up to 18m in length, while over 150m of
alongside berthing will accommodate Yacht Club
rallies and other maritime events.

FACILITIES AT A GLANCE

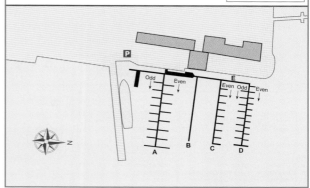

PORT SOLENT MARINA

Port Solent Marina
South Lockside, Portsmouth, PO6 4TJ
Tel: 023 9221 0765 Fax: 023 9232 4241
www.premiermarinas.com
Email: portsolent@premiermarinas.com

VHF   Ch 80
ACCESS H24

Port Solent Marina is located
to the north east of Portsmouth
Harbour, not far from the historic
Portchester Castle. Accessible
via a 24-hour lock, this purpose
built marina offers a full range
of facilities. The Boardwalk
comprises an array of shops and
restaurants, while close by is a
David Lloyd Health Centre and a
large Odeon cinema.

No visit to Portsmouth Harbour is complete
without a trip to the Historic Dockyard, home to
Henry VIII's *Mary Rose*, Nelson's HMS *Victory*
and the first iron battleship, HMS *Warrior*, built
in 1860.

FACILITIES AT A GLANCE

Key a Laundry, berth holders showers,
       toilets and baby change
     b Portsmouth Harbour YC
     c Chandlery, marine engineers
     d Under cover boat shed
     e Berth holders showers,
       toilets and public toilets,
       baby change
     f David Lloyd Health and
       Fitness Club
     g The Boardwalk -
       bars/restaurants
     h Odeon cinema
     i Marina control and
       Port Solent reception
     j Residential building

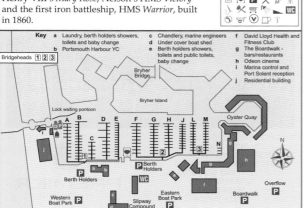

SOUTHSEA MARINA

Southsea Marina
Fort Cumberland Road, PO4 9RJ
Tel: 02392 822719 Fax: 02392 822220
Email: southsea@premiermarinas.com
www.premiermarinas.com

VHF   Ch 80
ACCESS HW±3

Southsea Marina is a small
and friendly marina located
on the western shore of
Langstone Harbour, an
expansive tidal bay situated
between Hayling Island and
Portsmouth. The channel
is clearly marked by seven
starboard and nine port hand
markers. A tidal gate allows

unrestricted movement in and out of the marina up
to 3 hours either side of HW operates the entrance.
The minimum depth in the marina entrance
during this period is 1.6m and a waiting pontoon
is available. There are excellent on site facilities
including a bar, restaurant and chandlery.

FACILITIES AT A GLANCE

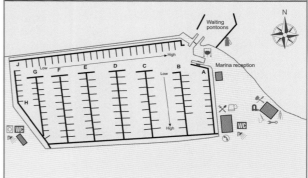

SPARKES MARINA

Sparkes Marina
38 Wittering Road, Hayling Island, Hampshire, PO11 9SR
Tel: 023 9246 3572 Fax: 023 9246 5741
Email: sparkes@mdlmarinas.co.uk www.sparkesmarina.co.uk

VHF Ch 80
ACCESS H24

Just inside the entrance to Chichester Harbour, on the eastern shores of Hayling Island, lies Sparkes Marina. One of two marinas in Chichester to have full tidal access, its facilities include 24-hour showers and toilets, a laundry room, an office/reception, and the Piranha Bar & Restaurant.

In addition to its berthing and marina services, Sparkes has many skilled professionals on site, including specialists in engineering, outboard engines, glass fibre repairs, rigging, sails and covers, marine carpentry, electrical, boat management and valeting. There is storage ashore for over 200 boats and a 40 ton mobile crane (lifting capacity 15 tons).

FACILITIES AT A GLANCE

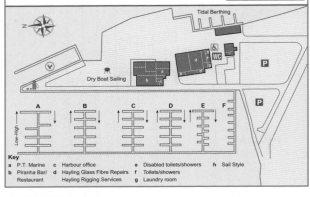

Key
a	P.T. Marine	c	Harbour office	h	Sail Style
b	Piranha Bar/	d	Hayling Glass Fibre Repairs		
	Restaurant		Hayling Rigging Services		
		e	Disabled toilets/showers		
		f	Toilets/showers		
		g	Laundry room		

NORTHNEY MARINA

Northney Marina
Northney Road, Hayling Island, Hampshire, PO11 0NH
Tel: 023 9246 6321 Fax: 023 9246 1467
Email: northney@mdlmarinas.co.uk
www.northneymarina.co.uk

VHF Ch 80
ACCESS H24

One of two marinas in Chichester Harbour to be accessible at all states of the tide, Northney Marina is on the northern shore of Hayling Island in the well marked Sweare Deep Channel, which branches off to port almost at the end of the Emsworth Channel.

Offering excellent boatyard facilities, the marina incorporates a provisions store and laundry area as well as fantastic ablution facilities plus wi-fi and 24/7 staff cover. There is also an events area for rallies.

FACILITIES AT A GLANCE

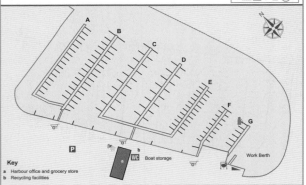

Key
a Harbour office and grocery store
b Recycling facilities

2

EMSWORTH YACHT HARBOUR

Emsworth Yacht Harbour Ltd
Thorney Road, Emsworth, Hants, PO10 8BP
Tel: 01243 377727 Fax: 01243 373432
Email: info@emsworth-marina.co.uk
www.emsworth-marina.co.uk

VHF	
ACCESS	HW±2

Accessible about one and a half to two hours either side of high water, Emsworth Yacht Harbour is a sheltered site, offering good facilities to yachtsmen.

Created in 1964 from a log pond, the marina is within easy walking distance of the pretty little town of Emsworth, which boasts at least 10 pubs, several high quality restaurants and two well-stocked convenience stores.

FACILITIES AT A GLANCE

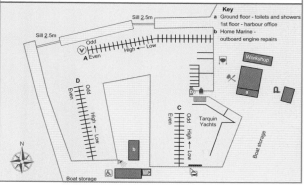

Key
a Ground floor - toilets and showers
   1st floor - harbour office
b Home Marine - outboard engine repairs

CHICHESTER MARINA

Chichester Marina
Birdham, Chichester, West Sussex, PO20 7EJ
Tel: 01243 512731 Fax: 01243 513472
Email: chichester@premiermarinas.com
www.premiermarinas.com

VHF	Ch 80
ACCESS	HW±5

Chichester Marina, nestling in an enormous natural harbour, has more than 1,000 berths, making it one of the largest in the UK. Its approach channel can be easily identified by the CM SHM pile. The channel was dredged to 0.5m below CD in 2004, giving access of around five hours either side of HW at springs. Besides the wide ranging marine facilities, there are also a restaurant and small convenience store on site. Chichester, which is only about a five minute bus or taxi ride away, has several places of interest, the most notable being the cathedral.

FACILITIES AT A GLANCE

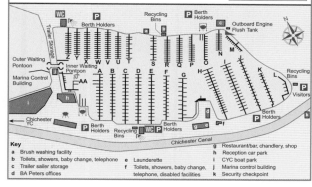

Key
a Brush washing facility
b Toilets, showers, baby change, telephone
c Trailer sailer storage
d BA Peters offices
e Launderette
f Toilets, showers, baby change, telephone, disabled facilities
g Restaurant/bar, chandlery, shop
h Reception car park
i CYC boat park
j Marina control building
k Security checkpoint

BIRDHAM POOL MARINA

Birdham Pool Marina
Birdham Pool, Chichester, Sussex
Tel: 01243 512310 Fax: 01243 513163
Email: info@birdhampool.co.uk www.birdhampool.co.uk

VHF	Ch 80
ACCESS	HW±3

Birdham Pool must be among Britain's most charming and rustic marinas. Its recently dredged channel allows access for up to four hours either side of HW via a lock. Any visiting yachtsman will not be disappointed by its unique and picturesque setting. The marina boasts a boatyard with skilled craftsmen offering a wide range of services as well as fuel. The channel is marked by green piles that should be left no more than 3m to starboard.

FACILITIES AT A GLANCE

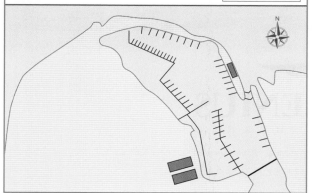

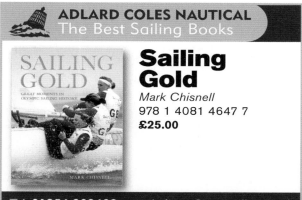

PANTAENIUS YACHT INSURANCE

Safety first. The same should apply for **you** and **your insurance** cover.

PANTAENIUS
Yacht Insurance

Germany · Great Britain* · Monaco · Denmark · Austria · Spain · Sweden · USA** · Australia

Plymouth · Phone +44 17 52 22 36 56

www.pantaenius.co.uk

*Pantaenius UK Limited is authorised and regulated by the Financial Services Authority (Authorised No. 308688)
**Pantaenius America Ltd. is a licensed insurance agent licensed in all 50 states. It is an independent corporation incorporated under the laws of New York and is a separate and distinct entity from any entity of the Pantaenius Group.

Key to Marina Plans symbols

Bottled gas		P	Parking
Chandler			Pub/Restaurant
Disabled facilities			Pump out
Electrical supply			Rigging service
Electrical repairs			Sail repairs
Engine repairs			Shipwright
First Aid			Shop/Supermarket
Fresh Water			Showers
Fuel - Diesel			Slipway
Fuel - Petrol		WC	Toilets
Hardstanding/boatyard			Telephone
Internet Café	@		Trolleys
Laundry facilities		V	Visitors berths
Lift-out facilities			Wi-Fi

Area 3 - South East England

MARINAS
Telephone Numbers
VHF Channel
Access Times

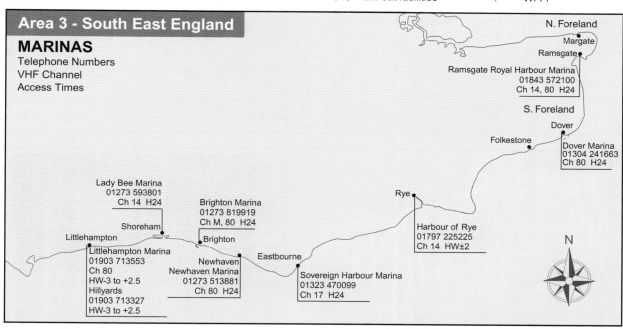

N. Foreland
Margate
Ramsgate
Ramsgate Royal Harbour Marina
01843 572100
Ch 14, 80 H24

S. Foreland

Dover
Folkestone
Dover Marina
01304 241663
Ch 80 H24

Lady Bee Marina
01273 593801
Ch 14 H24

Brighton Marina
01273 819919
Ch M, 80 H24

Shoreham

Rye

Harbour of Rye
01797 225225
Ch 14 HW±2

Littlehampton

Brighton

Littlehampton Marina
01903 713553
Ch 80
HW-3 to +2.5
Hillyards
01903 713327
HW-3 to +2.5

Newhaven
Newhaven Marina
01273 513881
Ch 80 H24

Eastbourne

Sovereign Harbour Marina
01323 470099
Ch 17 H24

N

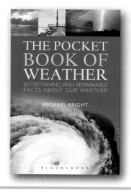
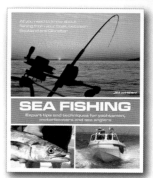

LITTLEHAMPTON MARINA

Littlehampton Marina
Ferry Road, Littlehampton, W Sussex
Tel: 01903 713553 Fax: 01903 732264
Email: sales@littlehamptonmarina.co.uk

VHF	Ch 80
ACCESS	HW-3 to +2.5

A typical English seaside town with funfair, promenade and fine sandy beaches, Littlehampton lies roughly midway between Brighton and Chichester at the mouth of the River Arun. It affords a convenient stopover for yachts either east or west bound, providing you have the right tidal conditions to cross the entrance bar with its charted depth of 0.7m. The marina lies about three cables above Town Quay and Fisherman's Quay, both of which are on the starboard side of the River Arun, and is accessed via a retractable footbridge that opens on request to the HM (note that you should contact him by 1630 the day before you require entry).

FACILITIES AT A GLANCE

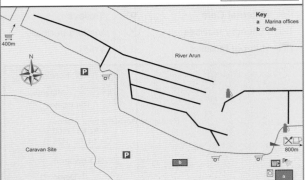

Key
a Marina offices
b Cafe

THE SHIPYARD

The Shipyard
Rope Walk, Littlehampton, West Sussex, BN17 5DG
Tel: 01903 713327
Email: info@littlehamptonshipyard.co.uk

VHF	
ACCESS	HW-3 to +2.5

Formerly Hillyards, The Shipyard is a full service boatyard with moorings and storage for up to 50 boats. Based on the south coast within easy reach of London and the main yachting centres of the UK and Europe, The Shipyard provides a comprehensive range of marine services.

The buildings of the boatyard are on the River Arun, a short distance from the English Channel. They provide the ideal conditions to accommodate and service craft up to 36m in length and with a maximum draft 3.5m. There is also craning services for craft up to 40 tons and the facilities to slip vessels up to 27m. In addition there are secure facilities to accommodate vessels up to 54m in dry dock.

FACILITIES AT A GLANCE

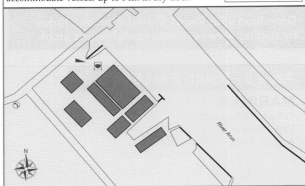

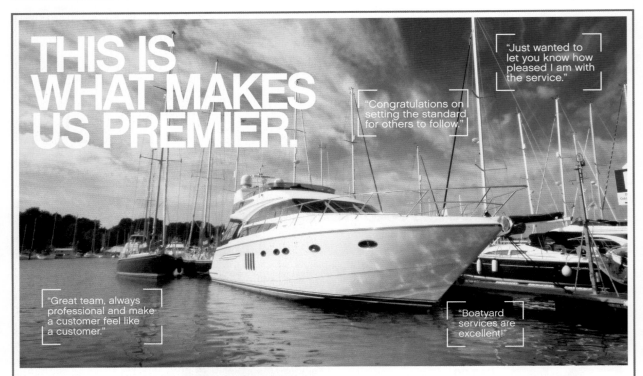

LADY BEE MARINA

**Lady Bee Marina
138-140 Albion Street, Southwick
West Sussex, BN42 4EG
Tel: 01273 593801 Fax: 01273 870349**

VHF Ch 14
ACCESS H24

Shoreham, only five miles west of Brighton, is one of the South Coast's major commercial ports handling, among other products, steel, grain, tarmac and timber. On first impressions it may seem that Shoreham has little to offer the visiting yachtsman, but once through the lock and into the eastern arm of the River Adur, the quiet Lady Bee Marina, with its Spanish waterside restaurant, can make this harbour an interesting alternative to the lively atmosphere of Brighton Marina. Run by the Harbour Office, the marina meets all the usual requirements, although fuel is available in cans from Southwick garage or from Corral's diesel pump situated in the western arm.

FACILITIES AT A GLANCE

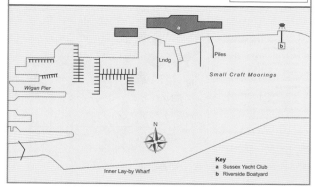

Key
a Sussex Yacht Club
b Riverside Boatyard

Wigan Pier
Lndg   Piles
Small Craft Moorings
Inner Lay-by Wharf
N

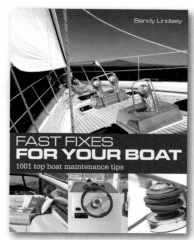
BRIGHTON MARINA

**Brighton Marina
West Jetty, Brighton, East Sussex, BN2 5UP
Tel: 01273 819919 Fax: 01273 675082
Email: brighton@premiermarinas.com
www.premiermarinas.com**

VHF Ch M, 80
ACCESS H24

Brighton Marina is the largest marina in the country and with its extensive range of shops, restaurants and facilities, is a popular and convenient stop-over for east and west-going passagemakers. Note, however, that it is not advisable to attempt entry in strong S to SE winds.

Only half a mile from the marina is the historic city of Brighton itself, renowned for being a cultural centre with a cosmopolitan atmosphere. Among its numerous attractions are the exotic Royal Pavilion, built for King George IV in the 1800s, and the Lanes, with its multitude of antiques shops.

FACILITIES AT A GLANCE

Key
a David Lloyd Heath & Fitness Club
b Bowling alley
c Casino/night club
d Multiplex cinema
e Yacht club
f Petrol station
g Mariners Quay
h Marina reception

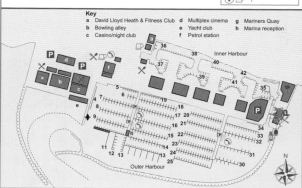

Inner Harbour
Outer Harbour
N

NEWHAVEN MARINA

Newhaven Marina
The Yacht Harbour, Fort Road, Newhaven
East Sussex, BN9 9BY
Tel: 01273 513881 Fax: 01273 510493
Email: john.stirling@seacontainers.com

VHF	Ch 80
ACCESS	H24

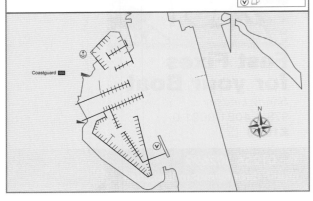

Some seven miles from Brighton, Newhaven lies at the mouth of the River Ouse. With its large fishing fleet and regular ferry services to Dieppe, the harbour has over the years become progressively commercial, therefore care is needed to keep clear of large vessels under manoeuvre. The marina lies approximately quarter of a mile from the harbour entrance on the west bank and was recently dredged to allow full tidal access except on LWS.

FACILITIES AT A GLANCE

SOVEREIGN HARBOUR MARINA

Sovereign Harbour Marina
Pacific Drive, Eastbourne, East Sussex, BN23 5BJ
Tel: 01323 470099 Fax: 01323 470077
Email: sovereignharbour@premiermarinas.com
www.premiermarinas.com

VHF	Ch 17
ACCESS	H24

Opened in 1993 and taken over by Premier Marinas in 2007, Sovereign Harbour is situated at the eastern end of Eastbourne and is accessible at all states of the tide and weather except for in strong NE to SE'ly winds. Entered via a lock at all times of the day or night, the Five Gold Anchor Award marina is part of one of the largest waterfront complexes in the UK, enjoying close proximity to shops, restaurants and a multiplex cinema. A short bus or taxi ride takes you to Eastbourne, where you will find shops and eating places to suit all tastes and budgets.

FACILITIES AT A GLANCE

Key
a   The Waterfront, shops, restaurants, pubs and offices
b   Harbour office - weather information and visitor's information
c   Cinema
d   Retail park - supermarket and post office
e   Restaurant
f   Toilets, showers, launderette and disabled facilities
g   24 hr fuel pontoon (diesel, petrol and holding tank pump out)
h   Recycling centre
i   Boatyard, boatpark, marine engineers, riggers and electricians
NB Berth numbering runs from low outer to high inner

HARBOUR OF RYE

Harbour of Rye
New Lydd Road, Camber, E Sussex, TN31 7QS
Tel: 01797 225225
Email: rye.harbour@environment-agency.gov.uk
www.environment-agency.gov.uk/harbourofrye

VHF	Ch 14
ACCESS	HW±2

The Strand Quay moorings are located in the centre of the historic town of Rye with all of its amenities a short walk away. The town caters for a wide variety of interests with the nearby Rye Harbour Nature Reserve, a museum, numerous antique shops and plentiful pubs, bars and restaurants. Vessels, up to a length of 15 metres, wishing to berth in the soft mud in or near the town of Rye should time their arrival at the entrance for not later than one hour after high water. Larger vessels should make prior arrangements with the Harbour Master. Fresh water, electricity, shower and toilet facilities are available.

FACILITIES AT A GLANCE

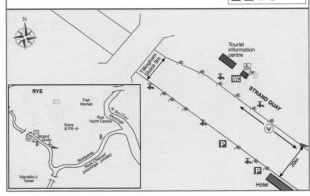

DOVER MARINA

Dover Harbour Board
Harbour House, Dover, Kent, CT17 9TF
Tel: 01304 241663 Fax: 01304 242549
Email: marina@doverport.co.uk www.doverport.co.uk/marina

VHF Ch 80
ACCESS H24

Nestling under the famous White Cliffs, Dover sits between South Foreland to the NE and Folkestone to the SW. Boasting a maritime history stretching back as far as the Bronze Age, Dover is today one of Britain's busiest commercial ports, with a continuous stream of ferries and cruise liners plying to and from their European destinations. However, over the past years the harbour has made itself more attractive to the cruising yachtsman, with the marina, set well away from the busy ferry terminal, offering three sheltered berthing options in the Tidal Harbour, Granville Dock and Wellington Dock.

FACILITIES AT A GLANCE

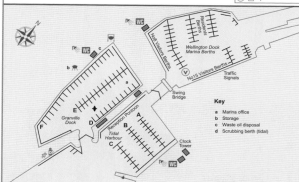

Key
a Marina office
b Storage
c Waste oil disposal
d Scrubbing berth (tidal)

ROYAL HARBOUR MARINA

Royal Harbour Marina, Ramsgate
Harbour Office, Military Road, Ramsgate, Kent, CT11 9LQ
Tel: 01843 572100 Fax: 01843 590941
Email: portoframsgate@thanet.gov.uk
www.portoframsgate.co.uk

VHF Ch 14, 80
ACCESS H24

Steeped in maritime history, Ramsgate was awarded 'Royal' status in 1821 by George IV in recognition of the warm welcome he received when sailing from Ramsgate to Hanover with the Royal Squadron. Offering good shelter and modern facilities, the Royal Harbour comprises an inner marina, entered approximately HW±2. Permission to enter or leave the Royal Harbour must be obtained from Port Control on channel 14 and berthing instructions can be obtained from the Dockmaster on channel 80.

FACILITIES AT A GLANCE

Key
a Harbour office
b Port Control (VHF 14)
c Dock office
d Showers/toilets laundry
e RNLI
f Dockmasters office
g Fuel barge (VHF 14)
h Museum

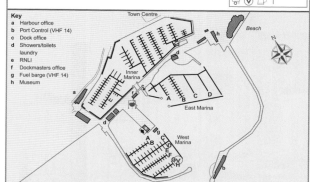

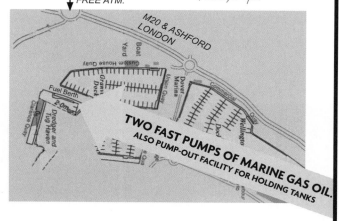

Port of Ramsgate

Royal Harbour Marina

SAIL IN & SEE US

Have you considered a permanent mooring at the Royal Harbour Marina, Ramsgate?

- Kent's premier marina offering safe mooring 365 days a year with superb facilities
- 24 hour security, CCTV and foot patrols
- 40 tonne boat hoist
- Good road access

Please visit our website at www.portoframsgate.co.uk for our fees and charges

Contact us on: 01843 572100 or email portoframsgate@thanet.gov.uk

Key to Marina Plans symbols

Bottled gas		P	Parking
Chandler			Pub/Restaurant
Disabled facilities			Pump out
Electrical supply			Rigging service
Electrical repairs			Sail repairs
Engine repairs			Shipwright
First Aid			Shop/Supermarket
Fresh Water			Showers
Fuel - Diesel			Slipway
Fuel - Petrol		WC	Toilets
Hardstanding/boatyard			Telephone
Internet Café			Trolleys
Laundry facilities		V	Visitors berths
Lift-out facilities			Wi-Fi

4

Area 4 - East England

MARINAS
Telephone Numbers, VHF Channel, Access Times

Gallions Pt Marina 020 7476 7054 Ch M, 80 HW±5
South Dock Marina 020 7252 2244 Ch M HW-2½ to +1½
Poplar Dock Marina 020 7308 9930 Ch 13 HW±1
St Katharine Haven 020 7264 5312 Ch 80 HW-2 to +1½
Chelsea Harbour 020 7225 9157 Ch 80 HW±1½
Brentford Dock Marina 020 8232 8941 HW±2½
Penton Hook Marina 01932 568681 Ch 80 H24
Windsor Marina 01753 853911 Ch 80 H24
Bray Marina 01628 623654 Ch 80 H24

Suffolk Yacht Hbr 01473 659240 Ch 80 H24
Royal Harwich YC Marina 01473 780319 Ch 77 H24
Woolverstone Marina 01473 780206 Ch 80 H24
Fox's Marina 01473 689111 Ch 80 H24
Neptune Marina 01473 215204 Ch M, 80 H24
Ipswich Haven Marina 01473 236644 Ch M, 68, 80 H24

Burnham Yacht Harbour 01621 782150 Ch 80 H24
Essex Marina 01702 258531 Ch 80 H24
Bridgemarsh Marina 01621 740414 Ch 80 HW±4
Fambridge Yacht Haven 01621 740370 Ch M, 80 H24

Limehouse Marina 020 7308 9930 Ch 80 HW±3

Hoo Marina 01634 250311 Ch 80 HW±3

Chatham Maritime Marina 01634 899200

Gt Yarmouth
Lowestoft
Royal Norfolk & Suffolk YC 01520 566726 Ch 14, 80 H24
Lowestoft Haven Marina 01520 580300 Ch M, 80 H24
Lowestoft Cruising Club 07913 391950, H24
Southwold
Shotley Marina 01473 788982 Ch 80 H24
Orford
Ipswich
Harwich
Titchmarsh Marina 01255 672185 Ch 80 HW±5
Walton Yacht Basin 01255 675873 Ch 80 HW-¾ to +¼
Bradwell Marina 01621 776235 Ch M, 80 HW±4½
Blackwater Marina 01621 740264 Ch M HW±2
Tollesbury Marina 01621 869202 Ch 80 HW±2
Heybridge Basin 01621 853506 Ch 80 HW±1
R Thames
N. Foreland
Gillingham Marina 01634 280022 Ch 80 HW±4½
Ramsgate

N

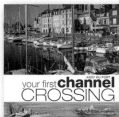

GILLINGHAM MARINA

Gillingham Marina
173 Pier Road, Gillingham, Kent, ME7 1UB
Tel: 01634 280022 Fax: 01634 280164
Email: berthing@gillingham-marina.co.uk
www.gillingham-marina.co.uk

VHF | Ch 80
ACCESS | HW±4.5

Gillingham Marina comprises a locked basin, accessible four and a half hours either side of high water, and a tidal basin upstream which can be entered approximately two hours either side of high water. Deep water moorings in the river cater for yachts arriving at other times.

Visiting yachts are usually accommodated in the locked basin, although it is best to contact the marina ahead of time. Lying on the south bank of the River Medway, the marina is approximately eight miles from Sheerness, at the mouth of the river, and five miles downstream of Rochester Bridge. Facilities include a well-stocked chandlery, brokerage and an extensive workshop.

FACILITIES AT A GLANCE

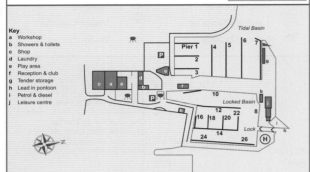

Key
a Workshop
b Showers & toilets
c Shop
d Laundry
e Play area
f Reception & club
g Tender storage
h Lead in pontoon
i Petrol & diesel
j Leisure centre

HOO MARINA

Hoo Marina
Vicarage Lane, Hoo, Rochester, Kent, ME3 9LE
Tel: 01634 250311 Fax: 01634 251761
Email: jcmarine@btconnect.com

VHF | Ch 80
ACCESS | HW±3

Hoo is a small village on the Isle of Grain, situated on a drying creek on the north bank of the River Medway approximately eight miles inland from Sheerness. Its marina was the first to be constructed on the East Coast and comprises finger berths supplied by all the usual services. It can be approached either straight across the mudflats near HW or, for a 1.5m draught, three hours either side of HW via a creek known locally as Orinoco. The entrance to this creek, which is marked by posts that must be left to port, is located a mile NW of Hoo Ness.

Grocery stores can be found either in the adjacent chalet park or else in Hoo Village, while the Hoo Ness Yacht Club welcomes visitors to its bar and restaurant. There are also frequent bus services to the nearby town of Rochester.

FACILITIES AT A GLANCE

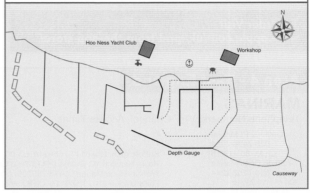

CHATHAM MARITIME MARINA

Chatham Maritime Marina, The Lock Building,
Leviathan Way, Chatham Maritime, Chatham, Medway, ME4 4LP
Tel: 01634 899200 Fax: 01634 899201
Email: chatham@mdlmarinas.co.uk www.marinas.co.uk

VHF Ch 80
ACCESS H24

Chatham Maritime Marina
is situated on the banks of
the River Medway in Kent,
providing an ideal location
from which to explore the
surrounding area. There are
plenty of secluded anchorages in
the lower reaches of the Medway
Estuary, while the river is
navigable for some 13 miles from
its mouth at Sheerness right up
to Rochester, and even beyond
for those yachts drawing less than 2m. Only 45
minutes from London by road, the marina is part of a
multi-million pound leisure and retail development,
currently accommodating 300 yachts.

FACILITIES AT A GLANCE

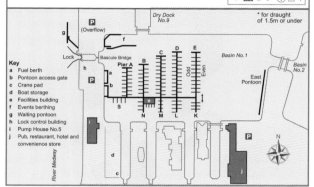

Key
a Fuel berth
b Pontoon access gate
c Crane pad
d Boat storage
e Facilities building
f Events berthing
g Waiting pontoon
h Lock control building
i Pump House No.5
j Pub, restaurant, hotel and
  convenience store

LIMEHOUSE MARINA

Limehouse Marina
46 Goodhart Place, London, E14 8EG
Tel: 020 7308 9930 Fax: 020 7363 0428
www.bwml.co.uk

VHF Ch 80
ACCESS HW±3

Limehouse Marina, situated
where the canal system
meets the Thames, is now
considered the 'Jewel in the
Crown' of the British inland
waterways network. With
complete access to 2,000 miles
of inland waterway systems
and with access to the Thames
at most stages of the tide
except around low water, the
marina provides a superb
location for river, canal and
sea-going pleasure craft alike. Boasting a wide
range of facilities and up to 90 berths, Limehouse
Marina is housed in the old Regent's Canal Dock.

FACILITIES AT A GLANCE

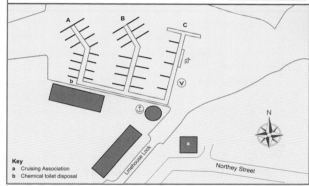

Key
a Cruising Association
b Chemical toilet disposal

THIS IS WHAT MAKES US PREMIER.

"We've sailed for
years, but never
had such good,
friendly and
helpful service."

"Great team, always
professional, make
a customer feel like
a customer."

GALLIONS POINT MARINA

Gallions Point Marina, Gate 14, Royal Albert Basin
Woolwich Manor Way, North Woolwich
London, E16 2QY. Tel: 020 7476 7054 Fax: 020 7474 7056
Email: info@gallionspointmarina.co.uk
www.gallionspointmarina.co.uk

VHF Ch M, 80
ACCESS HW±5

Gallions Point Marina
lies about 500 metres
down-stream of the
Woolwich Ferry
on the north side
of Gallions Reach.
Accessed via a lock
at the entrance to the
Royal Albert Basin,
the marina offers
deep water pontoon
berths as well as hard
standing. Future plans to improve facilities include
the development of a bar/restaurant, a chandlery
and an RYA tuition school.

FACILITIES AT A GLANCE

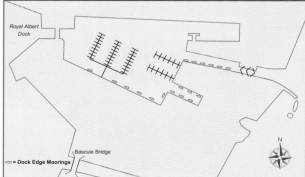

SOUTH DOCK MARINA

South Dock Marina
Rope Street, Off Plough Way
London, SE16 7SZ
Tel: 020 7252 2244 Fax: 020 7237 3806
Email: christopher.magro@southwark.gov.uk

VHF | Ch M
ACCESS | HW-2.5 to +1.5

South Dock Marina is housed in part of the old Surrey Dock complex on the south bank of the River Thames. Its locked entrance is immediately downstream of Greenland Pier, just a few miles down river of Tower Bridge. For yachts with a 2m draught, the lock can be entered HW-2½ to HW+1½ London Bridge, although if you arrive early there is a holding pontoon on the pier. The marina can be easily identified by the conspicuous arched rooftops of Baltic Quay, a luxury waterside apartment block. Once inside this secure, 200-berth marina, you can take full advantage of all its facilities as well as enjoy a range of restaurants and bars close by or visit historic maritime Greenwich.

FACILITIES AT A GLANCE

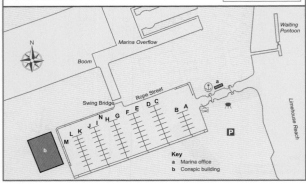

Key
a Marina office
b Conspic building

CHELSEA HARBOUR MARINA

Chelsea Harbour Marina
Estate Managements Office
C2-3 The Chambers, London, SW10 0XF
Tel: 07770 542783 Fax: 020 7352 7868
Email: harbourmaster@chelsea-harbour.co.uk

VHF |
ACCESS | HW±1.5

Chelsea Harbour is widely thought of as one of London's most significant maritime sites. It is located in the heart of SW London, therefore enjoying easy access to the amenities of Chelsea and the West End. On site is the Chelsea Harbour Design Centre, where 80 showrooms exhibit the best in British and International interior design, offering superb waterside views along with excellent cuisine in the Wyndham Grand.

The harbour lies approximately 48 miles up river from Sea Reach No 1 buoy in the Thames Estuary and is accessed via the Thames Flood Barrier in Woolwich Reach. With its basin gate operating one and a half hours either side of HW (+ 20 minutes at London Bridge), the marina welcomes visiting yachtsmen.

FACILITIES AT A GLANCE

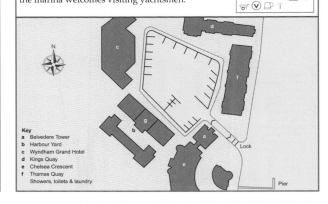

Key
a Belvedere Tower
b Harbour Yard
c Wyndham Grand Hotel
d Kings Quay
e Chelsea Crescent
f Thames Quay
Showers, toilets & laundry

ST KATHARINE DOCKS

St Katharine's Marina Ltd
50 St Katharine's Way, London, E1W 1LA
Tel: 020 7264 5312 Fax: 020 7702 2252
Email: marina.reception@skdocks.co.uk
www.skdocks.co.uk

VHF | Ch 80
ACCESS | HW -2 to +1.5

St Katharine's Marina is a 160 berth full service marina located in central London next to Tower Bridge.

St Katharine Docks is a unique marina benefiting from waterside dining, boutique shops and excellent transport links to the West End. Visitors are welcomed all year round and the marina provides its own calendar of events details of which can be found on the website and social media pages.

The marina is ideally situated for visiting the Tower of London, Tower Bridge, *HMS Belfast* and the City of London all of which can be reached on foot. A short river bus service away is Greenwich and the Cutty Sark and to the west the Shard and London Eye.

FACILITIES AT A GLANCE

Key
a Ivory House
b Dickens Inn
c Marina office
d Tower Hotel

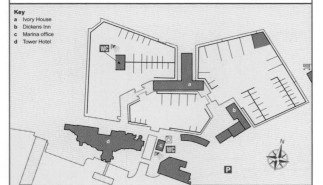

BRENTFORD DOCK MARINA

Brentford Dock Marina
2 Justin Close, Brentford, Middlesex, TW8 8QE
Tel: 020 8232 8941 Mob: 07970 143 987
E-mail: brentforddockmarina@gmail.com

VHF |
ACCESS | HW±2.5

Brentford Dock Marina is situated on the River Thames at the junction with the Grand Union Canal. Its hydraulic lock is accessible for up to two and a half hours either side of high water, although boats over 9.5m LOA enter on high water by prior arrangement. There is a grocery store on site. The main attractions within the area are the Royal Botanic Gardens at Kew and the Kew Bridge Steam Museum at Brentford.

FACILITIES AT A GLANCE

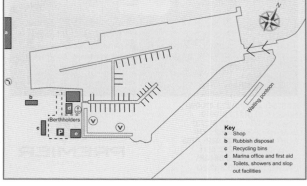

Key
a Shop
b Rubbish disposal
c Recycling bins
d Marina office and first aid
e Toilets, showers and slop out facilities

PENTON HOOK MARINA

Penton Hook Marina
Staines Road, Chertsey, Surrey, KT16 8PY
Tel: 01932 568681 Fax: 01932 567423
Email: pentonhook@mdlmarinas.co.uk
www.marinas.co.uk

VHF Ch 80
ACCESS H24

Penton Hook, the largest inland marina in Europe, is situated on what is considered to be one of the most attractive reaches of the River Thames; close to Chertsey and about a mile downstream of Runnymede.

Providing unrestricted access to the River Thames through a deep water channel below Penton Hook Lock, the marina can accommodate ocean-going craft of up to 30m LOA and is ideally placed for a visit to Thorpe Park, reputedly one of the country's most popular family leisure attractions.

FACILITIES AT A GLANCE

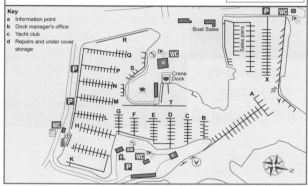

Key
a   Information point
b   Dock manager's office
c   Yacht club
d   Repairs and under cover storage

WINDSOR MARINA

Windsor Marina
Maidenhead Road, Windsor
Berkshire, SL4 5TZ
Tel: 01753 853911
Email: windsor@mdlmarinas.co.uk www.marinas.co.uk

VHF Ch 80
ACCESS H24

Situated on the outskirts of Windsor town on the south bank of the River Thames, Windsor Marina enjoys a peaceful garden setting. On site is the Windsor Yacht Club and fuel (diesel and petrol), enabling you to fill up as and when you need.

A trip to the town of Windsor, comprising beautiful Georgian and Victorian buildings, would not be complete without a visit to Windsor Castle. With its construction inaugurated over 900 years ago by William the Conqueror, it is the oldest inhabited castle in the world and accommodates a priceless art and furniture collection.

FACILITIES AT A GLANCE

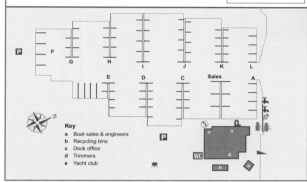

Key
a   Boat sales & engineers
b   Recycling bins
c   Dock office
d   Trimmers
e   Yacht club

4

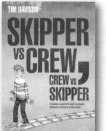

BRAY MARINA

Bray Marina
Monkey Island Lane, Bray
Berkshire, SL6 2EB
Tel: 01628 623654 Fax: 01628 773485
Email: bray@mdlmarinas.co.uk www.marinas.co.uk

VHF Ch 80
ACCESS H24

Bray Marina is situated in a country park setting among shady trees, providing berth holders with a delightfully tranquil mooring. From the marina there is direct access to the Thames and there are extensive well-maintained facilities available for all boat owners. Also on site is the highly acclaimed Riverside Brasserie. Twice winner of the AA rosette award for culinary excellence and short-listed for the Tatler best country restaurant, the Brasserie is especially popular with Club Outlook members who enjoy a 15% discount. The 400-berth marina boasts an active club, which holds social functions as well as boat training lessons and handling competitions, a small chandlery and engineering services.

FACILITIES AT A GLANCE

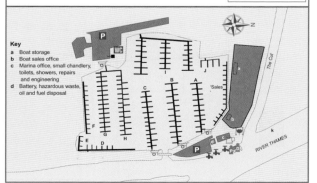

Key
a   Boat storage
b   Boat sales office
c   Marina office, small chandlery, toilets, showers, repairs and engineering
d   Battery, hazardous waste, oil and fuel disposal

BURNHAM YACHT HARBOUR MARINA

Burnham Yacht Harbour Marina Ltd
Burnham-on-Crouch, Essex, CM0 8BL
Tel: 01621 782150 Fax: 01621 785848
Email: admin@burnhamyachtharbour.co.uk

VHF	Ch 80
ACCESS	H24

Boasting four major yacht clubs, each with comprehensive racing programmes, Burnham-on-Crouch has come to be regarded by some as 'the Cowes of the East Coast'. At the western end of the town lies Burnham Yacht Harbour, dredged 2.2m below datum. Offering a variety of on site facilities, its entrance can be easily identified by a yellow pillar buoy with an 'X' topmark.

The historic town, with its 'weatherboard' and early brick buildings, elegant quayside and scenic riverside walks, exudes plenty of charm. Among its attractions are a sports centre, a railway museum and a two-screen cinema.

FACILITIES AT A GLANCE

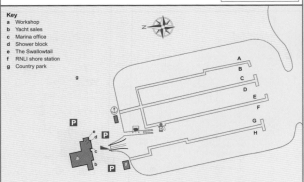

Key
a Workshop
b Yacht sales
c Marina office
d Shower block
e The Swallowtail
f RNLI shore station
g Country park

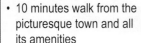

ESSEX MARINA

Essex Marina
Wallasea Island, Essex, SS4 2HF
Tel: 01702 258531 Fax: 01702 258227
Email: info@essexmarina.co.uk
www.essexmarina.co.uk

VHF	Ch 80
ACCESS	H24

Surrounded by beautiful countryside, Essex Marina is situated in Wallasea Bay, about half a mile up river of Burnham on Crouch. Boasting 500 deep water berths, including 50 swinging moorings, the marina can be accessed at all states of the tide. On site are a 70 ton boat hoist, a chandlery and brokerage service as well as the Essex Marina Yacht Club.

Buses run frequently to Southend-on-Sea, just seven miles away, while a ferry service takes passengers across the river on weekends to Burnham, where you will find numerous shops and restaurants.

FACILITIES AT A GLANCE

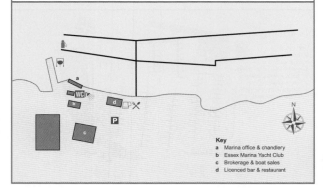

Key
a Marina office & chandlery
b Essex Marina Yacht Club
c Brokerage & boat sales
d Licenced bar & restaurant

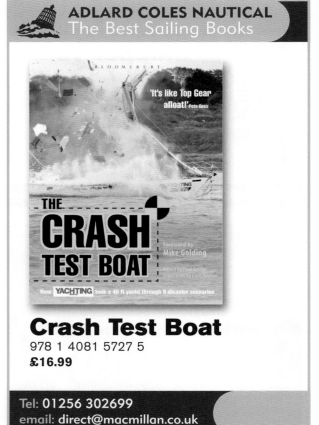

BRIDGEMARSH MARINA

Bridgemarsh Marine
Fairholme, Bridge Marsh Lane, Althorne, Essex
Tel: 01621 740414 Mobile: 07968 696815 Fax: 01621 742216

VHF Ch 80
ACCESS HW±4

On the north side of Bridgemarsh Island, just beyond Essex Marina on the River Crouch, lies Althorne Creek. Here Bridgemarsh Marine accommodates over 100 boats berthed alongside pontoons supplied with water and electricity. A red beacon marks the entrance to the creek, with red can buoys identifying the approach channel into the marina. Accessible four hours either side of high water, the marina has an on site yard with two docks, a slipway and crane. The village of Althorne is just a short walk away, from where there are direct train services (taking approximately one hour) to London.

FACILITIES AT A GLANCE

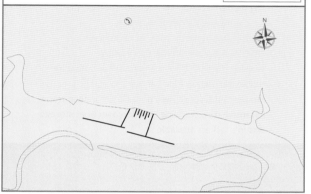

HEYBRIDGE BASIN

Heybridge Basin
Lock Hill, Heybridge Basin, Maldon, Essex, CM9 4RY
Tel: 01621 853506
Email: martin.maudsley@waterways.org.uk
www.essexwaterways.com

VHF Ch 80
ACCESS HW±1

Towards the head of the River Blackwater, not far from Maldon, lies Heybridge Basin. Situated at the lower end of the 14–mile long Chelmer and Blackwater Navigation Canal, it can be reached via a lock about one hour either side of HW for a yacht drawing around 2m. If you arrive too early, there is good holding ground in the river just outside the lock. Incorporating as many as 200 berths, the basin has a range of facilities, including shower and laundry amenities. It is strongly recommendedthat you book 24 hours in advance for summer weekends.

FACILITIES AT A GLANCE

4

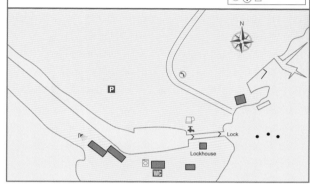

BRADWELL MARINA

Bradwell Marina, Port Flair Ltd, Waterside
Bradwell-on-Sea, Essex, CM0 7RB
Tel: 01621 776235 Fax: 01621 776393
Email: info@bradwellmarina.com
www.bradwellmarina.com

VHF Ch M, 80
ACCESS HW±4.5

Opened in 1984, Bradwell is a privately-owned marina situated in the mouth of the River Blackwater, serving as a convenient base from which to explore the Essex coastline or as a departure point for cruising further afield to Holland and Belgium.

The yacht basin can be accessed four and a half hours either side of HW and offers plenty of protection from all wind directions. With a total of 300 fully serviced berths, generous space has been allocated for manoeuvring between pontoons. Overlooking the marina is Bradwell Club House, incorporating a bar, restaurant, launderette and ablution facilities.

FACILITIES AT A GLANCE

Key
a Clubhouse
b Tower office

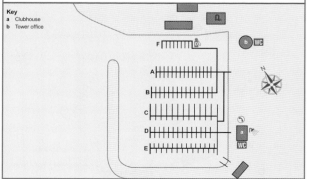

FAMBRIDGE YACHT HAVEN

**Fambridge Yacht Haven
Church Road, North Fambridge, Essex, CM3 6LR
Tel: 01621 740370 Fax: 01621 742359
Email: fambridge@yachthavens.com www.yachthavens.com**

VHF	Ch M, 80
ACCESS	H24

Just under a mile upstream of North Fambridge, Stow Creek branches off to the north of the River Crouch. The creek, marked with occasional starboard hand buoys and leading lights, leads to the entrance to Fambridge Yacht Haven, which enjoys an unspoilt, tranquil setting between saltings and farmland. Home to West Wick Yacht Club, the marina has 220 berths and can accommodate vessels up to 17m LOA.

The nearby village of North Fambridge features the Ferryboat Inn, a favourite haunt with the boating fraternity. Only six miles down river lies Burnham-on-Crouch, while the Essex and Kent coasts are within easy sailing distance.

FACILITIES AT A GLANCE

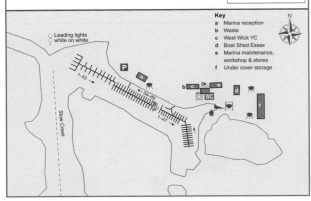

Key
a Marina reception
b Waste
c West Wick YC
d Boat Shed Essex
e Marina maintenance, workshop & stores
f Under cover storage

BLACKWATER MARINA

**Blackwater Marina
Marine Parade, Maylandsea, Essex
Tel: 01621 740264
Email: info@blackwater-marina.co.uk**

VHF	Ch M
ACCESS	HW±2

Blackwater Marina is a place where families in day boats mix with Smack owners and yacht crews; here seals, avocets and porpoises roam beneath the big, sheltering East Coast skies and here the area's rich heritage of working Thames Barges and Smacks remains part of daily life today.

But it isn't just classic sailing boats that thrive on the Blackwater. An eclectic mix of motor cruisers, open boats and modern yachts enjoy the advantages of a marina sheltered by its natural habitat, where the absence of harbour walls allows uninterrupted views of some of Britain's rarest wildlife and where the 21st century shoreside facilities are looked after by experienced professionals, who are often found sailing on their days off.

FACILITIES AT A GLANCE

Key
a Maylandsea Bay YC
b Harlow (Blackwater) Sailing Club
c Marina office

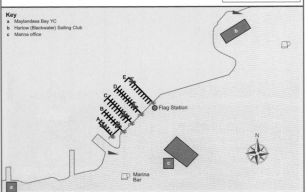

TOLLESBURY MARINA

**Tollesbury Marina
The Yacht Harbour, Tollesbury, Essex, CM9 8SE
Tel: 01621 869202 Fax: 01621 868489
email: marina@woodrolfe.com www.woodrolfe.com**

VHF	Ch 80
ACCESS	HW±2

Tollesbury Marina lies at the mouth of the River Blackwater in the heart of the Essex countryside. Within easy access from London and the Home Counties, it has been designed as a leisure centre for the whole family, with on-site activities comprising tennis courts and a covered heated swimming pool as well as a convivial bar and restaurant. Accommodating over 240 boats, the marina can be accessed two hours either side of HW and is ideally situated for those wishing to explore the River Crouch to the south and the Rivers Colne, Orwell and Deben to the north.

FACILITIES AT A GLANCE

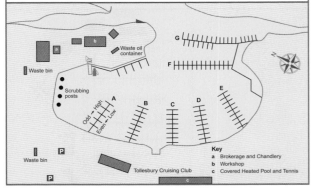

Key
a Brokerage and Chandlery
b Workshop
c Covered Heated Pool and Tennis

TITCHMARSH MARINA

Titchmarsh Marina Ltd
Coles Lane, Walton on the Naze, Essex, CO14 8SL
Tel: 01255 672185 Fax: 01255 851901
Email: info@titchmarshmarina.co.uk
www.titchmarshmarina.co.uk

VHF	Ch 80
ACCESS	HW±5

Titchmarsh Marina sits on the south side of The Twizzle in the heart of the Walton Backwaters. As the area is designated as a 'wetland of international importance', the marina has been designed and developed to function as a natural harbour. The 420 berths are well sheltered by the high-grassed clay banks, offering good protection in all conditions. Access to Titchmarsh is over a sill, which has a depth of about 1m at LWS, but once inside the basin, the depth increases to around 2m. Among the excellent facilities on site are the well stocked Marinestore Chandlery and Harbour Lights Restaurant & Bar serving carvery meals daily.

FACILITIES AT A GLANCE

Key
a Harbour master, chandlery (+ cycle hire marine engineers, marine electronics
b Hardstanding
c Harbour Lights - restaurant and bar

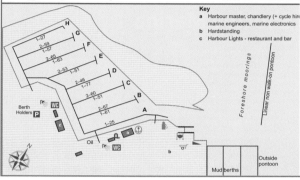

4

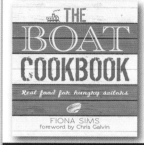
WALTON YACHT BASIN

Walton and Frinton Yacht Trust
Mill Lane, Walton on the Naze, CO14 8PF
Managed by Bedwell & Co Tel: 01255 675873
Fax: 01255 677405 After hours Tel: 01255 672655

VHF	
ACCESS	HW-0.75,HW+0.25

Walton Yacht Basin lies at the head of Walton Creek, an area made famous in Arthur Ransome's *Swallows & Amazons* and *Secret Waters*. The creek can only be navigated two hours either side of HW, although yachts heading for the Yacht Basin should arrive on a rising tide as the entrance gate is kept shut once the tide turns in order to retain the water inside. Before entering the gate, moor up against the Club Quay to enquire about berthing availability.

A short walk away is the popular seaside town of Walton, full of shops, pubs and restaurants. Its focal point is the pier which, overlooking superb sandy beaches, offers various attractions including a ten-pin bowling alley. Slightly further out of town, the Naze affords pleasant coastal walks with striking panoramic views.

FACILITIES AT A GLANCE

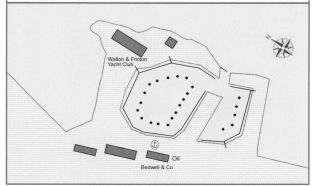

SUFFOLK YACHT HARBOUR

Suffolk Yacht Harbour Ltd
Levington, Ipswich, Suffolk, IP10 0LN
Tel: 01473 659240 Fax: 01473 659632
Email: info@syharbour.co.uk
www.syharbour.co.uk

VHF	Ch 80
ACCESS	H24

A friendly, independently-run marina on the East Coast of England, Suffolk Yacht Harbour enjoys a beautiful rural setting on the River Orwell, yet is within easy access of Ipswich, Woodbridge and Felixstowe. With approximately 500 berths, the marina offers extensive facilities while the Haven Ports Yacht Club provides a bar and restaurant.

FACILITIES AT A GLANCE

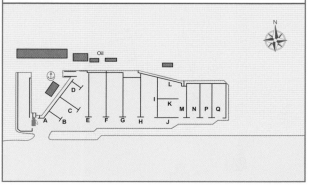

SHOTLEY MARINA

Shotley Marina Ltd
Shotley Gate, Ipswich, Suffolk, IP9 1QJ
Tel: 01473 788982 Fax: 01473 788868
Email: sales@shotleymarina.co.uk
www.shotleymarina.co.uk www.eastcoastmarinas.co.uk

VHF	Ch 80
ACCESS	H24

Based in the well protected Harwich Harbour where the River Stour joins the River Orwell, Shotley Marina is only eight miles from the county town of Ipswich. Entered via a lock at all states of the tide, its first class facilities include extensive boat repair and maintenance services as well as a well-stocked chandlery and on site bar and restaurant. The marina is strategically placed for sailing up the Stour to Manningtree, up the Orwell to Pin Mill or exploring the Rivers Deben, Crouch and Blackwater as well as the Walton Backwaters.

FACILITIES AT A GLANCE

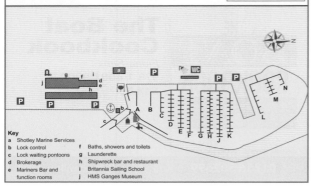

Key

a Shotley Marine Services
b Lock control
c Lock waiting pontoons
d Brokerage
e Mariners Bar and function rooms
f Baths, showers and toilets
g Launderette
h Shipwreck bar and restaurant
i Britannia Sailing School
j HMS Ganges Museum

ROYAL HARWICH YACHT CLUB MARINA

Royal Harwich Yacht Club Marina
Marina Road, Woolverstone, Suffolk, IP9 1BA
Tel: 01473 780319 Fax: 01473 780919
www.rhyc.demon.co.uk
Email: secretary@rhyc.demon.co.uk

VHF	Ch 77
ACCESS	H24

This 54 berth marina is ideally situated at a mid point on the Orwell between Levington and Ipswich. The facility is owned and run by the Royal Harwich Yacht Club and enjoys a full catering and bar service in the Clubhouse. The marina benefits from full tidal access, and can accommodate yachts up to 14.5m on the hammerhead. Within the immediate surrounds, there are boat repair services, and a well stocked chandlery. The marina is situated a mile's walk from the world famous Pin Mill and is a favoured destination with visitors from Holland, Belgium and Germany. The marina welcomes racing yachts and cruisers, and is able to accommodate multiple bookings.

FACILITIES AT A GLANCE

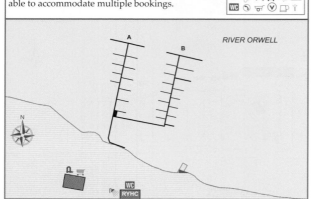

RIVER ORWELL

WOOLVERSTONE MARINA

Woolverstone Marina
Woolverstone, Ipswich, Suffolk, IP9 1AS
Tel: 01473 780206 Fax: 01473 780273
Email: woolverstone@mdlmarinas.co.uk www.marinas.co.uk

VHF	Ch 80
ACCESS	H24

Set in 22 acres of parkland, within close proximity to the Royal Harwich Yacht Club, Woolverstone Marina boasts 235 pontoon berths as well as 110 swinging moorings, all of which are served by a water taxi. Besides boat repair services, an on-site chandlery and excellent ablution facilities, the marina also incorporates a yacht brokerage and the Buttermans bar and restaurant, which overlooks the river and serves fine food using fresh local produce.

Woolverstone's location on the scenic R. Orwell makes it ideally placed for exploring the various cruising grounds along the East Coast, including the adjacent R. Stour, the Colne and Blackwater estuaries to the south and the R. Deben to the north.

FACILITIES AT A GLANCE

Key

a Marina office, toilets, showers, launderette and boat sales
b Buttermans Bar Restaurant
c Royal Harwich Yacht Club

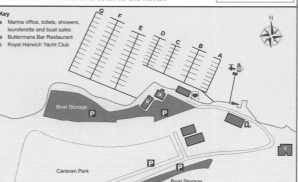

Boat Storage

Caravan Park

Boat Storage

PANTAENIUS YACHT INSURANCE

Safety first. The same should apply for **you** and **your insurance** cover.

PANTAENIUS
Yacht Insurance

Germany · Great Britain* · Monaco · Denmark · Austria · Spain · Sweden · USA** · Australia

Plymouth · Phone +44 17 52 22 36 56

www.pantaenius.co.uk

FOX'S MARINA

Fox's Marina & Boatyard
The Strand, Ipswich, Suffolk, IP2 8SA
Tel: 01473 689111 Fax: 01473 601737
Email: foxs@foxsmarina.com www.foxsmarina.com

VHF	Ch 80
ACCESS	H24

Located on the picturesque River Orwell, Fox's provides good shelter in all conditions and access at all states of tide. 100 pontoon berths and ashore storage for 200 vessels. A 70 tonne hoist provides the ability to handle boats up to 80ft in length.

The on-site chandlery is the largest on the east coast with a prominent position overlooking the marina. Fox's offer a full range of in-house boatyard services and with 10,000 sq ft of heated workshop space are specialists in repairs and refits of sailing yachts and motor boats. Other service on hand include experienced riggers and electronics engineers as well as marine engineers, and custom fabrication of stainless steel.

There are regular bus services to Ipswich, which is only about one to two miles away.

FACILITIES AT A GLANCE

Key
a Chandlery
b Harbourmaster office
c Yacht Club

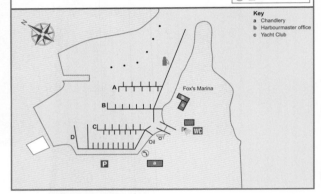

NEPTUNE MARINA

Neptune Marina Ltd
Neptune Quay, Ipswich, IP4 1QJ
Tel: 01473 215204 Fax: 01473 215206
Email: enquiries@neptune-marina.com

VHF	Ch M, 80
ACCESS	H±2.5

The Wet Dock at Ipswich, which was opened in 1850, became the largest in Europe and was in use right up until the 1930s. Now the dock incorporates Neptune Marina, situated at Neptune Quay on the Historic Waterfront, and ever increasing shoreside developments. This 26-acre dock is accessible through a 24-hr lock gate, with a waiting pontoon outside. The town centre is a 10 minute walk away, while Cardinal Park, a relatively new complex housing an 11-screen cinema and several eating places, is nearby. There are also a number of other excellent restaurants along the quayside and adjacent to the Marina. The Neptune Marina building occupies an imposing position in the NE corner of the dock with quality coffee shop and associated retail units.

FACILITIES AT A GLANCE

Key
a Old Custom House
b Conference centre
c Floating French restaurant
d Bistro
e Bellway apartments
f Neptune Marina office & facilities
g Marina storage yard

IPSWICH HAVEN MARINA

Ipswich Haven Marina
Associated British Ports
New Cut East, Ipswich, Suffolk, IP3 0EA
Tel: 01473 236644 Fax: 01473 236645
Email: ipswichhaven@abports.co.uk

VHF	Ch M, 68 & 80
ACCESS	H24

Lying at the heart of Ipswich, the Haven Marina enjoys close proximity to all the bustling shopping centres, restaurants, cinemas and museums that this County Town of Suffolk has to offer. The main railway station is only a 10-minute walk away, where there are regular connections to London, Cambridge and Norwich, all taking just over an hour to get to.

Within easy reach of Holland, Belgium and Germany, East Anglia is proving an increasingly popular cruising ground. The River Orwell, displaying breathtaking scenery, was voted one of the most beautiful rivers in Britain by the RYA.

FACILITIES AT A GLANCE

Boat Sales

Storage

Key
a Toilets, showers, laundry, office
b Licensed bistro
c R&J Marine Electronics
d Boat sales
e Fairline PDI Shed
f Future restaurant retail
g Burton Waters Repair Shop

HAMILTON DOCK

Hamilton Dock, c/o Lowestoft Haven Marina
School Road, Lowestoft, Suffolk, NR33 9NB
Tel: 01502 580300 Fax: 01502 581851
Email: lowestofhaven@abports.co.uk
www.lowestofthavenmarina.co.uk

VHF   Ch M, 80
ACCESS   H24

Lowestoft Haven Marina's Hamilton Dock is based in an old fish dock in the outer harbour and offers easy access to the open sea making it an ideal overnight location, whilst its in town position means all the facilities of the town centre are at your doorstep.

The marina's 47 berths can accommodate vessels from 10–28m and is especially geared up for club bookings. It offers a full range of modern facilities and is complimented by the main marina at School Road for boatyard facilities.

FACILITIES AT A GLANCE

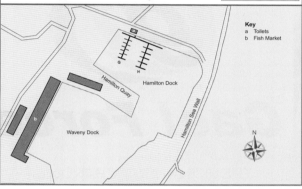

Key
a   Toilets
b   Fish Market

LOWESTOFT HAVEN MARINA

Lowestoft Haven Marina
School Road, Lowestoft, Suffolk, NR33 9NB
Tel: 01502 580300 Fax: 01502 581851
Email: lowestofhaven@abports.co.uk
www.lowestofthavenmarina.co.uk

VHF   Ch M, 80
ACCESS   H24

Lowestoft Haven Marina is based on Lake Lothing with easy access to both the open sea and the Norfolk Broads. The town centres of both Lowestoft and Oulton Broad are within a short distance of the marina.

The marina's 140 berths can accommodate vessels from 7–20m. Offering a full range of modern facilities the marina welcomes all visitors.

FACILITIES AT A GLANCE

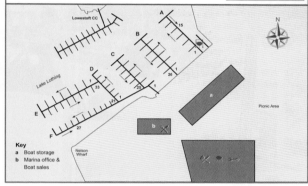

Key
a   Boat storage
b   Marina office & Boat sales

ROYAL NORFOLK & SUFFOLK YACHT CLUB

Royal Norfolk and Suffolk Yacht Club
Royal Plain, Lowestoft, Suffolk, NR33 0AQ
Tel: 01502 566726 Fax: 01502 5521735
Email: admin@rnsyc.org.uk www.msyc.net

VHF   Ch 14, 80
ACCESS   H24

With its entrance at the inner end of the South Pier, opposite the Trawl Basin on the north bank, the Royal Norfolk and Suffolk Yacht Club marina occupies a sheltered position in Lowestoft Harbour. Lowestoft has always been an appealing destination to yachtsmen due to the fact that it can be accessed

at any state of the tide, 24 hours a day. Note, however, that conditions just outside the entrance can get pretty lively when the wind is against tide. The clubhouse is enclosed in an impressive Grade 2 listed building overlooking the marina and its facilities include a bar and restaurant as well as a formal dining room with a full *à la carte* menu.

FACILITIES AT A GLANCE

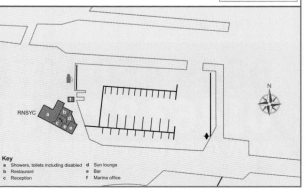

Key
a   Showers, toilets including disabled   d   Sun lounge
b   Restaurant   e   Bar
c   Reception   f   Marina office

LOWESTOFT CRUISING CLUB

Lowestoft Cruising Club
Off Harbour Road, Oulton Broad, Lowestoft, Suffolk, NR32 3LY
Tel: 07913 391950
www.lowestoftcruisingclub.co.uk

VHF
ACCESS   H24

Lowestoft Cruising Club welcomes visitors and can offer a friendly atmosphere, some of the finest moorings and at very competitive rates. Whatever the weather, these moorings provide a calm, safe haven for visiting yachts and with the Mutford lock only 250 metres away, easy access onto the Norfolk and Suffolk

Broads. Facilities include electricity and water, plus excellent showers, toilets and secure car parking. These moorings are the nearest ones to the railway stations (to Norwich and Ipswich), bus routes, shops, banks, pubs and restaurants in Oulton Broad.

FACILITIES AT A GLANCE

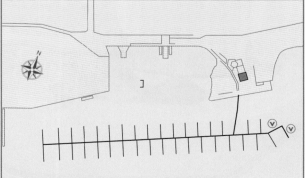

Key to Marina Plans symbols

ä	Bottled gas	P	Parking
Ⓐ	Chandler	✕	Pub/Restaurant
♿	Disabled facilities	⚓	Pump out
⚡	Electrical supply		Rigging service
⚡	Electrical repairs		Sail repairs
⚙	Engine repairs	✂	Shipwright
✚	First Aid	🛒	Shop/Supermarket
⚓	Fresh Water		Showers
D	Fuel - Diesel	▶	Slipway
P	Fuel - Petrol	WC	Toilets
🛠	Hardstanding/boatyard	☎	Telephone
@	Internet Café	🛒	Trolleys
▣	Laundry facilities	Ⓥ	Visitors berths
⚓	Lift-out facilities	Ⓨ	Wi-Fi

Area 5 - North East England **5**

MARINAS
Telephone Numbers
VHF Channel
Access Times

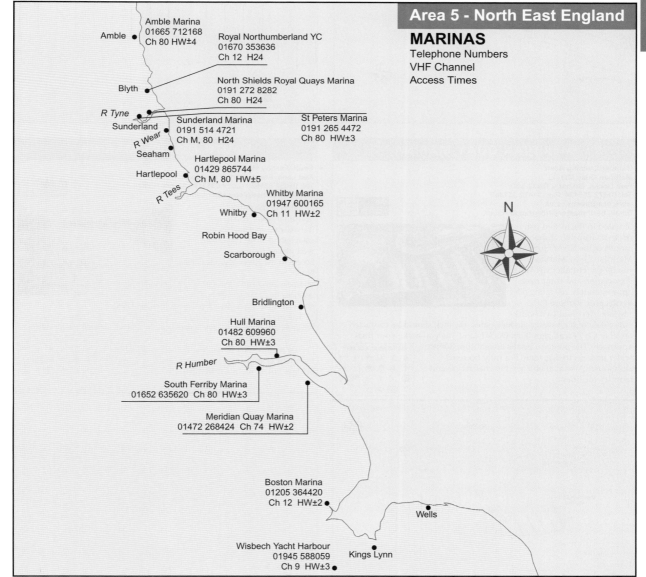

Amble Marina
01665 712168
Ch 80 HW±4

Amble

Royal Northumberland YC
01670 353636
Ch 12 H24

Blyth

North Shields Royal Quays Marina
0191 272 8282
Ch 80 H24

R Tyne

Sunderland Marina
0191 514 4721
Ch M, 80 H24

St Peters Marina
0191 265 4472
Ch 80 HW±3

Sunderland

R Wear

Seaham

Hartlepool Marina
01429 865744
Ch M, 80 HW±5

Hartlepool

R Tees

Whitby Marina
01947 600165
Ch 11 HW±2

Whitby

Robin Hood Bay

Scarborough

Bridlington

Hull Marina
01482 609960
Ch 80 HW±3

R Humber

South Ferriby Marina
01652 635620 Ch 80 HW±3

Meridian Quay Marina
01472 268424 Ch 74 HW±2

Boston Marina
01205 364420
Ch 12 HW±2

Wells

Wisbech Yacht Harbour
01945 588059
Ch 9 HW±3

Kings Lynn

N

WISBECH YACHT HARBOUR

Wisbech Yacht Harbour
Harbour Master, Harbour Office, Dock Cottage
Wisbech, Cambridgeshire PE13 3JJ
Tel: 01945 588059 Fax: 01945 580589
Email: cdorrington@fenland.gov.uk www.fenland.gov.uk

VHF Ch 9
ACCESS HW±3

Regarded as the capital of the English Fens, Wisbech is situated about 25 miles north east of Peterborough and is a market town of considerable character and historical significance. Rows of elegant houses line the banks of the River Nene, with the North and South Brink still deemed two of the finest Georgian streets in England.

Wisbech Yacht Harbour, linking Cambridgeshire with the sea, is proving increasingly popular as a haven for small craft, despite the busy commercial shipping. In recent years the facilities have been developed and improved upon and the HM is always on hand to help with passage planning both up or downstream.

FACILITIES AT A GLANCE

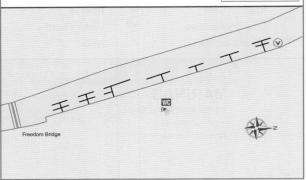
Freedom Bridge

BOSTON MARINA

Boston Marina
5/7 Witham Bank East, Boston, Lincs, PE21 9JU
Tel: 01205 364420 Fax: 01205 364420
Email: bostonmarina@5witham.fsnet www.bostonmarina.net

VHF Ch 12
ACCESS H±2

Boston Marina, located near Boston Grand Sluice in Lincolnshire, is an ideal location for both seagoing vessels and for river boats wanting to explore the heart of the Fens. The on site facilities include a fully-stocked chandlery and brokerage service, while nearby is the well-established and recently refurbished Witham bar and restaurant.

The old maritime port of Boston has numerous modern-day and historical attractions, one of the most notable being St Botolph's Church, better known as the 'Boston Stump'.

FACILITIES AT A GLANCE

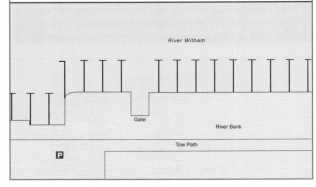
River Witham
Gate
River Bank
Tow Path

MERIDIAN QUAY MARINA

Humber Cruising Assn
Meridian Quay Marina
Fish Docks, Grimsby, DN31 3SD
Tel: 01472 268424 Fax: 01472 351869
www.hcagrimsby.co.uk
Email: berthmaster@hcagrimsby.co.uk

VHF Ch 74
ACCESS HW±2

Situated in the locked fish dock of Grimsby, at the mouth of the River Humber, Meridian Quay Marina is run by the Humber Cruising Association and comprises approximately 200 alongside berths plus 30 more for visitors. Accessed two hours either side of high water via lock gates, the lock should be contacted on VHF Ch 74 (call sign 'Fish Dock Island') as you make your final approach. The pontoon berths are equipped with water and electricity; there is a fully licensed clubhouse. Also available are internet access and laundry facilities.

FACILITIES AT A GLANCE

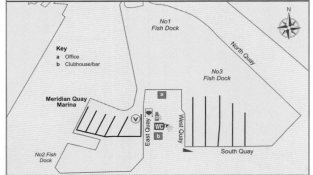
No1 Fish Dock
North Quay
No3 Fish Dock
Key
a Office
b Clubhouse/bar
Meridian Quay Marina
East Quay
West Quay
South Quay
No2 Fish Dock

SOUTH FERRIBY MARINA

South Ferriby Marina
Red Lane, South Ferriby, Barton on Humber, Lincs, DN18 6JH
Tel: 01652 635620 (Lock 635219) Mobile: 07828 312071
Email: enquiries@southferribymarina.com

VHF Ch 74
ACCESS HW±3

Situated at the entrance to the non-tidal River Ancholme the existing marina has been established since 1966 and is well placed to provide easy access to the River Humber and North Sea. This is a family run business providing a range of services including a boatyard and chandlery. Access is by way of lock at HW±3.

The marina has excellent road and rail services within easy reach, while South Ferriby village has two pubs and a Post Office/Spar Shop just a short walk away.

The picturesque River Ancholme is navigable for about 17 miles; the maximum headroom under bridges is 4.42 metres (14ft 6ins).

FACILITIES AT A GLANCE

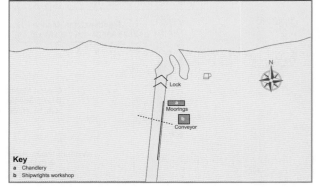
Lock
Moorings
Conveyor
Key
a Chandlery
b Shipwrights workshop

HULL MARINA

Hull Marina
W 13, Kingston Street, Hull, HU1 2DQ
Tel: 01482 609960 Fax: 01482 224148
Email: carolyn.murray@bwml.co.uk
www.bwml.co.uk

VHF	Ch 80
ACCESS	HW±3

Situated on the River Humber, Hull Marina is literally a stone's throw from the bustling city centre with its array of arts and entertainments. Besides the numerous historic bars and cafés surrounding the marina, there are plenty of traditional taverns to be sampled in the Old Town, while also found here is the Street Life Museum, vividly depicting the history of the city.

Yachtsmen enter the marina via a tidal lock, operating HW±3, and should try to give 15 minutes' notice of arrival via VHF Ch 80; if arriving between 2100-0700 from Oct-Mar, 24 hrs notice is required. Hull is perfectly positioned for exploring the Trent, Ouse and the Yorkshire coast as well as across the North Sea to Holland or Belgium.

FACILITIES AT A GLANCE

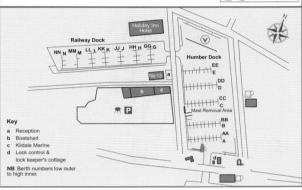

Key
a   Reception
b   Boatshed
c   Kildale Marine
d   Lock control &
     lock keeper's cottage
NB Berth numbers low outer
to high inner.

Hull Marina

- Fully serviced pontoons
- Visitors welcome
- Fully serviced boatyard with 50 tonne hoist

Hull Marina is a proud member of the TransEurope Marinas group

BWML

T: 01482 609960
F: 01482 224148
bwml.co.uk/ra-hull

Warehouse 13, Kingston Street,
Hull, Yorkshire HU1 2DQ
carolyn.murray@bwml.co.uk

5

WHITBY MARINA

Whitby Marina
Whitby Harbour Office, Endeavour Wharf
Whitby, North Yorkshire YO21 1DN
Harbour Office: 01947 602354 Marina: 01947 600165
Email: port.services@scarborough.gov.uk

VHF Ch 11
ACCESS HW±2

The only natural harbour between the Tees and the Humber, Whitby lies some 20 miles north of Scarborough on the River Esk. The historic town is said to date back as far as the Roman times, although it is better known for its abbey, which was founded over 1,300 years ago by King Oswy of Northumberland. Another place of interest is the Captain Cook Memorial Museum, a tribute to Whitby's greatest seaman.

A swing bridge divides the harbour into upper and lower sections, with the marina being in the Upper Harbour. The bridge opens on request (VHF Ch 11) each half hour for two hours either side of high water.

FACILITIES AT A GLANCE

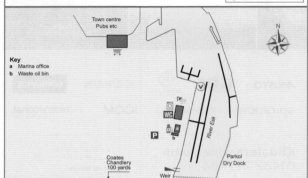

Key
a Marina office
b Waste oil bin

HARTLEPOOL MARINA

Hartlepool Marina
Lock Office, Slake Terrace, Hartlepool, TS24 0RU
Tel: 01429 865744
Email: enquiries@hartlepool-marina.com

VHF Ch M, 80
ACCESS HW±5

Hartlepool Marina is a modern boating facility on the NE coast. Nestling on the Tees Valley the multi award winning marina promotes up to 500 pontoon berths alongside a variety of reputable services all surrounded by an exciting array of on water activities, a cosmopolitan mix of bistros, bars, restaurants, shopping, hotels and entertainment options.

Beautiful cruising waters and golden sands to the North and South of the marina approach which is channel dredged to chart datum and accessible 5 hours either side of high water via a lock: vessels wishing to enter should contact the Marina Lock Office on VHF Ch 37/80 before arrival.

FACILITIES AT A GLANCE

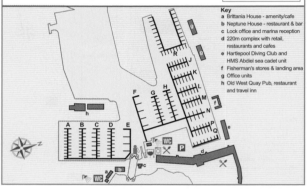

Key
a Brittania House - amenity/cafe
b Neptune House - restaurant & bar
c Lock office and marina reception
d 220m complex with retail, restaurants and cafes
e Hartlepool Diving Club and HMS Abdiel sea cadet unit
f Fisherman's stores & landing area
g Office units
h Old West Quay Pub, restaurant and travel inn

SUNDERLAND MARINA

The Marine Activities Centre
Sunderland Marina, Sunderland, SR6 0PW
Tel: 0191 514 4721 Fax: 0191 514 1847
Email: mervyn.templeton@marineactivitiescentre.co.uk

VHF	Ch M, 80
ACCESS	H24

Sunderland Marina sits on bank of the River Wear and is easily accessible through the outer breakwater at all states of the tide. Among the extensive range of facilities on site are a newsagent, café, hairdresser and top quality Italian restaurant. Other pubs, restaurants, hotels and cafés are located nearby on the waterfront.

Both the Wear Boating Association and the Sunderland Yacht Club are also located in the vicinity and welcome yachtsmen to their respective bars and lounges.

FACILITIES AT A GLANCE

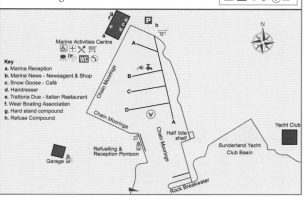

Key
a. Marina Reception
b. Marine News - Newsagent & Shop
c. Snow Goose - Café
d. Hairdresser
e. Trattoria Due - Italian Restaurant
f. Wear Boating Association
g. Hard stand compound
h. Refuse Compound

NORTH SHIELDS ROYAL QUAYS MARINA

North Shields Royal Quays Marina
Coble Dene Road, North Shields, NE29 6DU
Tel: 0191 272 8282 Fax: 0191 272 8288
www.quaymarinas.com
Email: royalquaysmarina@quaymarinas.com

VHF	Ch 80
ACCESS	H24

North Shields Royal Quays Marina enjoys close proximity to the entrance to the River Tyne, allowing easy access to and from the open sea as well as being ideally placed for cruising further up the Tyne. Just over an hour's motoring upstream brings you to the heart of the city of Newcastle,

where you can tie up on a security controlled visitors' pontoon right outside the Pitcher and Piano Bar.

With a reputation for a high standard of service, the marina accommodates 300 pontoon berths, all of which are fully serviced. It is accessed via double sector lock gates which operate at all states of the tide and 24 hours a day.

FACILITIES AT A GLANCE

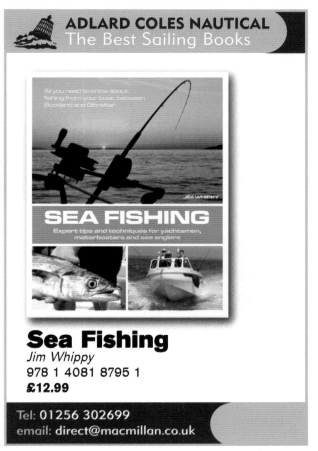

Key
a Marina office
   Toilets/showers
   Laundry
   Payphone
   Lock control
   Brokerage
b Refuse compound
c Chandlery & boat sales
d Access bridge & trolley park
e Boat sales & brokerage
f Bar/restaurant
g Waste oil disposal

ST PETERS MARINA

St Peters Marina, St Peters Basin
Newcastle upon Tyne, NE6 1HX
Tel: 0191 2654472 Fax: 0191 2762618
Email: info@stpetersmarina.co.uk
www.stpetersmarina.co.uk

VHF	Ch 80
ACCESS	HW±3

Nestling on the north bank of the River Tyne, some eight miles upstream of the river entrance, St Peters Marina is a fully serviced, 150-berth marina with the capacity to accommodate large vessels of up to 37m LOA. Situated on site is the Bascule Bar and Bistro, while a few minutes away is the centre of Newcastle. This city, along

with its surrounding area, offers an array of interesting sites, among which are Hadrian's Wall, the award winning Gateshead Millennium Bridge and the Baltic Art Centre.

FACILITIES AT A GLANCE

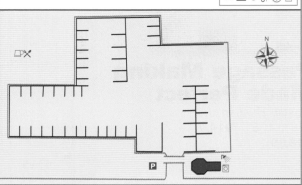

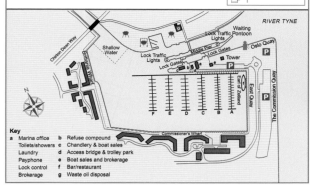

ROYAL NORTHUMBERLAND YACHT CLUB

Royal Northumberland Yacht Club
South Harbour, Blyth, Northumberland, NE24 3PB
Tel: 01670 353636

VHF	Ch 12
ACCESS	H24

The Royal Northumberland Yacht Club is based at Blyth, a well-sheltered port that is accessible at all states of the tide and in all weathers except for when there is a combination of low water and strong south-easterly winds. The yacht club is a private club with some 75 pontoon berths and a further 20 fore and aft moorings.

Visitors usually berth on the north side of the most northerly pontoon and are welcome to use the clubship, HY *Tyne* – a wooden lightship built in 1880 which incorporates a bar, showers and toilet facilities. The club also controls its own boatyard, providing under cover and outside storage space plus a 20 ton boat hoist.

FACILITIES AT A GLANCE

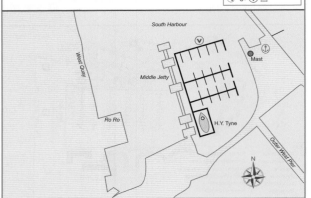

AMBLE MARINA

Amble Marina Ltd
Amble, Northumberland, NE65 0YP
Tel: 01665 712168
Email: marina@amble.co.uk   www.amble.co.uk

VHF	Ch 80
ACCESS	HW±4

Amble Marina is a small family run business offering peace, security and a countryside setting at the heart of the small town of Amble. It is located on the banks of the beautiful River Coquet and at the start of the Northumberland coast's area of outstanding natural beauty. Amble Marina has 250 fully serviced berths for residential and visiting yachts. Cafés, bars, restaurants and shops are all within a short walk.

From your berth watch the sun rise at the harbour entrance and set behind Warkworth Castle or walk on wide, empty beaches. There is so much to do or if you prefer simply enjoy the peace, tranquillity and friendliness at Amble Marina.

FACILITIES AT A GLANCE

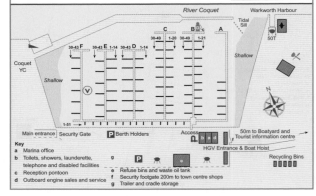

Key
a   Marina office
b   Toilets, showers, launderette, telephone and disabled facilities
c   Reception pontoon
d   Outboard engine sales and service
e   Refuse bins and waste oil tank
f   Security footgate 200m to town centre shops
g   Trailer and cradle storage

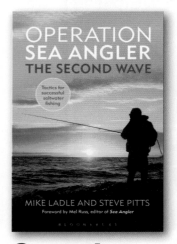
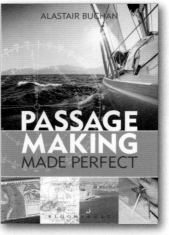

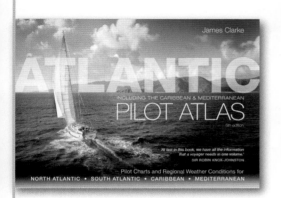
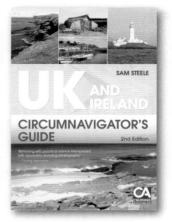
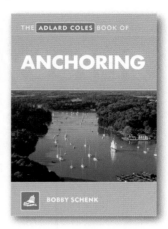

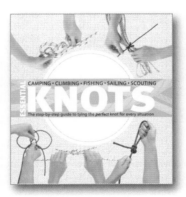
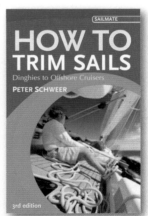

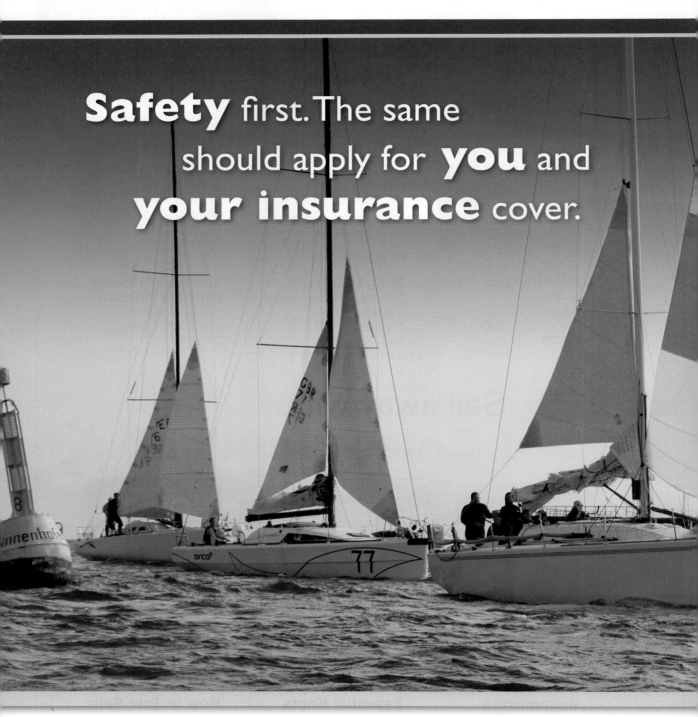

SOUTH EAST SCOTLAND – Eyemouth to Rattray Head

Key to Marina Plans symbols

Bottled gas		Parking	
Chandler		Pub/Restaurant	
Disabled facilities		Pump out	
Electrical supply		Rigging service	
Electrical repairs		Sail repairs	
Engine repairs		Shipwright	
First Aid		Shop/Supermarket	
Fresh Water		Showers	
Fuel - Diesel		Slipway	
Fuel - Petrol		Toilets	
Hardstanding/boatyard		Telephone	
Internet Café		Trolleys	
Laundry facilities		Visitors berths	
Lift-out facilities		Wi-Fi	

6

Area 6 - South East Scotland

MARINAS
Telephone Numbers
VHF Channel
Access Times

Aberdeen
Stonehaven
Montrose
Arbroath Harbour 01241 872166 Ch 11, 16 HW±3
Arbroath
Tayport
Port Edgar Marina 0131 3313330 Ch 80 H24
Port Edgar
Granton
Dunbar
Berwick-upon-Tweed

N

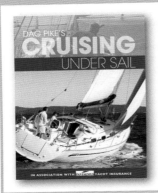
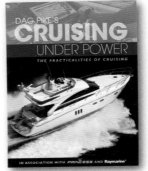

PORT EDGAR MARINA

Port Edgar Marina
Shore Road, South Queensferry
West Lothian, EH3 9SX
Tel: 0131 331 3330 Fax: 0131 331 4878
Email: admin.pe@edinburghleisure.co.uk

VHF	Ch 80
ACCESS	H24

Port Edgar is a large watersports centre and marina found on the south bank of the sheltered Firth of Forth. Situated in the village of South Queensferry, just west of the Forth Road Bridge, it is managed by Edinburgh Leisure on behalf of the City of Edinburgh Council and is reached via a deep water channel just west of the suspension bridge.

The nearby village offers a sufficient range of shops and restaurants, while Port Edgar is only a 20-minute walk from Dalmeny Station from where trains run regularly to Edinburgh.

FACILITIES AT A GLANCE

Key
a Changing rooms and toilets
b Landing and trolleys
c Port Edgar Yacht Club
d Sail loft
e Cafe
f Marina office
g Ferry Marine
h Blue V
i Bosuns Locker

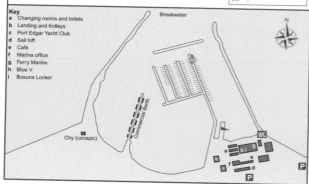

ARBROATH HARBOUR

Arbroath Harbour
Harbour Office, Arbroath, DD11 1PD
Tel: 01241 872166 Fax: 01241 878472
Email: harbourmaster@angus.gov.uk

VHF	Ch 11
ACCESS	HW±3

Arbroath harbour has 59 floating pontoon berths with security entrance which are serviced with electricity and fresh water to accommodate all types of leisure craft. Half height dock gates with walkway are located between the inner and outer harbours, which open and close at half tide, maintaining a minimum of 2.5m of water in the inner harbour.

The town of Arbroath offers a variety of social and sporting amenities to visiting crews and a number of quality pubs, restaurants, the famous twelfth century Abbey and Signal Tower Museum are located close to the harbour. Railway and bus stations are only 1km from the harbour with direct north and south connections.

FACILITIES AT A GLANCE

Key
a Signal Tower Museum
b Tourist Information
c RNLI
d Harbourmaster
e Harbour gates & walkway

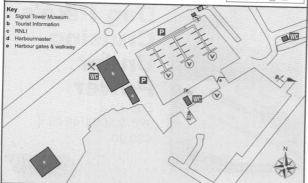

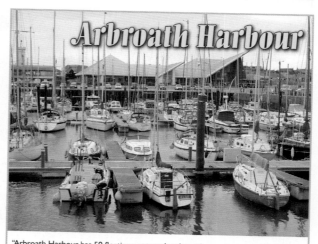

Arbroath Harbour

"Arbroath Harbour has 59 floating pontoon berths with security entrance which are serviced with electricity and fresh water to accommodate all types of leisure craft. Half height dock gates with a walkway are located between the inner and outer harbours, which open and close at half tide, maintaining a minimum of 2.5m of water in the inner harbour.

Other facilities in the harbour include free partking, toilets and showers, a crew room, fueling facilities, a nearby chandlery shop and boat builders' yard.

The town of Arbroath also offers a variety of social and sporting amenities to visiting crews and a number of quality pubs, restaurants, the famous twelfth century Abbey and Signal Tower Museum are located close to the harbour. The railway and bus stations are only 1km from the harbour with direct north and south connections."

Arbroath Harbour
Harbour Office . Arbroath . DD11 1PD

Harbour Master: Bruce Fleming
Tel: 01241 872166
Fax: 01241 878472
Email: harbourmaster@angus.gov.uk

Angus Council

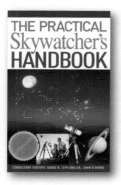

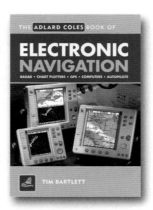
EN

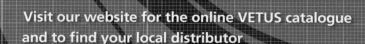

NORTH EAST SCOTLAND – Peterhead to Cape Wrath & Orkney & Shetland Is

Key to Marina Plans symbols

🝰	Bottled gas	P	Parking
	Chandler	✕	Pub/Restaurant
♿	Disabled facilities		Pump out
	Electrical supply		Rigging service
	Electrical repairs		Sail repairs
	Engine repairs		Shipwright
✚	First Aid		Shop/Supermarket
	Fresh Water		Showers
	Fuel - Diesel		Slipway
	Fuel - Petrol	WC	Toilets
	Hardstanding/boatyard		Telephone
@	Internet Café		Trolleys
	Laundry facilities	Ⓥ	Visitors berths
	Lift-out facilities		Wi-Fi

Area 7 - North East Scotland

MARINAS
Telephone Numbers
VHF Channel
Access Times

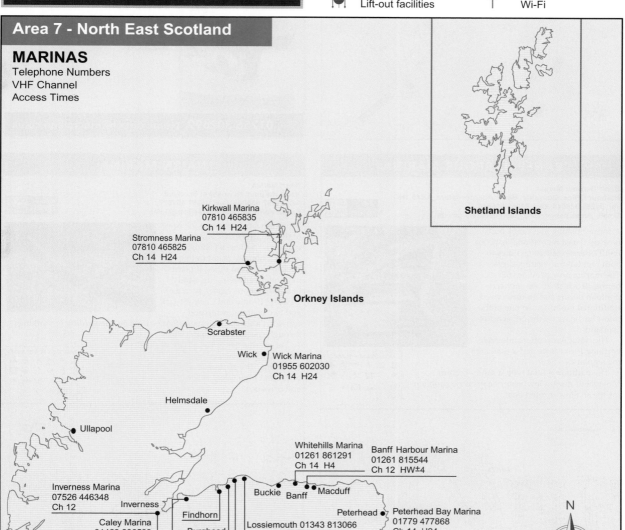

Shetland Islands

7

Kirkwall Marina
07810 465835
Ch 14 H24

Stromness Marina
07810 465825
Ch 14 H24

Orkney Islands

Scrabster

Wick • Wick Marina
01955 602030
Ch 14 H24

Helmsdale

Ullapool

Whitehills Marina
01261 861291
Ch 14 H4

Banff Harbour Marina
01261 815544
Ch 12 HW±4

Inverness Marina
07526 446348
Ch 12

Inverness

Buckie Banff Macduff

Findhorn

Caley Marina
01463 236539
Ch 74 H24
Seaport Marina
01463 725500
Ch 74 HW±4

Burghead

Nairn Marina
01667 456008
Ch 10 HW±2

Hopeman

Lossiemouth 01343 813066
Ch 12 HW±4

Peterhead • Peterhead Bay Marina
01779 477868
Ch 14 H24

Mallaig

Aberdeen

N

PETERHEAD BAY MARINA

Peterhead Port Authority
Harbour Office, West Pier, Peterhead, AB42 1DW
Tel: 01779 477868/483600
Email: marina@peterheadport.co.uk
www.peterheadport.co.uk

VHF	Ch 14
ACCESS	H24

Based in the south west corner of Peterhead Bay Harbour, the marina provides one of the finest marine leisure facilities in the east of Scotland. In addition to the services on site, there are plenty of nautical businesses in the vicinity, ranging from ship chandlers and electrical servicing to boat repairs and surveying.

Due to its easterly location, Peterhead affords an ideal stopover for those yachts heading to or from Scandinavia as well as for vessels making for the Caledonian Canal.

FACILITIES AT A GLANCE

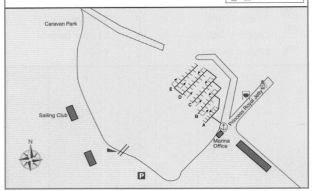

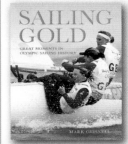
BANFF HARBOUR MARINA

Banff Harbour Marina
Harbour Office, Quayside, Banff, Aberdeenshire, AB45 1HQ
Tel: 01261 815544 Fax: 01261 815544
Email: james.henderson@aberdeenshire.gov.uk

VHF	Ch 12
ACCESS	HW±4

A former fishing and cargo port now used as a recreational harbour. Banff offers excellent facilities to both regular and visiting users. The marina now provides 92 berths, of which 76 are serviced pontoon berths and 16 unserviced, traditional moorings, in one of the safest harbours on the NE coast of Scotland.

The outer basin offers adequate berthing for visitors and a tidal area for regulars.

The harbour is tidal with a sandy bottom. Movement during low water neaps is no problem for the shallow drafted boat.

FACILITIES AT A GLANCE

Key
a Harbourmasters Office

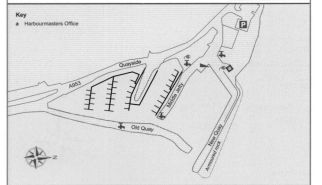

NAIRN MARINA

Nairn Marina
Nairn Harbour, Nairnshire, Scotland
Tel: 01667 456008 Fax: 01667 452877
Email: nairn.harbourmaster@virgin.net

VHF	Ch 10
ACCESS	HW±2

Nairn is a small town on the coast of the Moray Firth. Formerly renowned both as a fishing port and as a holiday resort dating back to Victorian times, it boasts miles of award-winning, sandy beaches, famous castles such as Cawdor, Brodie and Castle Stuart, and two championship golf courses. Other recreational activities include horse riding or walking through spectacular countryside.

The marina lies at the mouth of the River Nairn, entry to which should be avoided in strong N to NE winds. The approach is made from the NW at or around high water as the entrance is badly silted and dries out.

FACILITIES AT A GLANCE

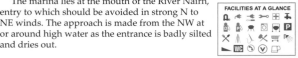

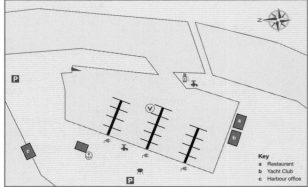

Key
a Restaurant
b Yacht Club
c Harbour office

WHITEHILLS MARINA

Whitehills Harbour Commissioners
Whitehills, Banffshire AB45 2NQ
Tel: 01261 861291
www.whitehillsharbour.co.uk
Email: harbourmaster@whitehillsharbour.co.uk

VHF	Ch 14
ACCESS	H24

Built in 1900, Whitehills is a Trust Harbour fully maintained and run by nine commissioners elected from the village. It was a thriving fishing port up until 1999, but due to changes in the fishing industry, was converted into a marina during 2000.

Three miles west of Banff Harbour the marina benefits from good tidal access – although there is just 1.5m at springs – comprising 38 serviced berths, with electricity, as well as eight non-serviced berths.

The nearby village of Whitehills boasts a selection of local stores and a couple of pubs. A coastal path leads from the marina to the top of the headland, affording striking views across the Moray Firth to the Caithness Hills.

FACILITIES AT A GLANCE

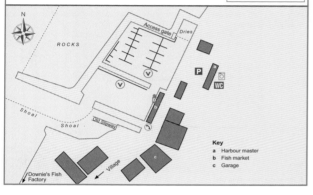

Key
a   Harbour master
b   Fish market
c   Garage

7

LOSSIEMOUTH MARINA

The Harbour Office
Lossiemouth, Moray, IV31 6TW
Tel: 01343 813066   Mobile: 07969 213513
Email: info@lossiemouthmarina.com

VHF	Ch 12
ACCESS	HW±4

Situated on the southern shore of the Moray Firth, Lossiemouth provides 88 serviced finger berths, 5 serviced dedicated visitor berths and 25 small boat berths. The Marina has full lift out facilities and a boat repair shed capable of handling 4 vessels at any one time with a marine engineer based on site.

The Marina is close to the town centre with a good range of shops and restaurants and also two championship golf courses. A regular bus service provides easy access to Elgin railway station (6 miles) and Inverness airport (35miles). Lossiemouth has miles of sandy beaches and is the ideal starting point for the Speyside Whisky trail.

FACILITIES AT A GLANCE

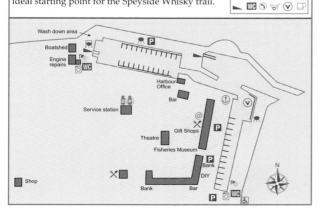

INVERNESS MARINA

Inverness Marina
Longman Drive, Inverness, IV1 1SU
Tel: 01463 220501
Email: info@invernessmarina.com
www.invernessmarina.com

VHF	Ch 12
ACCESS	H24

Inverness Marina is situated in the Inverness firth just one mile from the city centre and half a mile from the entrance to the Caledonian Canal. The marina has a minimum depth of 3m, 24hr access and 150 fully serviced berths. On site are a chandlery and services including rigging, engineering, electronics and boat repair.

Inverness is the capital of the highlands with transport networks including bus, train, and flights to the rest of the UK and Europe. Inverness is the gateway to the Highlands with best possible location as a base for touring with golf courses, historic sites and the Whisky Trail. The marina is a perfect base for cruising Orkney, Shetland and Scandinavia.

FACILITIES AT A GLANCE

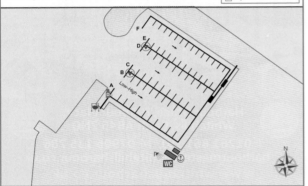

SEAPORT MARINA

Seaport Marina
Muirtown Wharf, Inverness, IV3 5LE
Tel: 01463 725500 Fax: 01463 710942
Email: enquiries.scotland@britishwaterways.co.uk
www.scottishcanals.co.uk

VHF	Ch 74
ACCESS	HW±4

Seaport Marina is based at Muirtown Basin at the eastern entrance of the Caledonian Canal; a 60 mile coast-to-coast channel slicing through the majestic Great Glen. Only a 15 minute walk from the centre of Inverness, the Marina is an ideal base for visiting the Highlands.

There are shops and amenities nearby, as well as chandlers, boat repair services and a slipway. The marina also offers a variety of winter mooring packages and details of transit and short term licences, including the use of the Caledonian Canal can be found on the above website.

FACILITIES AT A GLANCE

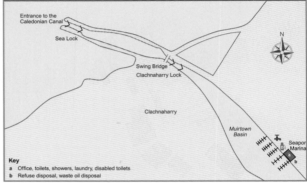

Key
a   Office, toilets, showers, laundry, disabled toilets
b   Refuse disposal, waste oil disposal

CALEY MARINA

Caley Marina
Canal Road, Inverness, IV3 8NF
Tel: 01463 236539 Fax: 01463 238323
Email: info@caleymarina.com
www.caleymarina.com

VHF	Ch 74
ACCESS	H24

Caley Marina is a family run business based near Inverness. With the four flight Muirtown locks and the Kessock Bridge providing a dramatic backdrop, the marina runs alongside the Caledonian Canal which, opened in 1822, is regarded as one of the most spectacular waterways in Europe. Built as a short cut between the North Sea and the Atlantic Ocean, thus avoiding the potentially dangerous Pentland Firth on the north coast of Scotland, the canal is around 60 miles long and takes about three days to cruise from east to west. With the prevailing winds behind you, it takes slightly less time to cruise in the other direction.

FACILITIES AT A GLANCE

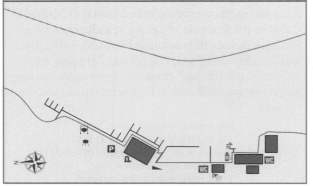

WICK MARINA

Wick Marina
Harbour Office, Wick, Caithness, KW1 5HA
Tel: 01955 602030 Fax: 01955 605936
Email: malcolm.bremner@wickharbour.co.uk

VHF	Ch 14, 16
ACCESS	H24

This is the most northerly marina on the British mainland and the last stop before the Orkney and Shetland Islands. Situated an easy five minutes walk from the town centre Wick Marina accommodates 70 fully serviced berths with all the support facilities expected in a modern marina including a boat lift.

This part of Scotland with its rugged coastline and rich history is easily accessible by air and a great starting point for cruising in the northern isles, Moray Firth, Caledonian Canal and Scandinavia, a comfortable 280-mile sail.

FACILITIES AT A GLANCE

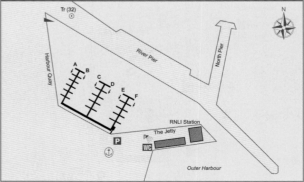

KIRKWALL MARINA

Kirkwall Marina
Harbour Street, Kirkwall, Orkney, KW15
Tel: 07810 465835 Fax: 01856 871313
Email: info@orkneymarinas.co.uk www.orkneymarinas.co.uk

VHF Ch 14
ACCESS H24

The Orkney Isles, comprising 70 islands in total, provides some of the finest cruising grounds in Northern Europe. The Main Island, incorporating the ancient port of Kirkwall, is the largest, although 16 others have lively communities and are rich in archaeological sites as well as spectacular scenery and wildlife.

Kirkwall Marina, an all year facility, is located within the harbour and just yards from the visitor attractions of this ancient port. Local shops, hotels and restaurants are all within walking distance.

FACILITIES AT A GLANCE

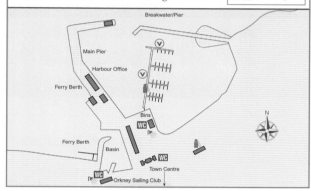

STROMNESS MARINA

Stromness Marina
Stromness, Orkney, KW16
Tel: 07810 465825 Fax: 01856 871313
Email: info@orkneymarinas.co.uk
www.orkneymarinas.co.uk

VHF Ch 14
ACCESS H24

Stromness lies on the south-western tip of the Orkney Isles' Mainland. Sitting beneath the rocky ridge known as Brinkie's Brae, it is considered one of Orkney's major seaports, with sailors first attracted to the fine anchorage provided by the bay of Hamnavoe.

Stromness offers comprehensive facilities including a chandlery and repair services. Also on hand are an internet café, a fitness suite and swimming pool as well as car and bike hire.

FACILITIES AT A GLANCE

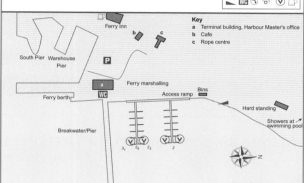

Key
a Terminal building, Harbour Master's office
b Cafe
c Rope centre

NORTH WEST SCOTLAND – Cape Wrath to Crinan Canal

Key to Marina Plans symbols

🔔	Bottled gas	P	Parking
🔩	Chandler	✗	Pub/Restaurant
♿	Disabled facilities		Pump out
🔌	Electrical supply		Rigging service
🔌	Electrical repairs		Sail repairs
🔧	Engine repairs	✗	Shipwright
✚	First Aid	🛒	Shop/Supermarket
🚰	Fresh Water		Showers
D	Fuel - Diesel		Slipway
P	Fuel - Petrol	WC	Toilets
	Hardstanding/boatyard	✆	Telephone
@	Internet Café	🛒	Trolleys
🔲	Laundry facilities	V	Visitors berths
	Lift-out facilities	Y	Wi-Fi

Area 8 - North West Scotland

MARINAS
Telephone Numbers
VHF Channel
Access Times

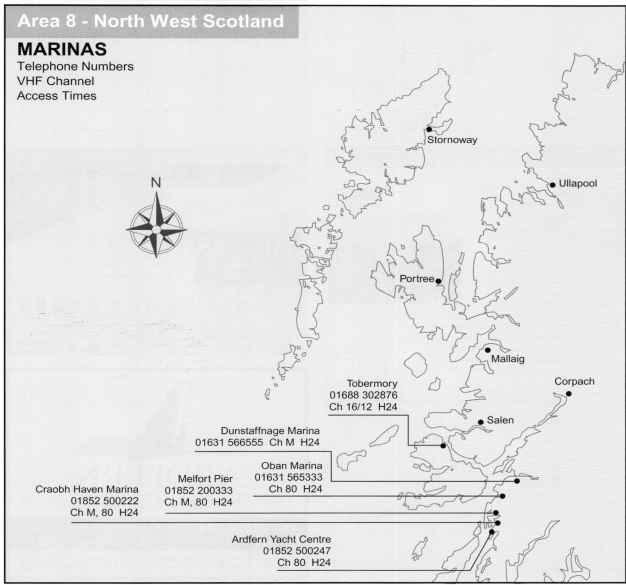

Stornoway

Ullapool

N

Portree

Mallaig

Corpach

Tobermory
01688 302876
Ch 16/12 H24

Salen

Dunstaffnage Marina
01631 566555 Ch M H24

Oban Marina
01631 565333
Ch 80 H24

Melfort Pier
01852 200333
Ch M, 80 H24

Craobh Haven Marina
01852 500222
Ch M, 80 H24

Ardfern Yacht Centre
01852 500247
Ch 80 H24

TOBERMORY

Tobermory Harbour Association
Taigh Solais, Tobermory, Isle of Mull, PA75 6NR
Tel: 01688 302876 Mob: 07917 832497
www.tobermoryharbour.co.uk
Email: jim.traynor@tobermoryharbour.co.uk

| VHF | Ch 16/12 |
| ACCESS | 0800–2000 |

Tobermory Harbour pontoons are located in the west shore of Tobermory Bay with access directly to the town. The THA offers a full range of facilities and services afloat and ashore. The THA also offers swinging moorings for hire.

Tobermory is the iconic Scottish west coast destination, a natural historic harbour and protected anchorage. Tobermory offers an exceptional array of shops, bars and and restaurants, most offering fresh local shellfish and all within easy walking distance. Tobermory has transport links to and from all mainland ferries or destination tours throughout the Island of Mull.

FACILITIES AT A GLANCE

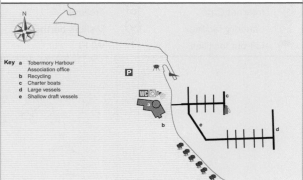

Key a Tobermory Harbour
         Association office
     b Recycling
     c Charter boats
     d Large vessels
     e Shallow draft vessels

DUNSTAFFNAGE MARINA

Dunstaffnage Marina Ltd
Dunbeg, by Oban, Argyll, PA37 1PX
Tel: 01631 566555 Fax: 01631 571044
Email: lizzy@dunstaffnage.sol.co.uk

| VHF | Ch M |
| ACCESS | H24 |

Located just two to three miles north of Oban, Dunstaffnage Marina has recently been renovated to include an additional 36 fully serviced berths, a new breakwater providing shelter from NE'ly to E'ly winds and an increased amount of hard standing. Also on site is the Wide Mouthed Frog, offering a convivial bar, restaurant and accomodation with spectacular views of the 13th century Dunstaffnage Castle.

The marina is perfectly placed to explore Scotland's stunning west coast and Hebridean Islands. Only 10 miles NE up Loch Linnhe is Port Appin, while sailing 15 miles S, down the Firth of Lorne, brings you to Puldohran where you can walk to an ancient hostelry situated next to the C18 Bridge Over the Atlantic.

FACILITIES AT A GLANCE

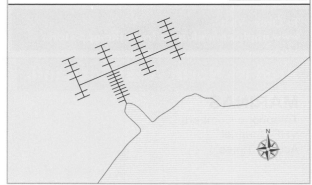

OBAN MARINA

Oban Marina & Yacht Services Ltd
Isle of Kerrera, Oban, Argyll, PA34 4SX
Tel: 01631 565333
Email: info@obanmarina.com

| VHF | Ch 80 |
| ACCESS | H24 |

Oban Marina is situated on the picturesque Isle of Kerrera. less than a mile from Oban town, the gateway to the western isles. This is a well-serviced marina popular with sailors and motorboats owners alike, offering one of the few facilities with all tides access on the west coast of Scotland.

For those travelling by land or sea, Kerrera is a short ride away from Oban itself in the marina's own complimentary shuttle, which can carry up to 65 people.

One of the many improvements undertaken by Oban Marina Ltd is the opening of the fully licensed Waypoint Bar & Grill serving a wide selection of island-produced seafood and meats available from start of May to the end of September.

FACILITIES AT A GLANCE

Key
a Reception
b Showers/toilets
c Bar & grill
d Shed

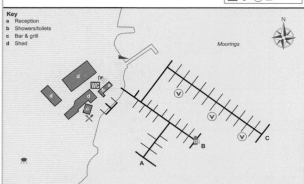

MELFORT PIER AND HARBOUR

Melfort Pier and Harbour
Kilmelford, by Oban, Argyll
Tel: 01852 200333 Fax: 01852 200329
Email: melharbour@aol.com www.mellowmelfort.com

VHF M, 80
ACCESS H24

Melfort Pier & Harbour is situated on the shores of Loch Melfort, one of the most peaceful lochs on the south west coast of Scotland. Overlooked by the Pass of Melfort and the Braes of Lorn, it lies approximately 18 miles north of Lochgilphead and 16 miles south of Oban. Its onsite facilities include showers, laundry, telephone, free Wi-Fi access and parking – pets welcome. Fuel, power and water are available at nearby Kilmelford Yacht Haven. There is an onsite restaurant, The Melfort Mermaid, serving freshly cooked local food. For those who want a few nights on dry land, Melfort Pier & Harbour offers lochside houses, each one equipped with a sauna, spa bath and balcony offering stunning views over the loch - available per night.

FACILITIES AT A GLANCE

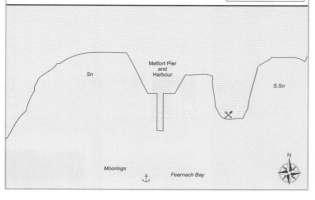

CRAOBH HAVEN MARINA

Craobh Haven Marina
By Lochgilphead, Argyll, Scotland, PA31 8UA
Tel: 01852 500222 Fax: 01852 500252
Email: info@craobhmarina.co.uk
www.craobhmarina.co.uk

VHF Ch M, 80
ACCESS H24

Craobh Marina is idyllically situated in the heart of Scotland's most sought after cruising grounds. Not only does Craobh offer ready access to a wonderful choice of scenic cruising throughout the western isles, the marina is conveniently close to Glasgow and its international transport hub.

Craobh Marina has been developed from a near perfect natural harbour, offering secure and sheltered berthing for up to 250 vessels to 22m LOA and with a draft of 4m. With an unusually deep and wide entrance Craobh Marina provides shelter and a warm welcome for all types of craft.

FACILITIES AT A GLANCE

Key
a Holiday cottages
b Village store
c Bar
d Gift shop
e Waste oil
f Boat shed
g Marina office

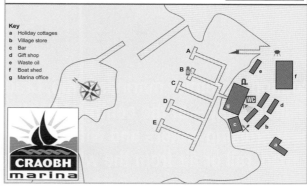

CRAOBH marina

ARDFERN YACHT CENTRE

Ardfern Yacht Centre
Ardfern, by Lochgilphead, Argyll, PA31 8QN
Tel: 01852 500247 Fax: 01852 500624
www.ardfernyacht.co.uk Email: office@ardfernyacht.co.uk

VHF Ch 80
ACCESS H24

Developed around an old pier once frequented by steamers, Ardfern Yacht Centre lies at the head of Loch Craignish, one of Scotland's most sheltered and picturesque sea lochs. With several islands and protected anchorages nearby, Ardfern is an ideal place from which to cruise the west coast of Scotland and the Outer Hebrides.

The Yacht Centre comprises pontoon berths and swinging moorings as well as a workshop, boat storage and well-stocked chandlery, while a grocery store and eating places can be found in the village. Among the onshore activities available locally are horse riding, cycling, and walking.

FACILITIES AT A GLANCE

Key
a Workshop
b Showers, toilets and launderette
c Chandlery and office

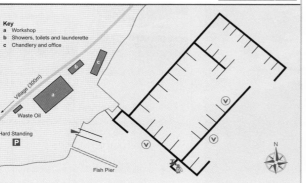

8

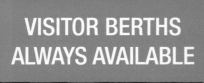

SOUTH WEST SCOTLAND – Crinan Canal to Mull of Galloway

Key to Marina Plans symbols

Bottled gas		P	Parking
Chandler			Pub / Restaurant
Disabled facilities			Pump out
Electrical supply			Rigging service
Electrical repairs			Sail repairs
Engine repairs			Shipwright
First Aid			Shop / Supermarket
Fresh Water			Showers
Fuel - Diesel			Slipway
Fuel - Petrol		WC	Toilets
Hardstanding/boatyard			Telephone
Internet Café			Trolleys
Laundry facilities		V	Visitors berths
Lift-out facilities			Wi-Fi

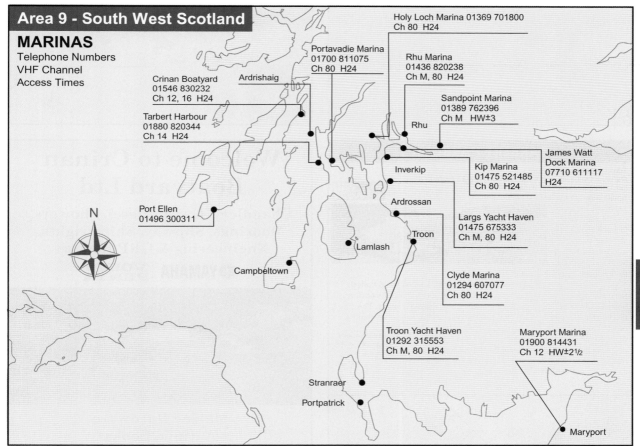

Area 9 - South West Scotland

MARINAS
Telephone Numbers
VHF Channel
Access Times

Holy Loch Marina 01369 701800
Ch 80 H24

Portavadie Marina
01700 811075
Ch 80 H24

Ardrishaig

Crinan Boatyard
01546 830232
Ch 12, 16 H24

Rhu Marina
01436 820238
Ch M, 80 H24

Tarbert Harbour
01880 820344
Ch 14 H24

Sandpoint Marina
01389 762396
Ch M HW±3

Rhu

James Watt
Dock Marina
07710 611117
H24

Inverkip

Kip Marina
01475 521485
Ch 80 H24

Port Ellen
01496 300311

Ardrossan

Largs Yacht Haven
01475 675333
Ch M, 80 H24

Troon

Lamlash

Clyde Marina
01294 607077
Ch 80 H24

Campbeltown

Troon Yacht Haven
01292 315553
Ch M, 80 H24

Maryport Marina
01900 814431
Ch 12 HW±2½

Stranraer

Portpatrick

Maryport

N

9

PORT ELLEN MARINA

Port Ellen Marina
Port Ellen, Islay, Argyll, PA42 7DB
Tel: 01496 302458 Fax: 01496 300302
Email: bertie66@btinternet.com www.portellenmarina.com

VHF
ACCESS H24

A safe and relaxed marina for visitors to the *Malt Whisky Island*. There are seven classic distilleries and yet another still (private) to start production soon. If you are planning a cruise to the north then superb sailing will take you onward via Craighouse on Jura. Meeting guests or short term storage is trouble free with the excellent air and ferry services connecting to Glasgow. Once on Islay you will be tempted to extend your stay so be warned, check www.portellenmarina.com for the many reasons to visit, from golf to music.

FACILITIES AT A GLANCE

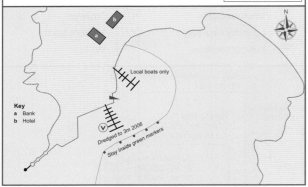

Key
a Bank
b Hotel

Local boats only

Dredged to 3m 2006

Stay inside green markers

CRINAN BOATYARD

Crinan Boatyard Ltd
Crinan, Lochgilphead, Argyll, PA31 8SW
Tel: 01546 830232 Fax: 01546 830281
Email: info@crinanboatyard.co.uk
www.crinanboatyard.co.uk

VHF Ch 12, 16
ACCESS H24

Situated at the westerly entrance of the scenic Crinan Canal, Crinan Boatyard offers swinging moorings nightly or longer term, a fuelling/loading berth, a well stocked Chandlery, heads, showers, laundry and an experienced work force for repair work all on site. A hotel and coffee shop, just a short walk away at the Canal basin, great walking and the historic Kilmartin Glen close by are some of the attractions on shore.

The nearby town of Lochgilphead 7 miles away offers shopping and good travel links to Glasgow (85 miles) and its International Airport.

FACILITIES AT A GLANCE

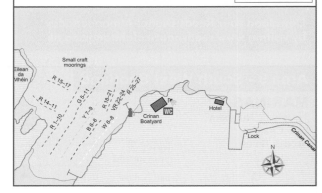

Small craft moorings

Eilean da Mhèin

R 15–17
R 14–11
G 5–11
Y 7–9
B 6–8
R 18–21
W 6–8
VR 22–24
R 25–27

R 1–10

Crinan Boatyard

Hotel

Lock

Crinan Canal

TARBERT HARBOUR

Tarbert Harbour Authority
Harbour Office, Garval Road, Tarbert, Argyll, PA29 6TR
Tel: 01880 820344 Fax: 01880 820719
Email: tarbertharbour@btconnect.com

VHF Ch 14
ACCESS H24

Tarbert is situated on the west side of Loch Fyne, at 70km the longest sea loch in Scotland opening to the south into the Firth of Clyde.

The harbour is a natural amphi-theatre with an easily navigated narrow entrance at the east side opening onto Loch Fyne. Its eastern boundary is a line between Garbhaird Pt and Rubha Loisgte. The Harbour is accessible at all states of the tide and is one of Scotland's most sheltered harbours making it an excellent place to stay or leave a vessel unattended.

There are visiting berths for 65–100 sailing and motor yachts of varying sizes. Fresh water and electricity are available on the pontoons.

FACILITIES AT A GLANCE

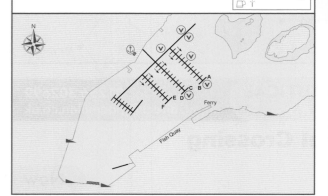

Ferry

Fish Quay

PORTAVADIE MARINA

Portavadie Marina
Portavadie, Loch Fyne, Argyll, PA21 2DA
Tel: 01700 811075 Fax: 01700 811074
Email: info@portavadiemarina.com

VHF Ch 80
ACCESS H24

Portavadie Marina offers deep and sheltered berthing to residential and visiting boats in an area renowned for its superb cruising waters. Situated on the east side of Loch Fyne in close proximity to several islands and the famous Kyles of Bute, Portavadie is within easy sailing distance of the Crinan Canal, giving access to the Inner and Outer Hebrides. The marina has 230 berths 60 of which are reserved for visitors, plus comprehensive on shore facilities, including a choice of restaurants, bars and self catering accommodation. There is also a shop and small chandlery overlooking the marina, a dedicated fuel berth for petrol and diesel and bike hire.

This unspoiled area of Argyll which is less than two hours by road from Glasgow offers an ideal base for boat owners looking for a safe and secure haven.

FACILITIES AT A GLANCE

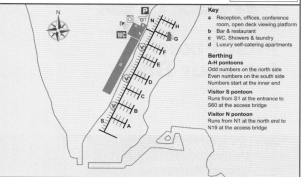

Key
a Reception, offices, conference room, open deck viewing platform
b Bar & restaurant
c WC, Showers & laundry
d Luxury self-catering apartments

Berthing
A-H pontoons
Odd numbers on the north side
Even numbers on the south side
Numbers start at the inner end

Visitor S pontoon
Runs from S1 at the entrance to S60 at the access bridge

Visitor N pontoon
Runs from N1 at the north end to N19 at the access bridge

HOLY LOCH MARINA

Holy Loch Marina
Rankin's Brae, Sandbank, Dunoon, PA23 8FE
Tel: 01369 701800 Fax: 01369 704749
Email: info@holylochmarina.co.uk

VHF Ch 80
ACCESS H24

Holy Loch Marina, the marine gateway to Loch Lomond and the Trossachs National Park, lies on the south shore of the loch, roughly half a mile west of Lazaretto Point. Holy Loch is among the Clyde's most beautiful natural harbours and, besides being a peaceful location, offers an abundance of wildlife, places of local historical interest as well as excellent walking and cycling through the Argyll Forest Park. The marina can be entered in all weather conditions and is within easy sailing distance of Loch Long and Upper Firth.

FACILITIES AT A GLANCE

Key
a Office/Harbourmaster
b Boat storage
c Holy Loch Sailing Club
d Pier

Sandbank Village

RHU MARINA

Rhu Marina
Rhu, Dunbartonshire, G84 8LH
Tel: 01436 820238 Fax: 01436 821039
Email: sbell@quaymarinas.com

VHF Ch M, 80
ACCESS H24

Located on the north shore of the Clyde Estuary, Rhu Marina is accessible at all states of the tide and can accommodate yachts up to 24m in length. It also operates 40 swinging moorings in the bay adjacent to the marina, with a ferry service provided.

Within easy walking distance of the marina is Rhu village, a conservation village incorporating a few shops, a pub and the beautiful Glenarn Gardens as well as the Royal Northern & Clyde Yacht Club. A mile or two to the east lies the holiday town of Helensburgh, renowned for its attractive architecture and elegant parks and gardens, while Glasgow city is just 25 miles away and can be easily reached by train.

FACILITIES AT A GLANCE

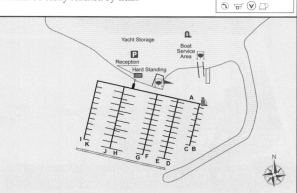

SANDPOINT MARINA

Sandpoint Marina Ltd
Sandpoint, Woodyard Road, Dumbarton, G82 4BG
Tel: 01389 762396 Fax: 01389 732605
Email: sales@sandpoint-marina.co.uk
www.sandpoint-marina.co.uk

VHF
ACCESS HW±3

Lying on the north bank of the Clyde estuary on the opposite side of the River Leven from Dumbarton Castle, Sandpoint Marina provides easy access to some of the most stunning cruising grounds in the United Kingdom. It is an independently run marina, offering a professional yet personal service to every boat owner. Among the facilities to hand are an on site chandlery, storage areas, a 40 ton travel hoist and 20 individual workshop units.

Within a 20-minute drive of Glasgow city centre, the marina is situated close to the shores of Loch Lomond, the largest fresh water loch in Britain.

FACILITIES AT A GLANCE

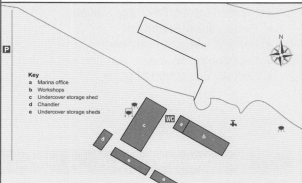

Key
a Marina office
b Workshops
c Undercover storage shed
d Chandler
e Undercover storage sheds

9

JAMES WATT DOCK MARINA

James Watt Dock Marina
East Hamilton Street
Greenock, Renfrewshire, PA15 2TD
Tel: 01475 729838
www.jwdmarina.co.uk Email: info@jwdmarina.co.uk

VHF	80
ACCESS	H24

Based in the historic James Watt Dock alongside the stunning Victorian Sugar Shed, this new marina opened in May 2011 and is the first step in establishing an exciting new River Clyde waterfront development only 23 miles from Glasgow and 15 miles from the airport. James Watt Dock will have all the usual amenities expected of a modern marina.

Within easy reach of Greenock's cinema, pool, ice rink, restaurants and shops, and with nearby transport connections, the marina will be a great location for both visitors and regular berthers.

FACILITIES AT A GLANCE

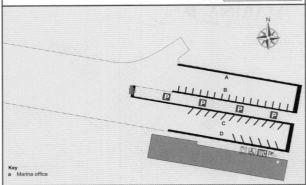

Key
a Marina office

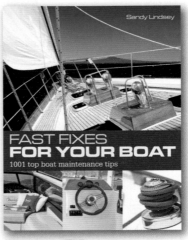

KIP MARINA

Kip Marina, The Yacht Harbour
Inverkip, Renfrewshire, Scotland, PA16 0AS
Tel: 01475 521485 Fax: 01475 521298
www.kipmarina.co.uk Email: enquire@kipmarina.co.uk

VHF Ch 80
ACCESS H24

Inverkip is a small village which lies on the south shores of the River Kip as it enters the Firth of Clyde. Once established for fishing, smuggling and, in the 17th century, witch-hunts, it became a seaside resort in the 1860s as a result of the installation of the railway. Today it is a yachting centre, boasting a state-of-the-art marina with over 600 berths and full boatyard facilities. With the capacity to accommodate yachts of up to 23m LOA, Kip Marina offers direct road and rail access to Glasgow and its international airport, therefore making it an ideal location for either a winter lay up or crew changeover.

FACILITIES AT A GLANCE

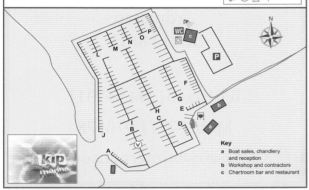

Key
a Boat sales, chandlery and reception
b Workshop and contractors
c Chartroom bar and restaurant

LARGS YACHT HAVEN

Largs Yacht Haven Ltd
Irvine Road, Largs, Ayrshire, KA30 8EZ
Tel: 01475 675333 Fax: 01475 672245
Email: largs@yachthavens.com www.yachthavens.com

VHF Ch M, 80
ACCESS H24

Largs Yacht Haven offers a superb location among lochs and islands, with numerous fishing villages and harbours nearby. Sheltered cruising can be enjoyed in the inner Clyde, while the west coast and Ireland are only a day's sail away. With a stunning backdrop of the Scottish mountains, Largs incorporates 700 fully serviced berths and provides a range of on site facilities including chandlers, sailmakers, divers, engineers, shops, restaurants and club.

A 20-minute coastal walk brings you to the town of Largs, which has all the usual amenities as well as good road and rail connections to Glasgow.

FACILITIES AT A GLANCE

9

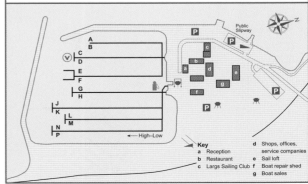

Key
a Reception
b Restaurant
c Largs Sailing Club
d Shops, offices, service companies
e Sail loft
f Boat repair shed
g Boat sales

CLYDE MARINA

Clyde Marina Ltd
The Harbour, Ardrossan, Ayrshire, KA22 8DB
Tel: 01294 607077 Fax: 01294 607076
www.clydemarina.com Email: info@clydemarina.com

VHF	Ch 80
ACCESS	H24

Situated on the Clyde Coast between Irvine and Largs, Clyde Marina is a modern bustling yacht harbour with boatyard, 50 Tonne hoist and active boat sales, set in a landscaped environment. A deep draft marina berthing vessels up to 30m LOA, draft up to 5m. Peviously accommodated vessels include tall ships and Whitbread 60s plus a variety of sail and power craft. Fully serviced pontoons plus all the yard facilities you would expect from a leading marina including boatyard and boatshed for repairs or storage. Good road and rail connections and only 30 minutes from Glasgow and Prestwick airports.

FACILITIES AT A GLANCE

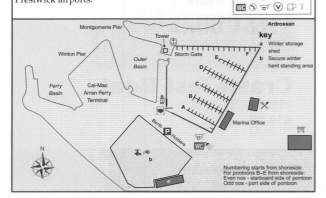

Jessail

SAIL REPAIRS
CANVAS WORK
UPHOLSTERY
INDUSTRIAL SEWING

58 Glasgow Street
Ardrossan
KA22 8EH

Tel/Fax: 01294 467311

Mob: 07771 970578

jessail@btinternet.com

TROON YACHT HAVEN

Troon Yacht Haven Ltd
The Harbour, Troon, Ayrshire, KA10 6DJ
Tel: 01292 315553 Fax: 01292 312836
Email: troon@yachthavens.com
www.yachthavens.com

VHF	Ch 80, M
ACCESS	H24

Troon Yacht Haven, situated on the Southern Clyde Estuary, benefits from deep water at all states of the tide. Tucked away in the harbour of Troon, it is well sheltered and within easy access of the town centre.

There are plenty of cruising opportunities to be had from here, whether it be hopping across to the Isle of Arran, with its peaceful anchorages and mountain walks, sailing round the Mull or through the Crinan Canal to the Western Isles, or heading for the sheltered waters of the Clyde.

FACILITIES AT A GLANCE

Key
a Main building
   Toilets
   Showers
   Baths
   Laundry
b Marina office

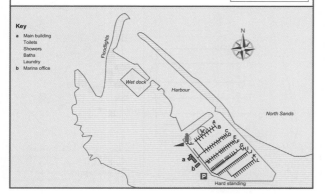

MARYPORT MARINA

Maryport Development Ltd
Marine Road, Maryport, Cumbria, CA15 8AY
Tel: 01900 814431
www.maryportmarina.com
Email: enquires@maryportmarina.com

VHF	Ch 12,16
ACCESS	HW±2.5

Maryport Marina is located in the historic Senhouse Dock, which was originally built for sailing clippers in the late 19th century. The old stone harbour walls provide good shelter to the 190 berths from the prevailing south westerlies.

Maryport town centre and its shops, pubs and other amenities is within easy walking distance from the marina. Maryport a perfect location from which to explore the west coast of Scotland as well as the Isle of Man and the Galloway Coast. For those who wish to venture inland, then the Lake District is only seven miles away.

FACILITIES AT A GLANCE

Key
a Marina Office
b Boat repair facility
c Coastguard building
d Fish handling building
e Wet fish shop
f Aquarium, cafe
g Play area
h Amenity block

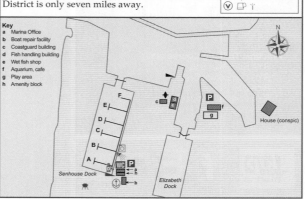

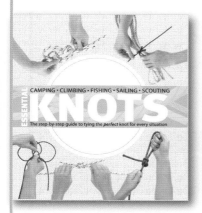

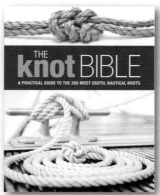
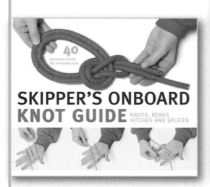

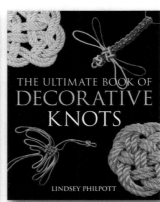

NW ENGLAND, ISLE OF MAN & N WALES – Mull of Galloway to Bardsey Is

Key to Marina Plans symbols

Bottled gas		Parking
Chandler		Pub/Restaurant
Disabled facilities		Pump out
Electrical supply		Rigging service
Electrical repairs		Sail repairs
Engine repairs		Shipwright
First Aid		Shop/Supermarket
Fresh Water		Showers
Fuel - Diesel		Slipway
Fuel - Petrol		Toilets
Hardstanding/boatyard		Telephone
Internet Café		Trolleys
Laundry facilities		Visitors berths
Lift-out facilities		Wi-Fi

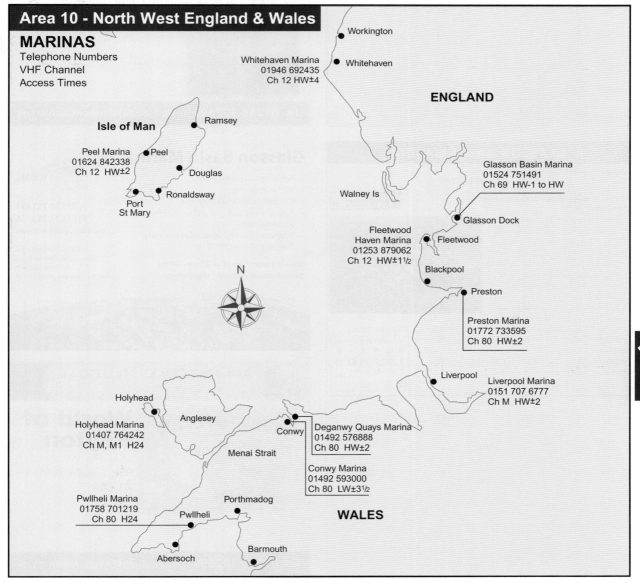

Area 10 - North West England & Wales

MARINAS
Telephone Numbers
VHF Channel
Access Times

Workington

Whitehaven Marina
01946 692435
Ch 12 HW±4

Whitehaven

ENGLAND

Isle of Man

Ramsey

Peel Marina
01624 842338
Ch 12 HW±2

Peel

Douglas

Ronaldsway

Port
St Mary

Glasson Basin Marina
01524 751491
Ch 69 HW-1 to HW

Walney Is

Glasson Dock

Fleetwood
Haven Marina
01253 879062
Ch 12 HW±1½

Fleetwood

Blackpool

Preston

Preston Marina
01772 733595
Ch 80 HW±2

N

Liverpool

Liverpool Marina
0151 707 6777
Ch M HW±2

Holyhead

Holyhead Marina
01407 764242
Ch M, M1 H24

Anglesey

Conwy

Deganwy Quays Marina
01492 576888
Ch 80 HW±2

Menai Strait

Conwy Marina
01492 593000
Ch 80 LW±3½

Pwllheli Marina
01758 701219
Ch 80 H24

Porthmadog

Pwllheli

WALES

Barmouth

Abersoch

10

WHITEHAVEN MARINA

Whitehaven Marina Ltd
Harbour Office, Bulwark Quay, Whitehaven, Cumbria, CA28 7HW
Tel: 01946 692435
Email: enquiries@whitehavenmarina.co.uk
www.whitehavenmarina.co.uk

VHF	Ch 12
ACCESS	HW±4

Whitehaven Marina can be found at the south-western entrance to the Solway Firth, providing a strategic departure point for those yachts heading for the Isle of Man, Ireland or Southern Scotland. The harbour is one of the more accessible ports of refuge in NW England, affording a safe entry in most weathers. The approach channel across the outer harbour is dredged to about 1.0m above chart datum, allowing entry into the inner harbour via a sea lock at around HW±4. Over 100 new walk ashore berths were installed in 2013.

Conveniently situated for visiting the Lake District, Whitehaven is an attractive Georgian town, renowned in the C18 for its rum and slave imports.

FACILITIES AT A GLANCE

GLASSON BASIN MARINA

BWML, Glasson Basin Marina
School Lane, Glasson Dock, Lancaster, LA2 0AW
Tel: 01524 751491 Fax: 01524 752626
Email: barnaby.hayward@bwml.co.uk
www.bwml.co.uk

VHF	Ch 69
ACCESS	HW-1 to HW

Glasson Dock Marina lies on the River Lune, west of Sunderland Point. Access is via the outer dock which opens 45 minutes before H. W.Liverpool and thence via BWB lock into the inner basin. It is recommended to leave Lune No. 1 Buoy approx 1.5 hrs before HW. Contact the dock on Channel 69. The Marina can only be contacted by telephone. All the necessary requirements can be found either on site or within easy reach of Glasson Dock, including boat, rigging and sail repair services as well as a launderette, ablution facilities, shops and restaurants.

FACILITIES AT A GLANCE

Key
a Marina office
b Glasson Sailing Club
c Harbour House

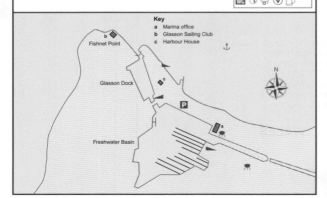

PEEL MARINA

Peel Marina
The Harbour Office, East Quay, Peel, IM5 1AR
Tel: 01624 842338 Fax: 01624 843610
www.gov.im/harbours/
Email: enquiries@harbours.dot.gov.im

VHF	Ch 12
ACCESS	HW±2

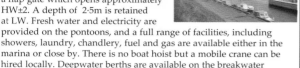

The Inner Harbour has recently been re-developed to provide a 120-berth marina in the southern end. Access is via a flap gate which opens approximately HW±2. A depth of 2·5m is retained at LW. Fresh water and electricity are provided on the pontoons, and a full range of facilities, including showers, laundry, chandlery, fuel and gas are available either in the marina or close by. There is no boat hoist but a mobile crane can be hired locally. Deepwater berths are available on the breakwater

Peel is the most active fishing port on the Isle of Man. The harbour is overlooked by its ancient castle, which also features the award-winning House of Manannan heritage centre. The town offers good shopping, banks, bars, a post office and chemist.

FACILITIES AT A GLANCE

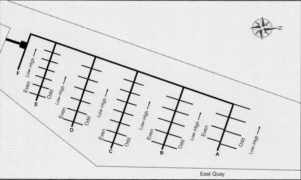

East Quay

FLEETWOOD HAVEN MARINA

Fleetwood Haven Marina
c/o ABP, Port & Marina Office, Fleetwood, FY7 8BP
Tel: 01253 879062 Fax: 01253 879063
Email: fleetwoodhaven@abports.co.uk

VHF	Ch 12
ACCESS	HW±1.5

Fleetwood Haven Marina provides a good location from which to cruise Morecambe Bay and the Irish Sea. To the north west is the Isle of Man, the north is the Solway Firth and the Clyde Estuary, while to the south west is Conwy, the Menai Straits and Holyhead.

Tucked away in a protected dock which dates to 1835, the marina has 420 full service berths and offers extensive facilities including a 75-tonne boat hoist, laundry and a first class shower/bathroom block.

Call Fleetwood Dock Radio on VHF Channel 12 (Tel 01253 872351) for permission to enter the dock channel.

FACILITIES AT A GLANCE

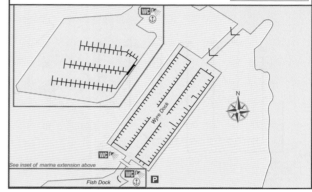

See inset of marina extension above

Wyre Dock

Fish Dock

PRESTON MARINA

Preston Marine Services Ltd
The Boathouse, Navigation Way, Preston, PR2 2YP
Tel: 01772 733595 Fax: 01772 731881
Email: info@prestonmarina.co.uk www.prestonmarina.co.uk

VHF	Ch 80
ACCESS	HW±2

Preston Marina forms part of the comprehensive Riversway Docklands development, meeting all the demands of modern day boat owners. With the docks' history dating back over 100 years, today the marina comprises 40 acres of fully serviced pontoon berths sheltered behind the refurbished original lock gates.

Lying 15 miles up the River Ribble, which itself is an interesting cruising ground with an abundance of wildlife, Preston is well placed for sailing to parts of Scotland, Ireland or Wales. The Docklands development includes a wide choice of restaurants, shops and cinemas as well as being in easy reach of all the cultural and leisure facilities provided by a large town.

FACILITIES AT A GLANCE

Key
a Riverway control building
b Marina HQ
c Pub/restaurant

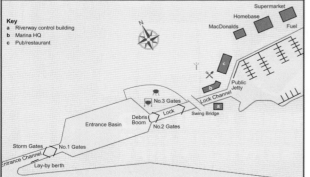

Supermarket
Homebase
MacDonalds
Fuel
Public Jetty
Lock Channel
No.3 Gates
Lock
Swing Bridge
Debris Boom
No.2 Gates
Entrance Basin
Storm Gates
No.1 Gates
Entrance Channel
Lay-by berth

LIVERPOOL MARINA

Liverpool Marina
Coburg Wharf, Sefton Street, Liverpool, L3 4BP
Tel: 0151 707 6777 Fax: 0151 707 6770
Email: mail@liverpoolmarina.co.uk

VHF	Ch M
ACCESS	HW±2

Liverpool Marina is ideally situated for yachtsmen wishing to cruise the Irish Sea. Access is through a computerised lock that opens two and a half hours either side of high water between 0600 and 2200 daily. Once in the marina, you can enjoy the benefits of the facilities on offer, including a first class club bar and restaurant.

Liverpool - recently announced Capital of Culture 2008 - is now a thriving cosmopolitan city, with attractions ranging from numerous bars and restaurants to museums, art galleries and the Beatles Story.

FACILITIES AT A GLANCE

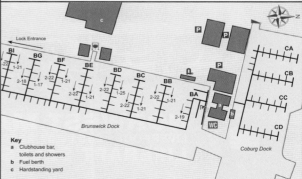

Lock Entrance
Brunswick Dock
Coburg Dock

Key
a Clubhouse bar,
   toilets and showers
b Fuel berth
c Hardstanding yard

10

CONWY MARINA

Conwy Marina
Conwy, LL32 8EP
Tel: 01492 593000 Fax: 01492 564828
Email: jroberts@quaymarinas.com
www.quaymarinas.com

⚓⚓⚓⚓

| VHF | Ch 80 |
| ACCESS | LW±3.5 |

Situated in an area of outstanding natural beauty, with the Mountains of Snowdonia National Park providing a stunning backdrop, Conwy is the first purpose-built marina to be developed on the north coast of Wales. Enjoying a unique site next to the 13th century Conwy Castle, the third of Edward I's great castles, it provides a convenient base from which to explore the cruising grounds of the North Wales coast. The unspoilt coves of Anglesey and the beautiful Menai Straits prove a popular destination, while further afield are the Llyn Peninsula and the Islands of Bardsey and Tudwells. The marina incorporates about 500 fully serviced berths which are accessible through a barrier gate between half tide and high water.

FACILITIES AT A GLANCE

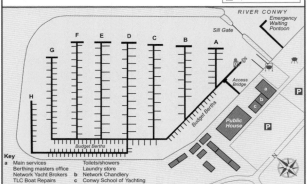

Key
a Main services
   Berthing masters office
   Network Yacht Brokers
   TLC Boat Repairs
   Toilets/showers
   Laundry store
b Network Chandlery
c Conwy School of Yachting

DEGANWY QUAYS MARINA

Deganwy Quays Marina
Deganwy, Conwy, LL31 9DJ
Tel: 01492 576888 Fax: 01492 580066
Email: jjones@quaymarinas.com www.quaymarinas.com

⚓⚓⚓⚓

| VHF | Ch 80 |
| ACCESS | HW±2 |

Deganwy Quays Marina is located in the centre of the north Wales coastline on the estuary of the Conwy River and sits between the river and the small town of Deganwy with the beautiful backdrop of the Vardre hills. The views from the Marina across the Conwy River are truly outstanding with the medieval walled town and Castle of Conwy outlined against the foothills of the Snowdonia National Park.

Deganwy Quays Marina opened in 2004 and has 165 fully serviced berths which are accessed via a tidal gate between half tide and high water.

FACILITIES AT A GLANCE

HOLYHEAD MARINA

Holyhead Marina Ltd
Newry Beach, Holyhead, Gwynedd, LL65 1YA
Tel: 01407 764242 Fax: 01407 769152
Email: info@holyheadmarina.co.uk

VHF Ch M
ACCESS H24

One of the few natural deep water harbours on the Welsh coast, Anglesey is conveniently placed as a first port of call if heading to North Wales from the North, South or West. Its marina at Holyhead, accessible at all states of the tide, is sheltered by Holyhead Mountain as well as an enormous harbour breakwater and extensive floating breakwaters, therefore offering good protection from all directions.

Anglesey boasts numerous picturesque anchorages and beaches in addition to striking views over Snowdonia, while only a tide or two away are the Isle of Man and Eire.

FACILITIES AT A GLANCE

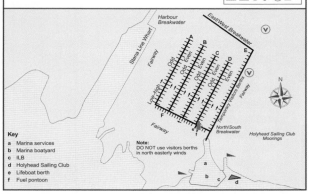

Key
a Marina services
b Marina boatyard
c ILB
d Holyhead Sailing Club
e Lifeboat berth
f Fuel pontoon

Note:
DO NOT use visitors berths in north easterly winds

PWLLHELI MARINA

Pwllheli Marina
Glan Don, Pwllheli, North Wales, LL53 5YT
Tel: 01758 701219 Fax: 01758 701443
Email: hafanpwllheli@gwynedd.gov.uk

VHF Ch 80
ACCESS

Pwllheli is an old Welsh market town providing the gateway to the Llyn Peninsula, which stretches out as far as Bardsey Island to form an 'Area of Outstanding Natural Beauty'. Enjoying the spectacular backdrop of the Snowdonia Mountains, Pwllheli's numerous attractions include an open-air market every Wednesday, 'Neuadd Dwyfor', offering a mix of live theatre and latest films, and beautiful beaches.

Pwllheli Marina is situated on the south side of the Llyn Peninsula. One of Wales' finest marinas and sailing centres, it has over 400 pontoon berths and excellent onshore facilities.

FACILITIES AT A GLANCE

Key
a Marina offices
   Toilets
   Showers
   Baby change
   Launderette
b Domestic refuse point
c Short stay boat park
d Pwllheli sailing club
e Chandlery
f Events pontoons

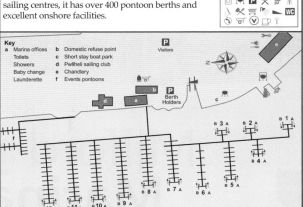

10

SOUTH WALES & BRISTOL CHANNEL – Bardsey Island to Land's End

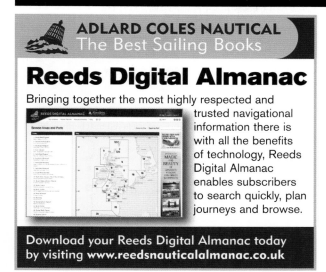
Key to Marina Plans symbols

🛢	Bottled gas	P	Parking
	Chandler	✕	Pub/Restaurant
♿	Disabled facilities		Pump out
	Electrical supply		Rigging service
	Electrical repairs		Sail repairs
	Engine repairs		Shipwright
✚	First Aid		Shop/Supermarket
	Fresh Water		Showers
	Fuel - Diesel		Slipway
	Fuel - Petrol	WC	Toilets
	Hardstanding/boatyard		Telephone
@	Internet Café		Trolleys
	Laundry facilities	Ⓥ	Visitors berths
	Lift-out facilities		Wi-Fi

Area 11 - South Wales & Bristol Channel

MARINAS
Telephone Numbers
VHF Channel
Access Times

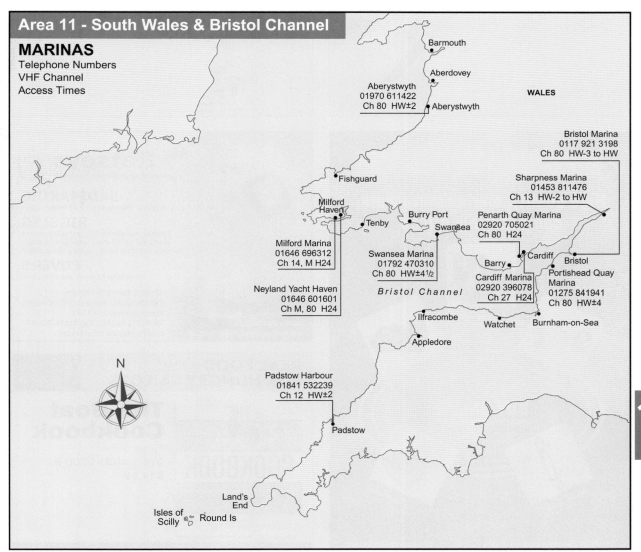

WALES

Barmouth

Aberdovey

Aberystwyth
01970 611422
Ch 80 HW±2
Aberystwyth

Bristol Marina
0117 921 3198
Ch 80 HW-3 to HW

Sharpness Marina
01453 811476
Ch 13 HW-2 to HW

Fishguard

Milford Haven

Burry Port

Penarth Quay Marina
02920 705021
Ch 80 H24

Tenby

Swansea

Milford Marina
01646 696312
Ch 14, M H24

Swansea Marina
01792 470310
Ch 80 HW±4½

Barry

Cardiff

Bristol

Portishead Quay Marina
01275 841941
Ch 80 HW±4

Cardiff Marina
02920 396078
Ch 27 H24

Neyland Yacht Haven
01646 601601
Ch M, 80 H24

Bristol Channel

Ilfracombe

Watchet

Burnham-on-Sea

Appledore

N

Padstow Harbour
01841 532239
Ch 12 HW±2

Padstow

Land's End

Isles of Scilly   Round Is

11

ABERYSTWYTH MARINA

Aberystwyth Marina, IMP Developments
Trefechan, Aberystwyth, Ceredigion, SY23 1AS
Tel: 01970 611422 Fax: 01970 624122
Email: enquiries@aberystwythmarina.com

VHF | Ch 80
ACCESS | HW±2

Aberystwyth is a picturesque university seaside town on the west coast of Wales. Its £9 million marina provides over 150 permanent pontoon berths and welcomes on average between 1,500 and 2,000 visiting yachts per year. Accessible two hours either side of high water, its facilities incorporate the usual marine services as well as an on-site pub and restaurant.

A short distance away are several pretty Welsh harbours, including Fishguard, Cardigan, Porthmadog and Abersoch, while the east coast of Ireland can be reached within a day's sail.

FACILITIES AT A GLANCE

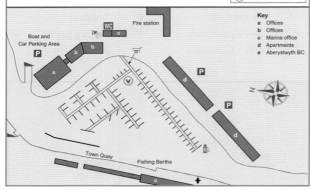

Key
a Offices
b Offices
c Marina office
d Apartments
e Aberystwyth BC

MILFORD MARINA

Milford Marina
Milford Docks, Milford Haven, Pembrokeshire, SA73 3AF
Tel: 01646 696312 Fax: 01646 696314
Email: enquiries@milfordmarina.com www.milfordmarina.com

VHF | Ch 14
ACCESS | H24

Set within one of the deepest natural harbours in the world, Milford Marina is situated in a non-tidal basin within the UK's only coastal National Park, the ideal base for discovering the fabulous coastline in Pembrokeshire, Wales and Ireland. Continued investment has meant that the marina provides safe, secure and sheltered boat berths with a full range of shoreside facilities in the heart of SW Wales.

Accessed via an entrance lock (with waiting pontoons both inside and outside the lock), the marina is perfect for exploring the picturesque upper reaches of the River Cleddau or cruising out beyond St Ann's Head to the unspoilt islands of Skomer, Skokholm and Grassholm.

FACILITIES AT A GLANCE

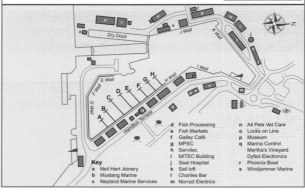

Key
a Neil Hart Joinery
b Mustang Marine
c Neyland Marine Services
d Fish Processing
e Fish Markets
f Galley Café
g MPSC
h Servitec
i MITEC Building
j Seal Hospital
k Sail loft
l Charlies Bar
m Norrad Electrics
n All Pets Vet Care
o Locks on Line
p Museum
q Marina Control
  Martha's Vineyard
  Dyfed Electronics
r Phoenix Bowl
s Windjammer Marine

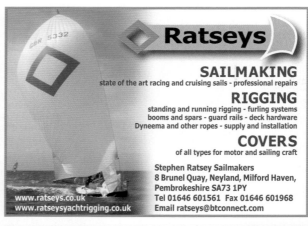

NEYLAND YACHT HAVEN

Neyland Yacht Haven Ltd
Brunel Quay, Neyland, Pembrokeshire, SA73 1PY
Tel: 01646 601601 Fax: 01646 600713
Email: neyland@yachthavens.com www.yachthavens.com

VHF	Ch M, 80
ACCESS	H24

Approximately 10 miles from the entrance to Milford Haven lies Neyland Yacht Haven. Tucked away in a well protected inlet just before the Cleddau Bridge, this marina has 420 berths and can accommodate yachts up to 25m LOA with draughts of up to 2.5m. The marina is divided into two basins, with the lower one enjoying full tidal access, while entry to the upper one is restricted by a tidal sill. Visitor and annual berthing enquiries welcome.

Offering a comprehensive range of services, Neyland Yacht Haven is within a five minute walk of the town centre where the various shops and takeaways cater for most everyday needs. The Yacht Haven is a member of the TransEurope Group.

FACILITIES AT A GLANCE

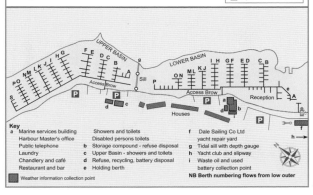

Key

a	Marine services building		Showers and toilets	f	Dale Sailing Co Ltd
	Harbour Master's office		Disabled persons toilets		yacht repair yard
	Public telephone	b	Storage compound - refuse disposal	g	Tidal sill with depth gauge
	Laundry	c	Upper Basin - showers and toilets	h	Yacht club and slipway
	Chandlery and café	d	Refuse, recycling, battery disposal	i	Waste oil and used
	Restaurant and bar	e	Holding berth		battery collection point

Weather information collection point

NB Berth numbering flows from low outer

11

SWANSEA MARINA

Swansea Marina
Lockside, Maritime Quarter, Swansea, SA1 1WG
Tel: 01792 470310 Fax: 01792 463948
www.swansea.gov.uk/swanseamarina
Email: swanmar@swansea.gov.uk

VHF	Ch 80
ACCESS	HW±4.5

At the hub of the city's recently redeveloped and award winning Maritime Quarter, Swansea Marina can be accessed HW±4½ hrs via a lock. Surrounded by a plethora of shops, restaurants and marine businesses to cater for most yachtsmen's needs, the marina is in close proximity to the picturesque Gower coast, where there is no shortage of quiet sandy beaches off which to anchor. It also provides the perfect starting point for cruising to Ilfracombe, Lundy Island, the North Cornish coast or West Wales.

Within easy walking distance of the marina is the city centre, boasting a covered shopping centre and market. For those who prefer walking or cycling, take the long promenade to the Mumbles fishing village from where there are plenty of coastal walks.

FACILITIES AT A GLANCE

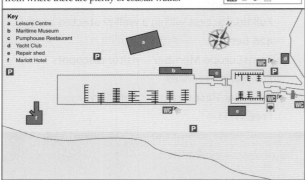

Key
a Leisure Centre
b Maritime Museum
c Pumphouse Restaurant
d Yacht Club
e Repair shed
f Mariott Hotel

PENARTH QUAYS MARINA

Penarth Quays Marina
Penarth, Vale of Glamorgan, CF64 1TQ
Tel: 02920 705021
Email: sjones@quaymarinas.com
www.quaymarinas.com

VHF	Ch 80
ACCESS	H24

Penarth Quays Marina has been established in the historic basins of Penarth Docks for over 20 years and is the premier boating facility in the region. The marina is Cardiff Bay's only 5 Gold Anchor marina and provides an ideal base for those using the Bay and the Bristol Channel. With 24hr access there is always water available for boating. Penarth and Cardiff boast an extensive range of leisure facilities, shops and restaurants making this marina an ideal base or destination. The marina has a blue flag and is a member of the TransEurope Group.

FACILITIES AT A GLANCE

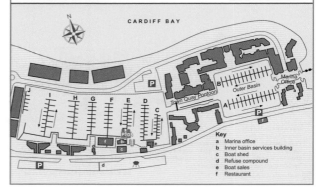

CARDIFF BAY

Key
a Marina office
b Inner basin services building
c Boat shed
d Refuse compound
e Boat sales
f Restaurant

CARDIFF MARINA

Cardiff Marina
Watkiss Way, Cardiff, CF11 0JL
Tel: 02920 396078 Fax: 02920 345116
Email: info@themarinegroup.co.uk
www.themarinegroup.co.uk

VHF	Ch M
ACCESS	H24

Cardiff Marina provides safe and sheltered moorings for motor-boats and yachts on the River Ely in the heart of Cardiff Bay. The 200 hectares of the bay make an attractive and approachable environment for all boat users with the Barrage allowing 24hr access to the Bristol Channel.

The location of the marina ensures plenty of activities within close proximity and excellent transport links for easy access to Cardiff and the wider country. As part of a fully integrated marine company, the marina is able to offer berth holders peace of mind by having the onsite expertise of its Marine Service Centre.

FACILITIES AT A GLANCE

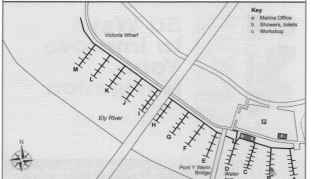

Key
a Marina Office
b Showers, toilets
c Workshop

Victoria Wharf

Ely River

Pont Y Werin Bridge

Water bus

SHARPNESS MARINA

Sharpness Marina
Berkeley, Gloucestershire GL13 9UN
Tel & fax: 01453 811476
Email: sharpness@f2s.com www.sharpnessmarina.co.uk

VHF	Ch 13
ACCESS	HW-2

Sharpness is a small port on the River Severn lying at the entrance to the Gloucester and Sharpness Canal. At the time of its completion in 1827, the canal was the largest and deepest ship canal in the world. However, although once an important commercial waterway, it is now primarily used by pleasure boats. Yachts approaching the marina from seaward can do so via a lock two hours before high water, but note that the final arrival should be timed as late as possible to avoid strong tides in the entrance. From the lock, a passage under two swing bridges and a turn to port brings you to the marina, where pontoon berths are equipped with electricity and water supplies.

FACILITIES AT A GLANCE

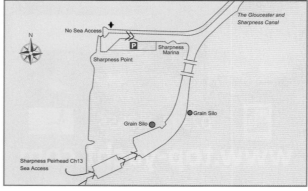

The Gloucester and Sharpness Canal

No Sea Access

Sharpness Marina

Sharpness Point

Grain Silo

Grain Silo

Sharpness Peirhead Ch13
Sea Access

BRISTOL MARINA

Bristol Marina Ltd
Hanover Place, Bristol, BS1 6TZ
Tel: 0117 921 3198 Fax: 0117 929 7672
Email: info@bristolmarina.co.uk

VHF	Ch 80
ACCESS	HW-3 to HW

Situated in the heart of the city, Bristol is a fully serviced marina providing over 100 pontoon berths for vessels up to 20m LOA. Among the facilities are a new fuelling berth and pump out station as well as an on site chandler and sailmaker. It is situated on the south side of the Floating Harbour, about eight miles from the mouth of the River Avon. Accessible from seaward via the Cumberland Basin, passing through both Entrance Lock and Junction Lock, it can be reached approximately three hours before HW.

Shops, restaurants, theatres and cinemas are all within easy reach of the marina, while local attractions include the SS *Great Britain*, designed by Isambard Kingdom Brunel, and the famous Clifton Suspension Bridge, which has an excellent visitors' centre depicting its fascinating story.

FACILITIES AT A GLANCE

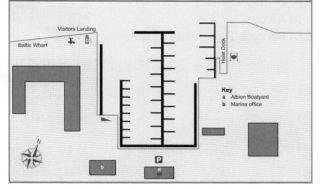

Key
a Albion Boatyard
b Marina office

PORTISHEAD QUAYS MARINA

Portishead Quays Marina
Newfoundland Way, Portishead, North Somerset, BS20 7DF
Tel: 01275 841941 Fax: 01275 841942
Email: portisheadmarina@quaymarinas.com
www.quaymarinas.com

VHF	Ch 80
ACCESS	HW±3.5

Portishead Marina is a popular destination for cruising in the Bristol Channel. Providing an excellent link between the inland waterways at Bristol and Sharpness and offering access to the open water and marinas down channel. The entrance to the Marina is via a lock, with a minimum access of HW+/- 3.5hrs. Contact the Marina on VHF Ch 80 ahead of time for next available lock. The Marina provides 250 fully serviced berths and can accommodate vessels up to 40m LOA, draft up to 5.5m. The marina has a 35 tonnes boat hoist and the boatyard offers all the facilities you would expect from a Quay Marinas site.

FACILITIES AT A GLANCE

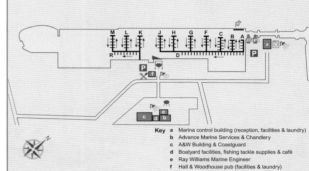

Key a Marina control building (reception, facilities & laundry)
b Advance Marine Services & Chandlery
c A&W Building & Coastguard
d Boatyard facilities, fishing tackle supplies & café
e Ray Williams Marine Engineer
f Hall & Woodhouse pub (facilities & laundry)

PADSTOW HARBOUR

Padstow Harbour Commissioners
The Harbour Office, Padstow, Cornwall, PL28 8AQ
Tel: 01841 532239 Fax: 01841 533346
Email: padstowharbour@btconnect.com
www.padstow-harbour.co.uk

VHF	Ch 12, 16
ACCESS	HW±2

Padstow is a small commercial port with a rich history situated 1.5 miles from the sea within the estuary of the River Camel. The inner harbour is serviced by a tidal gate – part of the 1988–1990 flood defence scheme, which is open approximately two hours either side of high water. A minimum of 3m of water is maintained in the inner harbour at all times. Onshore facilities are excellent, please enquire at the Harbour Office.

This is a thriving fishing port, so perhaps it wasn't surprising that celebrity chefs like Rick Stein and Jamie Oliver would set up shop in the town. This is a great resting point for everything Cornish from surf and coastal walks to fish and chips and cream teas.

FACILITIES AT A GLANCE

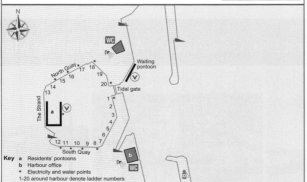

Key a Residents' pontoons
b Harbour office
* Electricity and water points
1-20 around harbour denote ladder numbers

11

SOUTH IRELAND – Malahide, clockwise to Liscannor Bay

Key to Marina Plans symbols

Bottled gas		P	Parking
Chandler			Pub/Restaurant
Disabled facilities			Pump out
Electrical supply			Rigging service
Electrical repairs			Sail repairs
Engine repairs			Shipwright
First Aid			Shop/Supermarket
Fresh Water			Showers
Fuel - Diesel			Slipway
Fuel - Petrol		WC	Toilets
Hardstanding/boatyard			Telephone
Internet Café	@		Trolleys
Laundry facilities		V	Visitors berths
Lift-out facilities			Wi-Fi

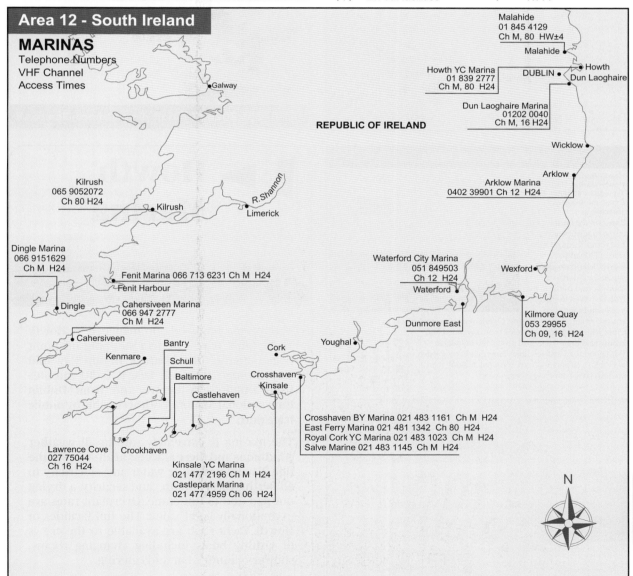

Area 12 - South Ireland

MARINAS

Telephone Numbers
VHF Channel
Access Times

REPUBLIC OF IRELAND

Galway

Limerick
R.Shannon

Malahide
01 845 4129
Ch M, 80 HW±4
Malahide

Howth YC Marina
01 839 2777
Ch M, 80 H24

DUBLIN
Howth
Dun Laoghaire

Dun Laoghaire Marina
01202 0040
Ch M, 16 H24

Wicklow

Arklow

Arklow Marina
0402 39901 Ch 12 H24

Kilrush
065 9052072
Ch 80 H24
Kilrush

Dingle Marina
066 9151629
Ch M H24

Fenit Marina 066 713 6231 Ch M H24
Fenit Harbour

Dingle

Cahersiveen Marina
066 947 2777
Ch M H24

Cahersiveen

Kenmare
Bantry
Schull
Baltimore
Castlehaven

Cork
Youghal

Crosshaven
Kinsale

Waterford City Marina
051 849503
Ch 12 H24
Waterford

Dunmore East

Wexford

Kilmore Quay
053 29955
Ch 09, 16 H24

Lawrence Cove
027 75044
Ch 16 H24

Crookhaven

Crosshaven BY Marina 021 483 1161 Ch M H24
East Ferry Marina 021 481 1342 Ch 80 H24
Royal Cork YC Marina 021 483 1023 Ch M H24
Salve Marine 021 483 1145 Ch M H24

Kinsale YC Marina
021 477 2196 Ch M H24
Castlepark Marina
021 477 4959 Ch 06 H24

N

12

MALAHIDE MARINA

Malahide Marina
Malahide, Co. Dublin
Tel: +353 1 845 4129 Fax: +353 1 845 4255
Email: info@malahidemarina.net
www.malahidemarina.net

VHF	Ch M, 80
ACCESS	HW±4

Malahide Marina, situated just 10 minutes from Dublin Airport and 20 minutes north of Dublin's city centre, is a fully serviced marina accommodating up to 350 yachts. Capable of taking vessels of up to 75m in length, its first class facilities include a boatyard with hard standing for approximately 170 boats and a 30-ton mobile hoist. Its on site restaurant provides a large seating area in convivial surroundings. The village of Malahide has plenty to offer the visiting yachtsmen, with a wide variety of eating places, nearby golf courses and tennis courts as well as a historic castle and botanical gardens.

FACILITIES AT A GLANCE

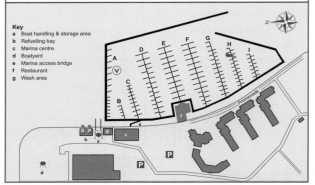

Key
a   Boat handling & storage area
b   Refuelling bay
c   Marina centre
d   Boatyard
e   Marina access bridge
f   Restaurant
g   Wash area

HOWTH MARINA

Howth Marina
Howth Marina, Harbour Road, Howth, Co. Dublin
Tel: +353 1 8392777 Fax: +353 1 8392430
Email: marina@hyc.ie
www.hyc.ie

VHF	Ch M, 80
ACCESS	H24

Based on the north coast of the rugged peninsula that forms the northern side of Dublin Bay, Howth Marina is ideally situated for north or south-bound traffic in the Irish Sea. Well sheltered in all winds, it can be entered at any state of the tide. Overlooking the marina is Howth Yacht Club, which has in recent years been expanded and is now said to be the largest yacht club in Ireland. With good road and rail links, Howth is in easy reach of Dublin's airport and ferry terminal, making it an obvious choice for crew changeovers.

FACILITIES AT A GLANCE

Key
a   Harbour office
b   RNLI boathouse
c   Clubhouse
d   Drying pad
e   Waiting pontoons (A&B)

Berth numbering starts
at hammerheads

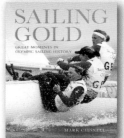

Howth Marina

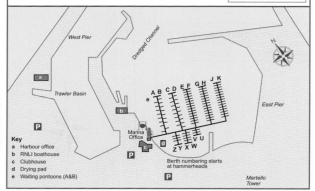

The marina is owned and managed by Howth Yacht Club. It is a perfect stopping off point being situated just north of Dublin Bay, mid way through the Irish Sea; it is 30 minutes from Dublin city centre and from Dublin International Airport, both accessible by public transport.

The marina is extremely safe in all weather conditions and there is access at all stages of the tide. Facilities include water and electricity to all berths, diesel pump, and security, a drying out pad and 15 ton crane. Overnight rates are exceptionally good value. The full facilities of Howth Yacht Club are available to the crews of visiting boats including changing rooms, showers, laundry, bar and catering.

DUN LAOGHAIRE MARINA

Dun Laoghaire Marina
Harbour Road, Dun Laoghaire, Co Dublin, Eire
Tel: +353 1 202 0040 Fax: +353 1 202 0043
Email: info@dlmarina.com   www.dlmarina.com

VHF | Ch M, 16
ACCESS | H24

Dun Laoghaire Marina – Gateway to Dublin and the first marina in the Republic of Ireland to be awarded five Gold anchors by THYA and also achieved the ICOMIA 'Clean Marina' accreditation – is the largest marina in Ireland. 24 hour access in all weather conditions. The town centre is located within 400m. Serviced berthing for 820 boats from 6m to 23m with visitors mainly on the hammerheads.

Larger vessels up to 30m and 80 tonne displacement can be accommodated alongside breakwater pontoons. Minimum draft is 3.6m LWS. With adjacent ferry terminal and rail station, Dublin 12kms and airport 35kms, the marina is an ideal location for crew change etc. Easy access to Dublin Bay, home to the biennial Dun Laoghaire Regatta.

FACILITIES AT A GLANCE

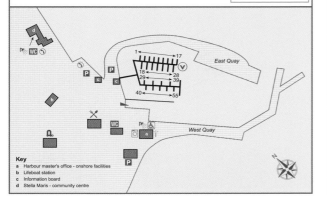

Key
a Royal Irish Yacht Club
b Marina office
c WC
d Royal St George Yacht Club
Berth numbering - odds to port, evens to starboard, increase inwards

---

ARKLOW MARINA

Arklow Marina
North Quay, Arklow, Co. Wicklow, Eire
Tel: +353 402 39901 Fax: +353 402 39902
Mobiles: 087 2375189 or 087 2588078
Email: technical@asl.ie
www.arklowmarina.com

VHF | Ch12
ACCESS | H24

Arklow is a popular fishing port and seaside town situated at the mouth of the River Avoca, 16 miles south of Wicklow and 11 miles north east of Gorey. The town is ideally placed for visiting the many beauty spots of County Wicklow including Glenmalure, Glendalough and Clara Lara, Avoca (Ballykissangel).

Arklow Marina is on the north bank of the river, just upstream of the commercial quays, with 42 berths in an inner harbour and 30 berths on pontoons outside the marina entrance. Vessels over 14m LOA should moor on the river pontoons.

FACILITIES AT A GLANCE

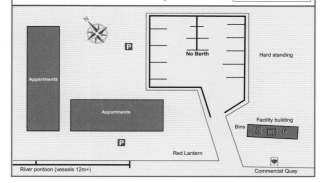

KILMORE QUAY

Kilmore Quay
Wexford, Ireland
Tel: +353 53 9129955 Fax: +353 53 9129915
Email: harbourmaster@wexfordcoco.ie   www.wexford.ie

VHF | Ch 09, 16
ACCESS | H24

Located in the SE corner of Ireland, Kilmore Quay is a small rural fishing village situated approximately 14 miles from the town of Wexford and 12 miles from Rosslare ferry port.

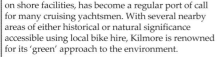

Its 55-berthed marina, offering shelter from the elements as well as various on shore facilities, has become a regular port of call for many cruising yachtsmen. With several nearby areas of either historical or natural significance accessible using local bike hire, Kilmore is renowned for its 'green' approach to the environment.

FACILITIES AT A GLANCE

Key
a Harbour master's office - onshore facilities
b Lifeboat station
c Information board
d Stella Maris - community centre

WATERFORD CITY MARINA

Waterford City Marina
Waterford, Ireland
Tel: +353 87 238 4944 Fax: +353 51 849763
Email: jcodd@waterfordcity.ie

VHF | Ch 12
ACCESS | H24

Famous for its connections with Waterford Crystal, manufactured in the city centre, Waterford is the capital of the SE region of Ireland. As a major city, it benefits from good rail links with Dublin, and Limerick, a regional airport with daily flights to Britain and an extensive bus service to

surrounding towns and villages. The marina is found on the banks of the River Suir, in the heart of this historic Viking city dating back to the ninth century. Yachtsmen can make the most of Waterford's wide range of shops, restaurants and bars without having to walk too far from their boats. With 150 fully serviced berths and first rate security, Waterford City Marina now provides shower, toilet and laundry facilities in its new reception building.

FACILITIES AT A GLANCE

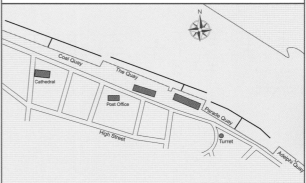

CROSSHAVEN BOATYARD MARINA

**Crosshaven Boatyard Marina
Crosshaven, Co Cork, Ireland
Tel: +353 214 831161 Fax: +353 214 831603
Email: info@crosshavenboatyard.com**

VHF **Ch M**
ACCESS **H24**

One of three marinas at Crosshaven, Crosshaven Boatyard was founded in 1950 and originally made its name from the construction of some of the most world-renowned yachts, including *Gypsy Moth* and Denis Doyle's *Moonduster*. Nowadays, however, the yard has diversified to provide a wide range of services to both the marine leisure and professional industries. Situated on a safe and sheltered river only 12 miles from Cork City Centre, the marina boasts 100 fully-serviced berths along with the capacity to accommodate yachts up to 35m LOA with a 4m draught. In addition, it is ideally situated for cruising the stunning south west coast of Ireland.

FACILITIES AT A GLANCE

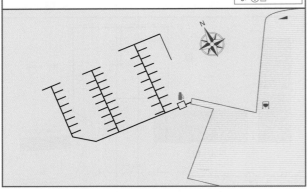

SALVE MARINE

**Salve Marine
Crosshaven, Co Cork, Ireland
Tel: +353 214 831 145 Fax: +353 214 831 747
Email: salvemarine@eircom.net**

VHF **Ch M**
ACCESS **H24**

Crosshaven is a picturesque seaside resort providing a gateway to Ireland's south and south west coasts. Offering a variety of activities to suit all types, its rocky coves and quiet sandy beaches stretch from Graball to Church Bay and from Fennell's Bay to nearby Myrtleville. Besides a selection of craft shops selling locally produced arts and crafts, there are plenty of pubs, restaurants and takeaways to suit even the most discerning of tastes. Lying within a few hundred metres of the village centre is Salve Marine, accommodating yachts up to 43m LOA with draughts of up to 4m. Its comprehensive services range from engineering and welding facilities to hull and rigging repairs.

FACILITIES AT A GLANCE

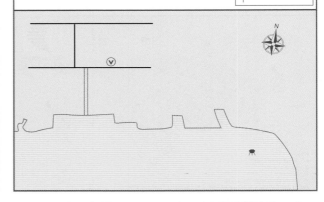

ROYAL CORK YACHT CLUB

**Royal Cork Yacht Club Marina
Crosshaven, Co Cork, Ireland
Tel: +353 21 483 1023 Fax: +353 21 483 1586
Email: mark@royalcork.com   www.royalcork.com**

VHF **Ch M**
ACCESS **H24**

Founded in 1720, the Royal Cork Yacht Club is one of the oldest and most prominent yacht clubs in the world. Organising, among many other events, the prestigious biennial Ford Cork Week, it boasts a number of World, European and National sailors among its membership.

The Yacht Club's marina is situated at Crosshaven, which nestles on the hillside at the mouth of the Owenabue River just inside the entrance to Cork Harbour. The harbour is popular with yachtsmen as it is accessible and well sheltered in all weather conditions. It also benefits from the Gulf Stream producing a temperate climate practically all year round.

FACILITIES AT A GLANCE

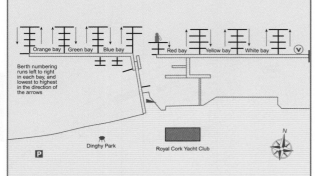

Orange bay | Green bay | Blue bay | Red bay | Yellow bay | White bay

Berth numbering runs left to right in each bay, and lowest to highest in the direction of the arrows

Dinghy Park

Royal Cork Yacht Club

EAST FERRY MARINA

**East Ferry Marina
Cobh, Co Cork, Ireland
Tel: +353 21 481 1342 Fax: +353 21 481 1342**

VHF **Ch 80**
ACCESS **H24**

East Ferry Marina lies on the east side of Great Island, one of three large islands in Cork Harbour which are now all joined by roads and bridges. Despite its remote, tranquil setting, it offers all the fundamental facilities including showers, water, fuel, electricity and that all important pub. The nearest town is Cobh, which is a good five mile walk away, albeit a pleasant one.

Formerly known as Queenstown, Cobh (pronounced 'cove') reverted back to its original Irish name in 1922 and is renowned for being the place from where thousands of Irish men and women set off to America to build a new life for themselves, particularly during the famine years of 1844–48.

FACILITIES AT A GLANCE

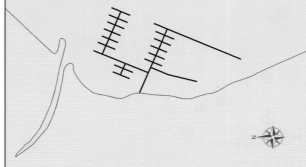

KINSALE YACHT CLUB MARINA

Kinsale Yacht Club Marina
Kinsale, Co Cork, Ireland
Tel: +353 21 4772196 Fax: +353 21 4774455
Email: kyc@iol.ie

VHF | Ch M
ACCESS | H24

Kinsale is a natural, virtually land-locked harbour on the estuary of the Bandon River, approximately 12 miles south west of Cork harbour entrance. Home to a thriving fishing fleet as well as frequented by commercial shipping, it boasts two fully serviced marinas, with the Kinsale Yacht Club & Marina being the closest to the town. Visitors to this marina automatically become temporary members of the club and are therefore entitled to make full use of the facilities, which include a fully licensed bar and restaurant serving evening meals on Wednesdays, Thursdays and Saturdays. Fuel, water and repair services are also available.

FACILITIES AT A GLANCE

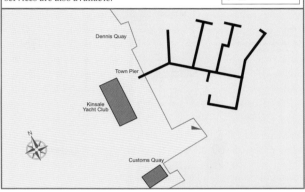

CASTLEPARK MARINA

Castlepark Marina Centre
Kinsale, Co Cork, Ireland
Tel: +353 21 4774959 Fax: +353 21 4773894
Email: tadgh@castleparkmarina.com

VHF | Ch 16, 14
ACCESS | H24

Situated on the south side of Kinsale Harbour, Castlepark is a small marina with deep water pontoon berths that are accessible at all states of the tide. Surrounded by rolling hills, it boasts its own beach as well as being in close proximity to the parklands of James Fort and a traditional Irish pub. The attractive town of Kinsale, with its narrow streets and slate-clad houses, lies just 1.5 miles away by road or five minutes away by ferry. Known as Ireland's 'fine food centre', it incorporates a number of gourmet food shops and high quality restaurants as well as a wine museum.

FACILITIES AT A GLANCE

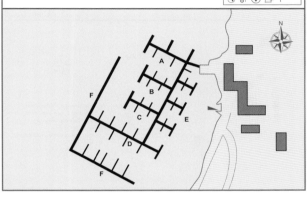

LAWRENCE COVE MARINA

Lawrence Cove Marina
Lawrence Cove, Bere Island, Co Cork, Ireland
Tel: +353 27 75044 Fax: +353 27 75044
Email: lcm@iol.ie
www.lawrencecovemarina.com

VHF | Ch 16
ACCESS | H24

Lawrence Cove enjoys a peaceful location on an island at the entrance to Bantry Bay. Privately owned and run, it offers sheltered and secluded waters as well as excellent facilities and fully serviced pontoon berths. A few hundred yards from the marina you will find a shop, pub and restaurant, while the mainland, with its various attractions, can be easily reached by ferry. Lawrence Cove lies at the heart of the wonderful cruising grounds of Ireland's south west coast and, just two hours from Cork airport, is an ideal place to leave your boat for long or short periods.

FACILITIES AT A GLANCE

CAHERSIVEEN MARINA

Cahersiveen Marina
The Pier, Cahersiveen, Co. Kerry, Ireland
Tel: +353 66 9472777 Fax: +353 66 9472993
Email: acard@eircom.net
www.cahersiveenmarina.ie

VHF | Ch M
ACCESS | H24

Situated two miles up Valentia River from Valentia Harbour, Cahersiveen Marina is well protected in all wind directions and is convenient for sailing to Valentia Island and Dingle Bay as well as for visiting some of the spectacular uninhabited islands in the surrounding area. Boasting a host of sheltered sandy beaches, the region is renowned for salt and fresh water fishing as well as being good for scuba diving.

Within easy walking distance of the marina lies the historic town of Cahersiveen, incorporating an array of convivial pubs and restaurants.

FACILITIES AT A GLANCE

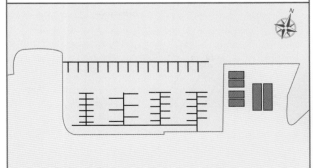

12

DINGLE MARINA

Dingle Marina
Strand Street, Dingle, Co Kerry, Ireland
Tel: +353 87 232 5844 Fax: +353 69 5152546
Email:dingleharbour@agriculture.gov.ie
www.dinglemarina.com

VHF	Ch M
ACCESS	H24

Dingle is Ireland's most westerly marina, lying at the heart of the sheltered Dingle Harbour, and is easily reached both day and night via a well buoyed approach channel. The surrounding area is an interesting and unfrequented cruising ground, with several islands, bays and beaches for the yachtsman to explore.

The marina lies in the heart of the old market town, renowned for its hospitality and traditional Irish pub music. Besides enjoying the excellent seafood restaurants and 52 pubs, other recreational pastimes include horse riding, golf, climbing and diving.

FACILITIES AT A GLANCE

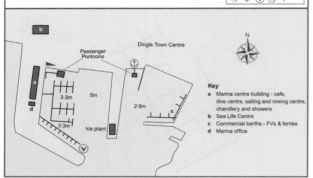

Key
a Marina centre building - cafe, dive centre, sailing and rowing centre, chandlery and showers
b Sea Life Centre
c Commercial berths - FVs & ferries
d Marina office

FENIT HARBOUR MARINA

Fenit Harbour & Marina
Fenit, Tralee, Co. Kerry, Republic of Ireland
Tel: +353 66 7136231 Fax: +353 66 7136473
Email: info@fenitharbour.com www.fenitharbour.com

VHF	Ch M
ACCESS	H24

Fenit Harbour Marina is tucked away in Tralee Bay, not far south of the Shannon Estuary. Besides offering a superb cruising ground, being within a day's sail of Dingle and Kilrush, the marina also provides a convenient base from which to visit inland attractions such as the picturesque tourist towns of Tralee and Killarney. This 120-berth marina accommodates boats up to 15m LOA and benefits from deep water at all states of the tide.

The small village of Fenit incorporates a grocery shop as well a several pubs and restaurants, while among the local activities are horse riding, swimming from one of the nearby sandy beaches and golfing.

FACILITIES AT A GLANCE

Key
a Warehouse
b Marina services, harbour office, lifeboat station

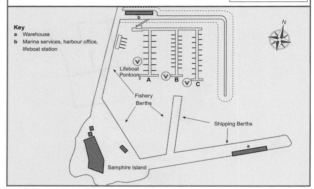

KILRUSH MARINA

Kilrush Marina Ltd
Kilrush, Co. Clare, Ireland
Tel: +353 65 9052072 Mobile: +353 86 2313870
Fax: +353 65 9051692 Email: hehirj@shannondevelopment.ie

VHF	Ch 80
ACCESS	H24

Kilrush Marina and boatyard is strategically placed for exploring the unspoilt west coast of Ireland, including Galway Bay, Dingle, W Cork and Kerry. It also provides a gateway to over 150 miles of cruising on Lough Derg, the R. Shannon and the Irish canal system. Accessed via lock gates, the marina lies at one end of the main street in Kilrush, the marina centre provides all the facilities for the visiting sailor. Kilrush is a vibrant market town with a long maritime history. A 15-minute ferry ride from the marina takes you to Scattery Is, once a 6th century monastic settlement but now only inhabited by wildlife. The Shannon Estuary is reputed for being the country's first marine Special Area of Conservation (SAC) and is home to Ireland's only known resident group of bottlenose dolphins.

FACILITIES AT A GLANCE

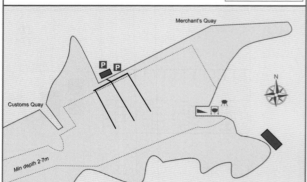

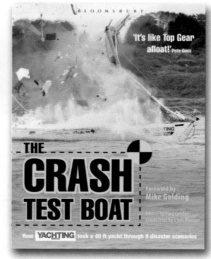

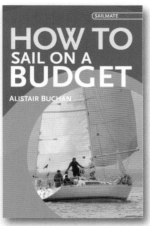
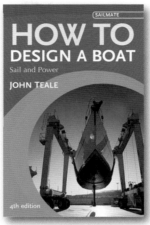
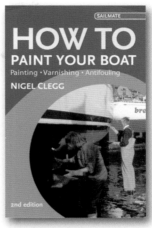
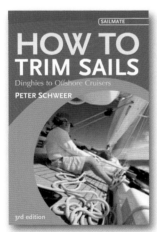
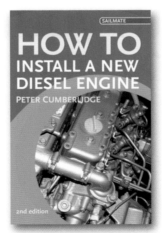
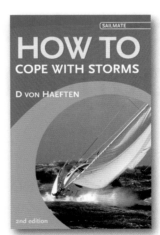

Are you completely satisfied with your accountant?

Bailey Oster offer
satisfaction guaranteed
or your money back.

Call Ben Oster on **0161 358 1212** quoting 'Reeds'

www.baileyoster.co.uk

NORTH IRELAND – Liscannor Bay, clockwise to Lambay Island

Key to Marina Plans symbols

	Bottled gas	P	Parking
	Chandler		Pub/Restaurant
	Disabled facilities		Pump out
	Electrical supply		Rigging service
	Electrical repairs		Sail repairs
	Engine repairs		Shipwright
	First Aid		Shop/Supermarket
	Fresh Water		Showers
D	Fuel - Diesel		Slipway
P	Fuel - Petrol	WC	Toilets
	Hardstanding/boatyard		Telephone
@	Internet Café		Trolleys
	Laundry facilities	V	Visitors berths
	Lift-out facilities		Wi-Fi

Area 13 - North Ireland

MARINAS
Telephone Numbers
VHF Channel
Access Times

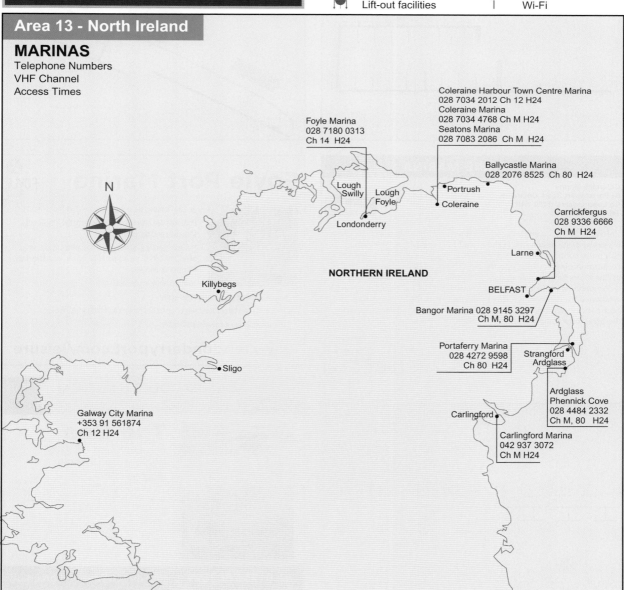

Coleraine Harbour Town Centre Marina
028 7034 2012 Ch 12 H24
Coleraine Marina
028 7034 4768 Ch M H24
Seatons Marina
028 7083 2086 Ch M H24

Foyle Marina
028 7180 0313
Ch 14 H24

Ballycastle Marina
028 2076 8525 Ch 80 H24

Lough Swilly
Lough Foyle

Portrush
Coleraine

Carrickfergus
028 9336 6666
Ch M H24

Londonderry

Larne

N

NORTHERN IRELAND

Killybegs

BELFAST

Bangor Marina 028 9145 3297
Ch M, 80 H24

Portaferry Marina
028 4272 9598
Ch 80 H24

Strangford
Ardglass

Sligo

Ardglass
Phennick Cove
028 4484 2332
Ch M, 80 H24

Galway City Marina
+353 91 561874
Ch 12 H24

Carlingford

Carlingford Marina
042 937 3072
Ch M H24

GALWAY CITY MARINA

Galway City Marina
Galway Harbour Co, Harbour Office, Galway, Ireland
Tel: +353 91 561874 Fax: +353 91 563738
Email: info@galwayharbour.com

VHF	Ch 12
ACCESS	HW-2 to HW

The Galway harbour Company operates a small marina in the confines of Galway Harbour with an additional 60m of pontoon-walkway. Freshwater and electrical power is available at the pontoons. Power cars can be purchased from the harbour office during the days and also from a local pub 'Bar 8' on dock located on dock road. A number of visitors pontoons are available for hire during the summer and for winter layup. Sailors intending to call to Galway Harbour should first make contact with the Harbour office to determine if a berth is available — advisable as demand is high in this quiet and beautiful part of Ireland.

FACILITIES AT A GLANCE

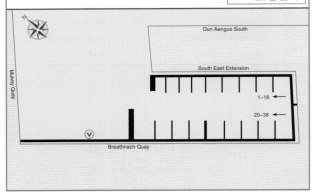

FOYLE MARINA

Foyle Marina
Londonderry Port, Lisahally, L'Derry, BT47 6FL
Tel: 02871 860313 Fax: 02871 861656
www.londonderryport.com/leisure
Email: info@londonderryport.com

VHF	Ch 14
ACCESS	H24

Foyle Marina lies in the heart of the city, 17M from the mouth of Lough Foyle, is accessible at any state of the tide and is sheltered from all directions of wind. Approach is via well-marked navigation channel with a maintained depth of 8m.

The marina has recently undergone extensive improvements with over 680m of secure pontoon mooring now available. Foyle Marina now offers full facilities to visiting vessels. Toilets and showers on site, water and electricity at each berth. Vessels up to 130m LOA can be accommodated. Craft can berth either side of the pontoons in depths of 5–7m at LW.

The pontoons are within easy walking distance of the city centre where you will find restaurants, bars, cinemas, shopping and a host of tourist attractions.

FACILITIES AT A GLANCE

Key a Council offices
        b Appartments
        c Doctor's surgery

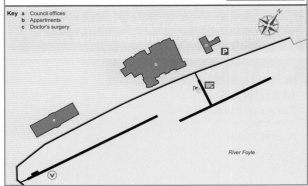

COLERAINE MARINA

Coleraine Marina
64 Portstewart Road, Coleraine,
Co Londonderry, BT52 1RR
Tel: 028 7034 4768

VHF	Ch M
ACCESS	H24

Coleraine Marina complex enjoys a superb location in sheltered waters just one mile north of the town of Coleraine and four and a half miles south of the River Bann Estuary and the open sea. Besides accommodating vessels up to 18m LOA, this modern marina with 105 berths offers hard standing, fuel, a chandlery and shower facilities.

Among one of the oldest known settlements in Ireland, Coleraine is renowned for its linen, whiskey and salmon. Its thriving commercial centre includes numerous shops, a four-screen cinema and a state-of-the-art leisure complex.

FACILITIES AT A GLANCE

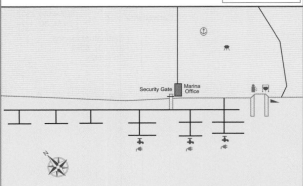

COLERAINE HARBOUR MARINA

Coleraine Harbour Town Centre Marina
Coleraine Harbour Office, 4 Riverside Road, Coleraine, BT52 1XA
Tel: 028 7034 2012　Fax: 028 7034 2000
Email: info@coleraineharbour.com
www.coleraineharbour.com

VHF	Ch 12
ACCESS	H24

The Marina lies upstream from about five miles from the sea ideally situated in the centre of the town, just a few minutes stroll from a selection of shops, restaurants and bars.

In addition to the pontoon berths there is a 40 tonne Roodberg slipway launch/recovery trailer. Hard standing and covered storage are available.

Coleraine is an ideal base for exploring the many nearby attractions including the Old Bushmills Distillery and the Giants Causeway.

FACILITIES AT A GLANCE

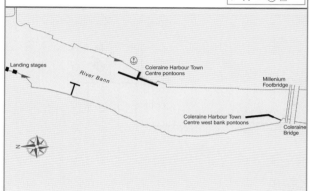

Coleraine Harbour Town Centre Marina

13

- The Best Sheltered Pontoon Berthing on the Lower Bann
- Situated in the Centre of the Town
- Water/Electricity on Berths
- Diesel Pump
- 24 Hour Security
- 40 Tonne Slipway Trailer

- Hard Standing/Undercover Storage
- Special Rates for Lift Out of up to 24 Hours for Survey, Power Wash, Repairs.

info@coleraineharbour.com
www.coleraineharbour.com

SEATONS MARINA

Seatons Marina
Drumslade Rd, Coleraine, Londonderry, BT52 1SE
Tel: 028 7083 2086　Mobile 07718 883099
Email: jill@seatonsmarina.co.uk　www.seatonsmarina.co.uk

VHF	Ch M
ACCESS	H24

Seatons Marina is a privately owned business on the north coast of Ireland, which was established by Eric Seaton in 1962. It lies on the east bank of the River Bann, approximately two miles downstream from Coleraine and three miles from the sea. Long term pontoon berths are available for yachts up to 11.5 with a maximum draft of 2.4m; fore and aft moorings are available for larger vessels. Lift out and mast stepping facilities are provided by a 12 tonne trailer hoist.

FACILITIES AT A GLANCE

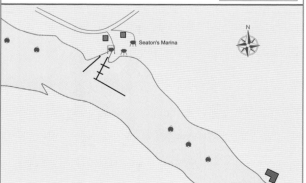

BALLYCASTLE MARINA

Ballycastle Marina
Bayview Road, Ballycastle, Northern Ireland
Tel: 028 2076 8525/07803 505084　Fax: 028 2076 6215
Email: info@moyle-council.org

VHF	Ch 80
ACCESS	H24

Ballycastle is a traditional seaside town situated on Northern Ireland's North Antrim coast. The 74-berthed, sheltered marina provides a perfect base from which to explore the well known local attractions such as the Giant's Causeway world heritage site, the spectacular Nine Glens of Antrim, and Rathlin, the only inhabited island in Northern Ireland. The most northern coastal marina in Ireland, Ballycastle, is accessible at all states of the tide, although yachts are required to contact the marina on VHF Ch 80 before entering the harbour. Along the seafront are a selection of restaurants, bars and shops, while the town centre is only about a five minute walk away.

FACILITIES AT A GLANCE

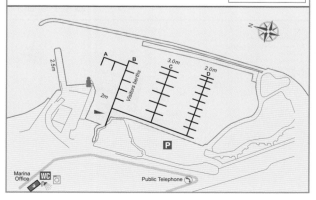

CARRICKFERGUS MARINA

Carrickferus Marina
3 Quayside, Carrickfergus, Co. Antrim, BT38 8BJ
Tel: 028 9336 6666 Fax: 028 9335 0505
Email: marinarec@carrickfergus.org
www.carrickfergus.org

VHF Ch M
ACCESS H24

Located on the north shore of
Belfast Lough, Carrickfergus
Marina and harbour incorporates
two sheltered areas suitable
for leisure craft. The harbour is
dominated by a magnificent 12th
century Norman Castle which,
recently renovated, includes
a film theatre, banqueting room and outdoor models depicting the
castle's chequered history.

With a wide range of services available to the
visitor, the marina is located 250m west of the
harbour and has become increasingly popular since
its opening in 1985. An interesting variety of shops
and restaurants along the waterfront caters for most
yachtsmen's needs.

FACILITIES AT A GLANCE

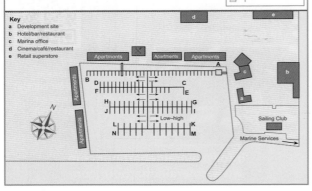

Key
a Development site
b Hotel/bar/restaurant
c Marina office
d Cinema/café/restaurant
e Retail superstore

BANGOR MARINA

Quay Marinas Limited
Bangor Marina, Bangor, Co. Down, BT20 5ED
Tel: 028 9145 3297 Fax: 028 9145 3450
Email: kbaird@quaymarinas.com
www.quaymarinas.com

VHF Ch 11, 80
ACCESS H24

Situated on the south shore of Belfast
Lough, Bangor is located close to
the Irish Sea cruising routes. The
Marina is right at the town's centre,
within walking distance of shops,
restaurants, hotels and bars. The
Tourist information centre is across
the road from marina reception
and there are numerous visitors'
attractions in the Borough. The Royal
Ulster Yacht Club and
the Ballyholme Yacht
Club are both nearby
and welcome visitors.

transeurope MARINAS

FACILITIES AT A GLANCE

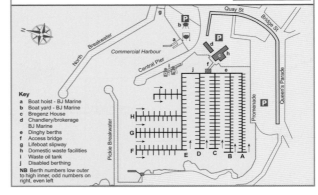

Key
a Boat hoist - BJ Marine
b Boat yard - BJ Marine
c Bregenz House
d Chandlery/brokerage
   BJ Marine
e Dinghy berths
f Access bridge
g Lifeboat slipway
h Domestic waste facilities
i Waste oil tank
j Disabled berthing
NB Berth numbers low outer
to high inner, odd numbers on
right, even left

CARLINGFORD MARINA

Carlingford Marina
Co. Louth, Ireland
Tel: +353 (0)42 937 3072   Fax: +353 (0)42 937 3075
Email: info@carlingfordmarina.ie
www.carlingfordmarina.ie

VHF Ch M
ACCESS H24

Carlingford Lough is an eight-
mile sheltered haven between the
Cooley Mountains to
the south and the Mourne
Mountains to the north.
The marina is situated on the
southern shore, about four miles
from Haulbowline Lighthouse,
and can be easily reached via a
deep water shipping channel.
Among the most attractive
destinations in the Irish Sea, Carlingford is only
60 miles from the Isle of Man and within a day's
sail from Strangford Lough and Ardglass. Full
facilities in the marina include a first class bar and
restaurant offering superb views across the water.

FACILITIES AT A GLANCE

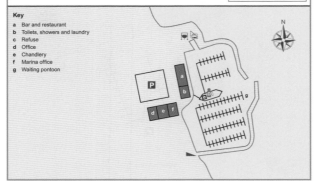

Key
a Bar and restaurant
b Toilets, showers and laundry
c Refuse
d Office
e Chandlery
f Marina office
g Waiting pontoon

ARDGLASS MARINA

Ardglass Marina
19 Quay Street, Ardglass, BT30 7SA
Tel & fax: 028 4484 2332
Email: ardglassmarina@tiscali.co.uk
www.ardglassmarina.co.uk

VHF Ch M, 80
ACCESS H24

Situated just south of
Strangford, Ardglass has the
capacity to accommodate
up to 33 yachts as well as
space for small craft. Despite
being relatively small
in size, the marina boasts an
extensive array of facilities,
either on site or close at hand.
Most of the necessary shops,
including grocery stores, a post office, chemist and off-licence, are
all within a five-minute walk from the marina.
Among the local onshore activities are golf,
mountain climbing in Newcastle, which is 18 miles
south, as well as scenic walks at Ardglass and
Delamont Park.

FACILITIES AT A GLANCE

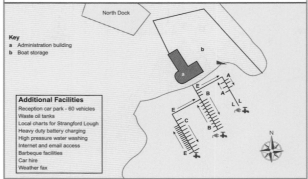

Key
a Administration building
b Boat storage

Additional Facilities
Reception car park - 60 vehicles
Waste oil tanks
Local charts for Strangford Lough
Heavy duty battery charging
High pressure water washing
Internet and email access
Barbeque facilities
Car hire
Weather fax

North Dock

PORTAFERRY MARINA

Portaferry Marina
1 Mill View, Portaferry, BT22 1LQ
Mobile: 07703 209780 Fax: 028 4272 9784
Email: info@portaferrymarina.co.uk

VHF	Ch 80
ACCESS	H24

Portaferry Marina lies on the east shore of the Narrows, the gateway to Strangford Lough on the north east coast of Ireland. A marine nature reserve of outstanding natural beauty, the Lough offers plenty of recreational activities.

The marina, which caters for draughts of up to 2.5m, is fairly small, accommodating around 30 yachts. The office is situated about 200m from the marina itself, where you will find ablution facilities along with a launderette.

Portaferry incorporates several pubs and restaurants as well as a few convenience stores, while one of its prime attractions is the Exploris Aquarium. Places of historic interest in the vicinity include Castleward, an 18th century mansion in Strangford, and Mount Stewart House & Garden in Newtownards.

FACILITIES AT A GLANCE

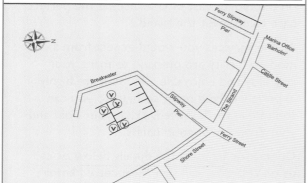

CHANNEL ISLANDS – Guernsey & Jersey

Key to Marina Plans symbols

🗲	Bottled gas	P	Parking
	Chandler	✕	Pub/Restaurant
♿	Disabled facilities		Pump out
⚡	Electrical supply		Rigging service
	Electrical repairs		Sail repairs
⚙	Engine repairs		Shipwright
✚	First Aid		Shop/Supermarket
	Fresh Water		Showers
D	Fuel - Diesel		Slipway
P	Fuel - Petrol	WC	Toilets
	Hardstanding/boatyard	☎	Telephone
@	Internet Café		Trolleys
▣	Laundry facilities	Ⓥ	Visitors berths
	Lift-out facilities		Wi-Fi

Area 14 - Channel Islands

MARINAS
Telephone Numbers
VHF Channel
Access Times

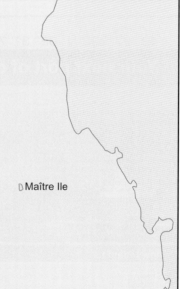

ALDERNEY

Beaucette Marina
01481 245000
Ch 80 HW±3

GUERNSEY

HERM

SARK

St Peter Port
Victoria Marina
01481 725987
Ch 12, Ch 80   HW±2½

Maître Ile

N

JERSEY

St Helier Marina
01534 447730
Ch 14   HW±3

BEAUCETTE MARINA

Beaucette Marina
Vale, Guernsey, GY3 5BQ
Tel: 01481 245000 Fax: 01481 247071
Mobile: 07781 102302
Email: info@beaucettemarina.com

VHF	Ch 80
ACCESS	HW±3

Situated on the north east tip of Guernsey, Beaucette enjoys a peaceful, rural setting in contrast to the more vibrant atmosphere of Victoria Marina. Now owned by a private individual and offering a high standard of service, the site was originally formed from an old quarry.

There is a general store close by, while the bustling town of St Peter Port is only 20 minutes away by bus.

FACILITIES AT A GLANCE

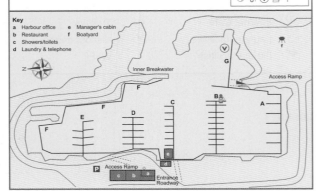

Key
a Harbour office
b Restaurant
c Showers/toilets
d Laundry & telephone
e Manager's cabin
f Boatyard

ST PETER PORT

Guernsey Harbours
PO Box 631, St Julian's Emplacement, St Peter Port
Tel: 01481 720229 Fax: 01481 714177
Email: guernsey.harbour@gov.gg

VHF	Ch 12, 80
ACCESS	HW±2.5

The harbour of St Peter Port comprises the Queen Elizabeth II Marina to the N and Victoria and Albert Marinas to the S, with visiting yachtsmen usually accommodated in Victoria Marina.

St Peter Port is the capital of Guernsey. Its regency architecture and picturesque cobbled streets filled with restaurants and boutiques help to make it one of the most attractive harbours in Europe. Among the places of interest are Hauteville House, home of the writer Victor Hugo, and Castle Cornet. There are regular bus services to all parts of the island for visitors to explore a rich heritage.

FACILITIES AT A GLANCE

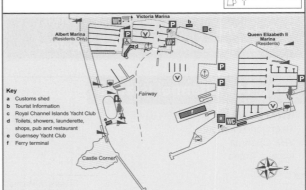

Key
a Customs shed
b Tourist Information
c Royal Channel Islands Yacht Club
d Toilets, showers, launderette, shops, pub and restaurant
e Guernsey Yacht Club
f Ferry terminal

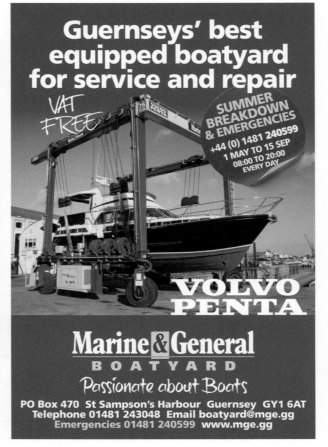

ST PETER PORT VICTORIA MARINA

Guernsey Harbours
PO Box 631, St Julian's Emplacement, St Peter Port
Tel: 01481 720229 Fax: 01481 714177
Email: guernsey.harbour@gov.gg

| VHF | Ch 80 |
| ACCESS | HW±2.5 |

Victoria Marina in St Peter Port accommodates some 300 visiting yachts. In the height of the season it gets extremely busy, but when full visitors can berth on 5 other pontoons in the Pool or pre-arrange a berth in the QE II or Albert marinas. There are no visitor moorings in the Pool. Depending on draught, the marina is accessible approximately two and a half hours either side of HW, with yachts crossing over a sill drying to 4.2m. The marina dory will direct you to a berth on arrival or else will instruct you to moor on one of the waiting pontoons just outside.

Guernsey is well placed for exploring the rest of the Channel Islands and nearby French ports.

FACILITIES AT A GLANCE

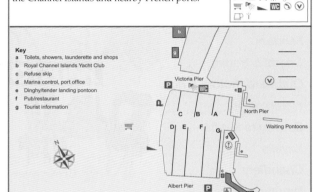

Key
a   Toilets, showers, launderette and shops
b   Royal Channel Islands Yacht Club
c   Refuse skip
d   Marina control, port office
e   Dinghy/tender landing pontoon
f   Pub/restaurant
g   Tourist information

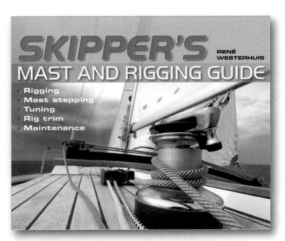
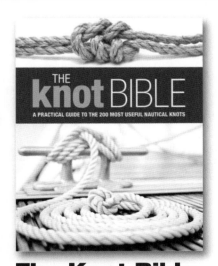

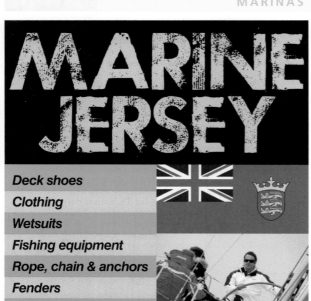

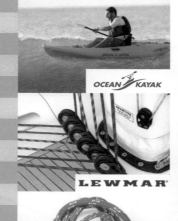

ST HELIER HARBOUR

St Helier Harbour
Maritime House, La Route du Port Elizabeth
St Helier, Jersey, JE1 1HB
Tel: 01534 447708
www.portofjersey.je Email: s.marina@gov.je

VHF Ch 14
ACCESS HW±3

Jersey is the largest of the Channel Islands, attracting the most number of tourists per year. Although St Helier can get very crowded in the height of the summer, if you hire a car and head out to the north coast in particular you will soon find isolated bays and pretty little fishing villages.

All visiting craft are directed to St Helier Marina, which may be entered three hours either side of HW via a sill. There is a long holding pontoon to port of the entrance accessible at any state of the tide. La Collette Yacht Basin is not for visitors but Elizabeth Marina may accept larger craft by prior arrangement.

FACILITIES AT A GLANCE

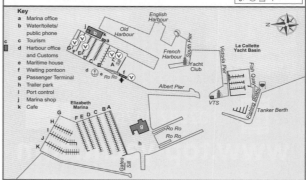

Key
a   Marina office
b   Water/toilets/ public phone
c   Tourism
d   Harbour office and Customs
e   Maritime house
f   Waiting pontoon
g   Passenger Terminal
h   Trailer park
i   Port control
j   Marina shop
k   Cafe

SECTION 2
MARINE SUPPLIES AND SERVICES GUIDE

ADLARD COLES NAUTICAL
The Best Sailing Books

Tel: 01256 302699
email: direct@macmillan.co.uk
or www.adlardcoles.com

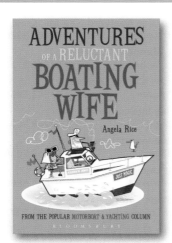

Adventures of a Reluctant Boating Wife

Angela Rice
978 1 4081 8204 8
£8.99

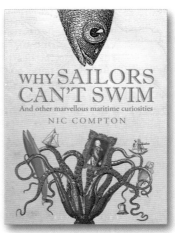

Why Sailors Can't Swim and Other Marvellous Maritime Curiosities

Nic Compton
978 1 4081 8805 7
£10.00

New

ADHESIVES

Casco Adhesives
Darwen   07710 546899

CC Marine Services Ltd
West Mersea   07751 734510

Industrial Self Adhesives Ltd
Nottingham   0115 9681895

Sika Ltd Garden City   01707 394444

Technix Rubber & Plastics Ltd
Southampton   01489 789944

Tiflex Liskeard   01579 320808

Trade Grade Products Ltd
Poole   01202 820177

UK Epoxy Resins
Burscough   01704 892364

Wessex Resins & Adhesives Ltd
Romsey   01794 521111

3M United Kingdom plc
Bracknell   01344 858315

ASSOCIATIONS/ AGENCIES

Cruising Association
London   020 7537 2828

**Fishermans Mutual Association
(Eyemouth) Ltd**
Eyemouth   01890 750373

Maritime and Coastguard Agency
Southampton   0870 6006505

Royal Institute of Navigation
London   020 7591 3130

Royal National Lifeboat Institution
Poole   01202 663000

**Royal Yachting Association
(RYA)** Southampton   0845 345 0400

BERTHS & MOORINGS

ABC Powermarine
Beaumaris   01248 811413

Aqua Bell Ltd Norwich   01603 713013

Ardfern Yacht Centre
Lochgilphead   01852 500247/500636

Ardmair Boat Centre
Ullapool   01854 612054

Arisaig Marine Ltd
Inverness-shire   01687 450224

Bristol Boat Ltd Bristol   01225 872032

British Waterways
Argyll   01546 603210

Burgh Castle Marine
Norfolk   01493 780331

Cambrian Marine Services Ltd
Cardiff   029 2034 3459

Chelsea Harbour Ltd
London   020 7225 9108

Clapson & Son (Shipbuilders) Ltd
Barton-on-Humber   01652 635620

Crinan Boatyard, Crinan 01546 830232

Dartside Quay Brixham 01803 845445

Douglas Marine
Preston   01772 812462

Dublin City Moorings
Dublin   +353 1 8183300

Emsworth Yacht Harbour
Emsworth   01243 377727

Exeter Ship Canal   01392 274306

HAFAN PWLLHELI
Glan Don, Pwllheli, Gwynedd LL53 5YT
Tel: (01758) 701219
Fax: (01758) 701443 VHF Ch80
Hafan Pwllheli has over 400 pontoon berths and offers access at virtually all states of the tide. Ashore, its modern purpose-built facilities include luxury toilets, showers, launderette, a secure boat park for winter storage, 40-ton travel hoist, mobile crane and plenty of space for car parking. Open 24-hours a day, 7 days a week.

Highway Marine
Sandwich   01304 613925

Iron Wharf Boatyard
Faversham   01795 537122

Jalsea Marine Services Ltd
Northwich   01606 77870

Jersey Harbours
St Helier   01534 447788

Jones (Boatbuilders), David
Chester   01244 390363

Lawrenny Yacht Station
Kilgetty   01646 651212

MacFarlane & Son
Glasgow   01360 870214

NEPTUNE MARINA LTD
Neptune Quay, Ipswich, Suffolk IP4 1AX
Tel: (01473) 215204
Fax: (01473) 215206
**e-mail:
enquiries@neptune-marina.com
www.neptune-marina.com**
The quay to the heart of Ipswich! Call Ipswich lock gates on Channel 68 and Neptune Marina on Channel 80. Bring your crew to the wonderful Ipswich waterfront, with plenty of watering holes and town centre activities. You won't want to leave!

Orkney Marinas Ltd
Kirkwall   07810 465835

V Marine
Shoreham-by-Sea   01273 461491

Sutton Harbour Marina
Plymouth   01752 204186

Wicor Marine Fareham   01329 237112

Winters Marine Ltd
Salcombe   01548 843580

Yarmouth Marine Service
Yarmouth   01983 760521

Youngboats
Faversham   01795 536176

BOAT BUILDERS & REPAIRS

ABC Hayling Island   023 9246 1968

ABC Powermarine
Beaumaris   01248 811413

Advance Yacht Systems
Southampton   023 8033 7722

Aqua-Star Ltd
St Sampsons   01481 244550

Ardoran Marine
Oban   01631 566123

Baumbach Bros Boatbuilders
Hayle   01736 753228

Beacon Boatyard
Rochester   01634 841320

Bedwell & Co
Walton on the Naze   01255 675873

Boyd Boat Building
Falmouth   07885 436722

Blackwell, Craig
Co Meath   +353 87 677 9605

Boatcraft
Ardrossan   01294 603047

Brennan, John
Dun Laoghaire   +353 1 280 5308

Burghead Boat Centre
Findhorn   01309 690099

Carrick Marine Projects
Co Antrim   02893 355884

Chapman & Hewitt Boatbuilders
Wadebridge   01208 813487

Chicks Marine Ltd
Guernsey   01481 723716

Clarence Boatyard
East Cowes   01983 294243

Cooks Maritime Craftsmen - Poliglow
Lymington   01590 675521

Creekside Boatyard (Old Mill Creek)
Dartmouth   01803 832649

CTC Marine & Leisure
Middlesbrough   01642 372600

Davies Marine Services
Ramsgate   01843 586172

Dickie International
Bangor   01248 363400

Dickie International
Pwllheli   01758 701828

East Llanion Marine Ltd
Pembroke Dock   01646 686866

Emblem Enterprises
East Cowes   01983 294243

Fairlie Quay Fairlie   01475 568267

Fairweather Marine
Fareham   01329 283500

Farrow & Chambers Yacht Builders
Humberston
            www.farrowand chambers.co.uk

Fast Tack Plymouth   01752 255171

Fergulsea Engineering
Ayr   01292 262978

Ferrypoint Boat Co
Youghal +353 24 94232

Floetree Ltd (Loch Lomond Marina)
Balloch 01389 752069

Freshwater Boatyard
Truro 01326 270443

Frogmore Boatyard
Kingsbridge 01548 531257

Furniss Boat Building
Falmouth 01326 311766

Gallichan Marine Ltd
Jersey 01534 746387

Garvel Clyde
Greenock 01475 725372

Goodchild Marine Services
Great Yarmouth 01493 782301

Gosport Boatyard
Gosport 023 9252 6534

Gweek Quay Boatyard
Helston 01326 221657

Halls
Walton on the Naze 01255 675596

Hardway Marine
Gosport 023 9258 0420

Harris Pye Marine
Barry 01446 720066

Haven Boatyard
Lymington 01590 677073

Hayling Yacht Company
Hayling Island 023 9246 3592

Hoare Ltd, Bob, Poole 01202 736704

Holyhead Boatyard
Holyhead 01407 760111

Jackson Marine
Lowestoft 01502 539772

Jackson Yacht Services
Jersey 01534 743819

JEP Marine
Canterbury 01227 710102

JWS Marine Services
Southsea 023 9275 5155

Kimelford Yacht Haven
Oban 01852 200248

Kingfisher Marine
Weymouth 01305 766595

Kingfisher Ultraclean UK Ltd
Tarporley 0800 085 7039

King's Boatyard
Pin Mill 01473 780258

Kinsale Boatyard
Kinsale +353 21477 4774

Kippford Slipway Ltd
Dalbeattie 01556 620249

Lavis & Son, CH
Exmouth 01395 263095

Lawrenny Yacht Station
Lawrenny 01646 651212

Lencraft Boats Ltd
Dungarvan +353 58 682220

Mackay Boatbuilders
Arbroath 01241 872879

Marine Services
Norwich 01692 582239

Mashford Brothers
Torpoint 01752 822232

Mayor & Co Ltd, J
Preston 01772 812250

Mears, HJ Axmouth 01297 23344

Mill, Dan, Galway +353 86 337 9304

Miller Marine
Tyne & Wear 01207 542149

Moody Yachts International Ltd
Swanwick 01489 885000

Morrison, A Killyleagh 028 44828215

Moss (Boatbuilders), David
Thornton-Cleveleys 01253 893830

Multi Marine Composites Ltd
Torpoint 01752 823513

Newing, Roy E
Canterbury 01227 860345

Noble and Sons, Alexander
Girvan 01465 712223

Northney Marine Services
Hayling Island 023 9246 9246

Northshore Sport & Leisure
King's Lynn 01485 210236

O'Sullivans Marine Ltd
Tralee +353 66 7124957

Oyster Marine Ltd
Ipswich 01473 688888

Pachol, Terry Brighton 01273 620192

Partington Marine Ltd, William
Pwllheli 01758 612808

Pasco's Boatyard
Truro 01326 270269

Penrhos Marine
Aberdovey 01654 767478

Penzance Marine Services
Penzance 01736 361081

PJ Bespoke Boat Fitters Ltd
Crewe 01270 812244

Preston Marine Services Ltd
Preston 01772 733595

Red Bay Boats Ltd
Cushendall 028 2177 1331

Reliance Marine
Wirral 0151 625 5219

Retreat Boatyard Ltd
Exeter 01392 874720/875934

Richardson Boatbuilders, Ian
Stromness 01856 850321

Richardson Yacht Services Ltd
Newport 01983 821095

Cordell Grove
Middlesbrough 01642 226226

Roberts Marine Ltd, S
Liverpool 0151 707 8300

Rothman Pantall & Co
Fareham 01329 280221

Rustler Yachts Falmouth 01326 310210

Salterns Boatyard
Poole 01202 707391

Sea & Shore Ship Chandler
Dundee 01382 450666

SEAFIT MARINE SERVICES LTD
Falmouth Marina, North Parade,
Falmouth, Cornwall TR11 2TD
Tel: (01326) 313713
Fax: (01326) 313713
Mob: 07971 196175
Email: mary.townsend@homecall.
co.uk
For installation maintenance and repair
work - electrical, plumbing, hulls, rigs etc.

Seamark-Nunn & Co
Felixstowe 01394 275327

Seapower
Woolverstone 01473 780090

Slipway Cooperative Ltd
Bristol 0117 907 9938

Smith, GB, & Sons
Rock 01208 862815

Spicer Boatbuilder, Nick
Weymouth Marina 01305 767118

Storrar Marine Store
Newcastle upon Tyne 0191 266 1037

TT Marine Ashwell 01462 742449

Waterfront Marine
Bangor 01248 352513

Way, A&R, Boat Building
Tarbert, Loch Fyne 01546 606657

WestCoast Marine
Troon 01292 318121

Western Marine
Dublin +353 1 280 0321

Wigmore Wright Marine Services
Penarth 029 2070 9983

Williams, Peter
Fowey 01726 870987

WQI Ltd
Bournemouth 01202 771292

Yarmouth Marine Service
01983 760521

Youngboats Faversham 01795 536176

BOATYARD SERVICES & SUPPLIES

A & P Ship Care
Ramsgate 01843 593140

ABC Marine
Hayling Island 023 9246 1968

Abersoch Boatyard Services Ltd
Abersoch   01758 713900

Amble Boat Co Ltd
Amble   01665 710267

Amsbrisbeg Ltd
Port Bannatyne   01700 831215

Ardmair Boat Centre
Ullapool   01854 612054

Ardmaleish Boat Building Co Rothesay
01700 502007

www.ardoran.co.uk
West coast Scotland. All marine
facilities.

Ardrishaig Boatyard
Lochgilphead   01546 603280

Arklow Slipway
Arklow   +353 402 33233

Baltic Wharf Boatyard
Totnes   01803 867922

Baltimore Boatyard
Baltimore   +353 28 20444

Bedwell and Co
Walton-on-the-Naze   01255 675873

Berthon Boat Co
Lymington   01590 673312

Birdham Shipyard
Chichester   01243 512310

BJ Marine Ltd Bangor   028 91271434

Blagdon, A
Plymouth   01752 561830

Boatcraft
Ardrossan   01294 603047

Boatworks + Ltd
St Peter Port   01481 726071

Brennan, John
Dun Laoghaire   +353 1 280 5308

Brighton Marina Boatyard
Brighton   01273 819919

Bristol Marina (Yard)
Bristol   0117 921 3198

Buckie Shipyard Ltd
Buckie   01542 831245

Bucklers Hard Boat Builders Ltd
Brockenhurst   01590 616214

C & J Marine Services
Newcastle Upon Tyne   0191 295 0072

Caley Marina Inverness   01463 236539

Cambrian Boat Centre
Swansea   01792 467263

Cambrian Marine Services Ltd
Cardiff   029 2034 3459

Cantell and Son Ltd
Newhaven   01273 514118

Canvey Yacht Builders Ltd
Canvey Island   01268 696094

Carroll's Ballyhack Boatyard
New Ross   +353 51 389164

Castlepoint Boatyard
Crosshaven   +353 21 4832154

Chabot, Gary
Newhaven   07702 006767

Chapman & Hewitt Boatbuilders
Wadebridge   01208 813487

Chippendale Craft Rye   01797 227707

Clapson & Son (Shipbuilders) Ltd
Barton on Humber   01652 635620

Clarence Boatyard
East Cowes   01983 294243

Coastal Marine Boatbuilders
(Berwick upon Tweed)
Eyemouth   01890 750328

Coastcraft Ltd
Cockenzie   01875 812150

Coates Marine Ltd
Whitby   01947 604486

Coombes, AA
Bembridge   01983 872296

Corpach Boatbuilding Company
Fort William   01397 772861

Craobh Marina
By Lochgilphead   01852 500222

Creekside Boatyard (Old Mill Creek)
Dartmouth   01803 832649

Crinan Boatyard
By Lochgilphead   01546 830232

Crosshaven Boatyard Co Ltd
Crosshaven   +353 21 831161

Dale Sailing Co Ltd
Neyland   01646 603110

Darthaven Marina
Kingswear   01803 752242

Dartside Quay Brixham   01803 845445

Dauntless Boatyard Ltd
Canvey Island   01268 793782

Davis's Boatyard Poole   01202 674349

Dinas Boat Yard Ltd
Y Felinheli   01248 671642

Dorset Yachts
Poole   01202 674531

Douglas Boatyard
Preston   01772 812462

Dover Yacht Co Dover   01304 201073

Dun Laoghaire Marina
Dun Laoghaire   +353 1 2020040

Elephant Boatyard
Southampton   023 8040 3268

Elton Boatbuilding Ltd
Kirkcudbright   01557 330177

Felixstowe Ferry Boatyard
Felixstowe   01394 282173

Ferguson Engineering
Wexford   +353 6568 66822133

Ferry Marine South
Queensferry   0131 331 1233

Findhorn Boatyard
Findhorn   01309 690099

Firmhelm Ltd Pwllheli   01758 612251

Fleming Engineering, J
Stornoway   01851 703488

Forrest Marine Ltd
Exeter   08452 308335

Fowey Boatyard
Fowey   01726 832194

Fox's Marina Ipswich   01473 689111

Frank Halls & Son
Walton on the Naze   01255 675596

Freeport Marine
Jersey   01534 888100

Furniss Boat Building
Falmouth   01326 311766

Garval Clyde
Greenock   01475 725372

Goodchild Marine Services
Great Yarmouth   01493 782301

Gosport Boatyard
Gosport   023 9252 6534

Gweek Quay Boatyard
Helston   01326 221657

Haines Boatyard
Chichester   01243 512228

Harbour Marine
Plymouth   01752 204691

Harbour Marine Services Ltd
Southwold   01502 724721

Harris Pye Marine
Barry   01446 720066

Hartlepool Marine Engineering
Hartlepool   01429 867883

Hayles, Harold
Yarmouth, IoW   01983 760373

Henderson, J Shiskine   01770 860259

Heron Marine
Whitstable   01227 361255

Hewitt, George
Binham   01328 830078

Holyhead Marina & Trinity Marine Ltd
Holyhead   01407 764242

Instow Marine Services
Bideford   01271 861081

Ipswich Haven Marina
Ipswich   01473 236644

Iron Wharf Boatyard
Faversham   01795 537122

Island Boat Services
Port of St Mary   01624 832073

Isle of Skye Yachts
Ardvasar   01471 844216

Jalsea Marine Services Ltd Weaver
Shipyard, Northwich   01606 77870

JBS Group
Peterhead   01779 475395

J B Timber Ltd
North Ferriby   01482 631765

Jersey Harbours Dept
St Helier   01534 885588

Kilnsale Boatyard
Kinsale   +353 21 4774774

Kilrush Marina & Boatyard – Ireland
     +353 65 9052072

Kingfisher Ultraclean UK Ltd
Tarporley   01928 787878

Kinsale Boatyard
Kinsale   +353 21477 4774

KPB Beaucette   07781 152581

Lake Yard Poole   01202 674531
Lallow, C Isle of Wight 01983 292112

Latham's Boatyard
Poole   01202 748029

Leonard Marine, Peter
Newhaven   01273 515987

Lincombe Marine
Salcombe   01548 843580

Lomax Boatbuilders
Cliffony   +353 71 66124

Lymington Yacht Haven
Lymington   01590 677071

MacDougalls Marine Services
Isle of Mull   01681 700294

Macduff Shipyard Ltd
Macduff   01261 832234

Madog Boatyard
Porthmadog   01766 514205/513435

Mainbrayce Marine
Alderney   01481 822772

Malakoff and Moore
Lerwick   01595 695544

Mallaig Boat Building and Engineering
Mallaig   01687 462304

Maramarine
Helensburgh   01436 810971

Marindus Engineering
Kilmore Quay   +353 53 29794

Mariners Farm Boatyard
Gillingham   01634 233179

McGruar and Co Ltd
Helensburgh   01436 831313

Mill, Dan, Galway   +353 86 337 9304

Mitchell's Boatyard
Poole   01202 747857

Mooney Boats
Killybegs   +353 73 31152/31388

Moore & Son, J
St Austell   01726 842964

Morrison, A Killyleagh 028 44828215

Moss (Boatbuilders), David
Thornton-Cleveleys   01253 893830

Mustang Marine
Milford Haven   01646 696320

New Horizons Rhu   01436 821555

Noble and Sons, Alexander
Girvan   01465 712223

North Pier (Oban)
Oban   01631 562892

North Wales Boat Centre
Conwy   01492 580740

Northam Marine
Brightlingsea   01206 302003

Northshore Yacht Yard
Chichester   01243 512611

Oban Yachts and Marine Services
By Oban   01631 565333

Pearn and Co, Norman
Looe   01503 262244

Penrhos Marine
Aberdovey   01654 767478

Penzance Dry Dock and Engineering Co Ltd Penzance   01736 363838

Philip & Son Dartmouth 01803 833351

Phillips, HJ Rye   01797 223234

Ponsharden Boatyard
Penryn   01326 372215

Powersail and Island Chandlers Ltd
East Cowes Marina   01983 299800

Priors Boatyard
Burnham-on-Crouch   01621 782160

R K Marine Ltd
Swanwick   01489 583572

Rat Island Sailboat Company (Yard) St
Mary's   01720 423399

Retreat Boatyard Ltd
Exeter   01392 874720/875934

Rice and Cole Ltd
Burnham-on-Crouch   01621 782063

Richardson Boatbuilders, Ian Stromness
01856 850321

Richardsons Boatbuilders
Binfield   01983 821095

Riverside Yard
Shoreham Beach   01273 592456

River Yar Boatyard
Yarmouth, IoW   01983 761000

Robertsons Boatyard
Woodbridge   01394 382305

Rossbrin Boatyard
Schull   +353 28 37352

Rossiter Yachts Ltd
Christchurch   01202 483250

Rossreagh Boatyard
Rathmullan   +353 74 9150182

Rudders Boatyard & Moorings
Milford Haven   01646 600288

Ryan & Roberts Marine Services
Askeaton   +353 61 392198

Rye Harbour Marina Rye
                         01797 227667

Rynn Engineering, Pat
Galway   +353 91 562568

Salterns Boatyard
Poole   01202 707391

Sandbanks Yacht Company
Poole   01202 611262

Scarborough Marine Engineering Ltd
Scarborough   01723 375199

Severn Valley Cruisers Ltd (Boatyard)
Stourport-on-Severn   01299 871165

Shepards Wharf Boatyard Ltd
Cowes   01983 297821

Shipshape
King's Lynn   01553 764058

Shotley Marina Ltd
Ipswich   01473 788982

Shotley Marine Services Ltd
Ipswich   01473 788913

Silvers Marina Ltd
Helensburgh   01436 831222

Skinners Boat Yard
Baltimore   +353 28 20114

Smith, GB, & Sons
Rock   01208 862815

Smith & Gibbs
Eastbourne   07802 582009

Sparkes Boatyard
Hayling Island   023 92463572

Spencer Sailing Services, Jim
Brightlingsea   01206 302911

Standard House Boatyard
Wells-next-the-Sea   01328 710593

Storrar Marine Store
Newcastle upon Tyne   0191 266 1037

Strand Shipyard Rye 01797 222070

Surry Boatyard
Shoreham-by-Sea   01273 461491

The Shipyard
Littlehampton   01903 713327

Titchmarsh Marina
Walton-on-the-Naze   01255 672185

Tollesbury Marina
Tollesbury   01621 869202

T J Rigging Conwy   07780 972411

Toms and Son Ltd, C
Fowey   01726 870232

Tony's Marine Service
Coleraine   028 7035 6422

Torquay Marina
Torquay   01803 200210

Trinity Marine & Holyhead Marina
Holyhead   01407 763855

Trouts Boatyard (River Exe)
Topsham   01392 873044

Upson and Co, RF
Aldeburgh   01728 453047

Versatility Workboats
Rye   01797 224422

Weir Quay Boatyard
Bere Alston   01822 840474

West Solent Boatbuilders
Lymington   01590 642080

Wicor Marine Fareham 01329 237112

Woodrolfe Boatyard
Maldon   01621 869202

Yarmouth Marine Services
Yarmouth, IoW   01983 760521

BOAT DELIVERIES & STORAGE

ABC Marine
Hayling Island   023 9246 1968

Abersoch Boatyard Services Ltd
Pwllheli   01758 713900

Ambrisbeg Ltd
Port Bannatyne   01700 502719

Arisaig Marine
Inverness-shire   01687 450224

Bedwell and Co	
Walton-on-the-Naze	01255 675873
Berthon Boat Company	
Lymington	01590 673312
Boat Shifters	
07733 344018/01326 210548	
C & J Marine Services	
Newcastle upon Tyne	0191 295 0072
Caley Marine	
Inverness	01463 233437
Carrick Marine Projects	
Co Antrim	02893 355884
Challenger Marine	
Penryn	01326 377222
Coates Marine Ltd	
Whitby	01947 604486
Convoi Exceptionnel Ltd	
Hamble	023 8045 3045
Creekside Boatyard (Old Mill Creek) Dartmouth	01803 832649
Crinan Boatyard Ltd	
Crinan	01546 830232
Dale Sailing Co Ltd	
Neyland	01646 603110
Dart Marina Ltd	
Dartmouth	01803 833351
Dartside Quay	
Brixham	01803 845445
Dauntless Boatyard Ltd	
Canvey Island	01268 793782
Debbage Yachting	
Ipswich	01473 601169
Douglas Marine Preston	01772 812462
East & Co, Robin	
Kingsbridge	01548 531257
East Coast Offshore Yachting	
	01480 861381
Emsworth Yacht Harbour	
Emsworth	01243 377727
Exeter Ship Canal	01392 274306
Exmouth Marina	01395 269314
Firmhelm Ltd Pwllheli	01758 612244
Forrest Marine Ltd	
Exeter	08452 308335
Fowey Boatyard	
Fowey	01726 832194
Freshwater Boatyard	
Truro	01326 270443
Hafan Pwllheli Pwllheli	01758 701219
Houghton Boat Transport	
Tewkesbury	07831 486710
Gweek Quay Boatyard	
Helston	01326 221657
Iron Wharf Boatyard	
Faversham	01795 537122
Jalsea Marine Services Ltd	
Northwich	01606 77870
KG McColl	
Oban	01852 200248
Latham's Boatyard	
Poole	01202 748029

Lavis & Son, CH	
Exmouth	01395 263095
Lincombe Boat Yard	
Salcombe	01548 843580
MCL Transboat	08455 201900
Marine Resource Centre Ltd	
Oban	01631 720291
Marine & General Engineers	
Guernsey	01481 245808
Milford Marina	
Milford Haven	01646 696312/3
Moonfleet Sailing	
Poole	01202 682269
Southerly	
Chichester	01243 512611
Pasco's Boatyard	
Truro	01326 270269
Pearn and Co, Norman	
Looe	01503 262244
Performance Yachting	
Plymouth	01752 565023
Peters & May Ltd	
Southampton	023 8048 0480
Ponsharden Boatyard	
Penryn	01326 372215
Portsmouth Marine Engineering	
Fareham	01329 232854
Priors Boatyard	
Burnham-on-Crouch	01621 782160
Reeder School of Seamanship, Mike	
Lymington	01590 674560
Rossiter Yachts	
Christchurch	01202 483250
Seafix Boat Transfer	
North Wales	0845 528 0139
Sealand Boat Deliveries Ltd	
Liverpool	01254 705225
Shearwater Sailing	
Southampton	01962 775213
Shepards Wharf Boatyard Cowes Harbour Commission	
Cowes	01983 297821
Silvers Marina Ltd	
Helensburgh	01436 831222
Southcoasting Navigators	
Devon	01626 335626
Waterfront Marine	
Bangor	01248 352513
West Country Boat Transport	
	01566 785651
Wicor Marine	
Fareham	01329 237112
Winters Marine Ltd	
Salcombe	01548 843580
Wolff, David	07659 550131**Yacht Solutions Ltd**
Portsmouth	023 9275 5155
Yarmouth Marine Service	
Yarmouth, IoW	01983 760521
Youngboats	
Faversham	01795 536176

BOOKS, CHARTS & PUBLISHERS

Adlard Coles Nautical	
London	020 7631 5600
Brown Son & Ferguson Ltd	
Glasgow	0141 429 1234
Cooke & Son Ltd, B Hull	01482 223454
Dubois Phillips & McCallum Ltd	
Liverpool	0151 236 2776
Imray, Laurie, Norie & Wilson	
Huntingdon	01480 462114
Kelvin Hughes	
Southampton	023 8063 4911
Lilley & Gillie Ltd, John	0191 257 2217
Marine Chart Services	
Wellingborough	01933 441629**Price & Co Ltd, WF**
Bristol	0117 929 2229
QPC	
Fareham	01329 287880
Stanford Charts	
Bristol	0117 929 9966
Stanford Charts	
London	020 7836 1321
Stanford Charts	0845 880 3730
Manchester	0870 890 3730
Wiley Nautical	
Chichester	01243 779777

BOW THRUSTERS

ARS Anglian Diesels Ltd	
Wakefield	01924 332492
Buckler's Hard Boat Builders Ltd	
Beaulieu	01590 616214
JS Mouldings International	
Bursledon	023 8063 4400

BREAKDOWN

BJ Marine Ltd	
Bangor, Ireland	028 9127 1434
Seafit Marine Services	
Falmouth	01326 313713

CHANDLERS

ABC Powermarine	
Beaumaris	01248 811413
Admiral Marine Supplies	
Bootle	01469 575909
Allgadgets.co.uk	
Exmouth	01395 227727
Alpine Room & Yacht Equipment	
Chelmsford	01245 223563
Aquatogs Cowes	01983 295071
Arbroath Fishermen's Association	
Arbroath	01241 873132
Ardfern Yacht Centre Ltd	
Argyll	01852 500247
Ardoran Marine	
Oban	01631 566123

Arthurs Chandlery
Gosport   023 9252 6522

Arun Canvas and Rigging Ltd
Littlehampton   01903 732561

Aruncraft Chandlers
Littlehampton   01903 713327

ASAP Supplies – Equipment & Spares Worldwide
Beccles   0845 1300870

Auto Marine
Southsea   02392 825601

Bayside Marine
Brixham   01803 856771

Bedwell and Co
Walton on the Naze   01255 675873

BJ Marine Ltd Bangor   028 9127 1434

Bluecastle Chandlers
Portland   01305 822298

Blue Water Marine Ltd
Pwllheli   01758 614600

Boatacs
Westcliffe on Sea   01702 475057

Boathouse, The
Penryn   01326 374177

Boston Marina   01205 364420

Bosun's Locker, The
Falmouth   01326 312212

Bosun's Locker, The
Ramsgate   01843 597158

Bosuns Locker, The
South Queensferry 0131 331 3875/4496

Bridger Marine, John
Exeter   01392 250970

Bristol Boat Ltd Bristol 01225 872032

Brixham Yacht Supplies Ltd
Brixham   01803 882290

Brunel Chandlery Ltd
Neyland   01646 601667

Bucklers Hard Boat Builders
Beaulieu   01590 616214

Burghead Boat Centre
Findhorn   01309 690099

Bussell & Co, WL
Weymouth   01305 785633

Buzzard Marine
Yarmouth   01983 760707

C & M Marine
Bridlington   01262 672212

Cabin Yacht Stores
Rochester   01634 718020

Caley Marina Inverness 01463 236539

Cambrian Boat Centre
Swansea   01792 467263

Cantell & Son Ltd
Newhaven   01273 514118

Carne (Sales) Ltd, David
Penryn   01326 374177

Carrickcraft
Malahide   +353 1 845 5438

Caters Carrick Ltd
Carrickfergus   028 93351919

CH Marine (Cork)
Cork   +353 21 4315700

CH Marine Skibbereen   +353 28 23190

Charity & Taylor Ltd
Lowestoft   01502 581529

Chertsey Marine Ltd
Penton Hook Marina   01932 565195

Chicks Marine Ltd
Guernsey   01481 723716

Christchurch Boat Shop
Christchurch   01202 482751

Clapson & Son (Shipbuilders) Ltd South
Ferriby Marina   01652 635620

Clarke, Albert, Marine
Newtownards   028 9187 2325

Clyde Chandlers
Ardrossan   01294 471444

Coastal Marine Boatbuilders Ltd
(Dunbar) Eyemouth   01890 750328

Coates Marine Ltd
Whitby   01947 604486

Collins Marine St Helier 01534 732415

Compass Marine
Lancing   01903 761773

Cosalt International Ltd
Aberdeen   01224 588327

Cosalt International Ltd
Southampton   023 8063 2824

Cotter, Kieran
Baltimore   +353 28 20106

Cox Yacht Charter Ltd, Nick
Lymington   01590 673489

C Q Chandlers Ltd
Poole   01202 682095

Crinan Boats Ltd
Lochgilphead   01546 830232

CTC Marine & Leisure
Middlesbrough   01642 372600

Dale Sailing Co Ltd
Milford Haven   01646 603110

Danson Marine
Sidcup   0208 304 5678

Dartmouth Chandlery
Dartmouth   01803 839292

Dartside Quay
Brixham   01803 845445

Dauntless Boatyard Ltd
Canvey Island   01268 793782

Davis's Yacht Chandler
Littlehampton   01903 722778

Denney & Son, EL
Redcar   01642 483507

Deva Marine Conwy   01492 572777

Dickie & Sons Ltd, AM
Bangor   01248 363400

Dickie & Sons Ltd, AM
Pwllheli   01758 701828

Dinghy Supplies Ltd/Sutton Marine Ltd
Sutton   +353 1 832 2312

Diverse Yacht Services
Hamble   023 80453399

Dixon Chandlery, Peter
Exmouth   01395 273248

Doling & Son, GW
Barrow In Furness   01229 823708

Dovey Marine Aberdovey 01654 767581

Down Marine Co Ltd
Belfast   028 9048 0247

Douglas Marine Preston 01772 812462

Dubois Phillips & McCallum Ltd
Liverpool   0151 236 2776

Duncan Ltd, JS Wick   01955 602689

Duncan Yacht Chandlers
Ely   01353 663095

East Anglian Sea School
Ipswich   01473 659992

Eccles Marine Co
Middlesbrough   01642 372600

Ely Boat Chandlers
Hayling Island   023 9246 1968

Emsworth Chandlery
Emsworth   01243 375500

Force 4 Chandlery
Stroud   0845 1300710

Exe Leisure Exeter   01392 879055

Express Marine Services
Chichester   01243 773788

Fairways Chandlery
Burnham-on-Crouch   01621 782659

Fairweather Marine
Fareham   01329 283500

Fal Chandlers
Falmouth Marina   01326 212411

Ferrypoint Boat Co
Youghal   +353 24 94232

Findhorn Marina & Boatyard
Findhorn   01309 690099

Firmhelm Ltd Pwllheli 01758 612244

Fisherman's Mutual Asssociation (Eyemouth) Ltd
Eyemouth   01890 750373

Floetree Ltd (Loch Lomond Marina)
Balloch   01389 752069

Force 4 (Deacons)
Bursledon   023 8040 2182

Force 4 Chichester   01243 773788

Force 4 Chandlery
Mail order   0845 1300710

Force 4 Chandlery
Plymouth   01752 252489

Force 4 (Hamble Point)
Southampton   023 80455 058

Force 4 (Mercury)
Southampton   023 8045 4849

Force 4 (Port Hamble)
Southampton   023 8045 4858

Force 4 (Shamrock)
Southampton   023 8063 2725

Force 4 (Swanwick)
Swanwick   01489 881825

Freeport Marine
Jersey   01534 888100

French Marine Motors Ltd Brightlingsea 01206 302133	**Jackson Yacht Services** Jersey 01534 743819	**Marine MegaStore** Morpeth 01670 516151
Furneaux Riddall & Co Ltd Portsmouth 023 9266 8621	**Jamison and Green Ltd** Belfast 028 9032 2444	**Marine Scene** Bridgend 01656 671822
Gallichan Marine Ltd Jersey 01534 746387	**Jeckells and Son Ltd** Lowestoft 01502 565007	**Marine Scene** Cardiff 029 2070 5780
Galway Marine Chandlers Ltd Galway +353 91 566568	**JF Marine Chandlery** Rhu 01436 820584	**Marine Services** Jersey 01534 626930
GB Attfield & Company Dursley 01453 547185	**JNW Services** Aberdeen 01224 594050	**Marine Store Wyatts** West Mersea 01206 384745
Gibbons Ship Chandlers Ltd Sunderland 0191 567 2101	**JNW Services** Peterhead 01779 477346	**Marine Store** Maldon 01621 854380
Goodwick Marine Fishguard 01348 873955	**JSB Ltd** Tarbert, Loch Fyne 01880 820180	**Marine Store** Titchmarsh Marina 01621 874495
Gorleston Marine Ltd Great Yarmouth 01493 661883	**Johnston Brothers** Mallaig 01687 462215	**Marine Store** Walton on the Naze 01255 679028
GP Barnes Ltd Shoreham 01273 591705/596680	**Johnstons Marine Stores** Lamlash 01770 600333	**Marine Superstore Port Solent Chandlery** Portsmouth 023 9221 9843
Great Outdoors Clarenbridge, Galway +353 87 2793821	**Kearon Ltd, George** Arklow +353 402 32319	**MarineCo** Torpoint 01752 816005
Green Marine, Jimmy Fore St Beer 01297 20744	**Kelpie Boats** Pembroke Dock 01646 683661	**Maryport Harbour and Marina** Maryport 01900 814431
Grimsby Rigging Services Ltd Grimsby 01472 362758	**Kelvin Hughes Ltd** Southampton 023 80634911	**Matchett Ltd, HC** Widnes 0151 423 4420
Gunn Navigation Services, Thomas Aberdeen 01224 595045	**Kildale Marine** Hull 01482 227464	**Matthews Ltd, D** Cork +353 214 277633
Hale Marine, Ron Portsmouth 023 92732985	**Kingfisher Marine** Weymouth 01305 766595	**McClean** Greenock 01475 728234
Harbour Marine Services Ltd (HMS) Southwold 01502 724721	**Kings Lock Chandlery** Middlewich 01606 737564	**McCready Sailboats Ltd** Holywood 028 9042 1821
Hardware & Marine Supplies Wexford +353 53 29791	**Kip Chandlery Inverkip** Greenock 01475 521485	**Moore, Kevin** Cowes 01983 289699
Hardway Marine Gosport 023 9258 0420	**Kirkcudbright Scallop Gear Ltd** Kirkcudbright 01557 330399	**Moore & Son, J** Mevagissey 01726 842964
Harris Marine (1984) Ltd, Ray Barry 01446 740924	**Kyle Chandlers** Troon 01292 311880	**Morgan & Sons Marine, LH** Brightlingsea 01206 302003
Hartlepool Marine Supplies Hartlepool 01429 862932	**Landon Marine, Reg** Truro 01872 272668	**Mount Batten Boathouse** Plymouth 01752 482666
Harwich Chandlers Ltd Harwich 01255 504061	**Largs Chandlers** Largs 01475 686026	**Murphy, Nicholas** Dunmore East +353 51 383259
Harwoods Yarmouth 01983 760258	**Lencraft Boats Ltd** Dungarvan +353 58 68220	**Mylor Chandlery & Rigging** Falmouth 01326 375482
Hawkins Marine Shipstores, John Rochester 01634 840812	**Lincoln Marina** Lincoln 01522 526896	**Nancy Black** Oban 01631 562550
Hayles, Harold Yarmouth 01983 760373	**Looe Chandlery** West Looe 01503 264355	**Nautical World** Bangor 028 91460330
Herm Seaway Marine Ltd St Peter Port 01481 726829	**Lynch Ltd, PA** Morpeth 01670 512291	**New World Yacht Care** Helensburgh 01436 820586
Highway Marine Sandwich 01304 613925	**Mackay Boatbuilders (Arbroath) Ltd** Aberdeen 01241 872879	**Newhaven Chandlery** Newhaven 01273 612612
Hoare Ltd, Bob Poole 01202 736704	**Mackay Marine Services** Aberdeen 01224 575772	**Nifpo** Ardglass 028 4484 2144
Hornsey (Chandlery) Ltd, Chris Southsea 023 9273 4728	**Mailspeed Marine** Burnham-on-Crouch 01342 710618	**Norfolk Marine** Great Yarmouth 01692 670272
Hunter & Combes Cowes 01983 299599	**Mailspeed Marine** Essex Marina 01342 710618	**Norfolk Marine Chandlery Shop** Norwich 01603 783150
Iron Stores Marine St Helier 01534 877755	**Mailspeed Marine** Warrington 01342 710618	**Northshore Sport & Leisure** Brancaster Staithe 01485 210236
Isles of Scilly Steamship Co St Mary's 01720 422710	**Mainbrayce Chandlers** Braye, Alderney 01481 822772	**Ocean Leisure Ltd** London 020 7930 5050
	Manx Marine Ltd Douglas 01624 674842	**One Stop Chandlery** Maldon 01621 853558
	Marine & Leisure Europe Ltd Plymouth 01752 268826	**O'Sullivans Marine Ltd** Tralee +353 66 7124957
	Marine MegaStore Hamble 023 8045 4400	**Partington Marine Ltd, William** Pwllheli 01758 612808

Pascall Atkey & Sons Ltd
Isle of Wight   01983 292381

Pennine Marine Ltd
Skipton   01756 792335

Penrhos Marine
Aberdovey   01654 767478

Penzance Marine Services
Penzance   01736 361081

Perry Marine, Rob
Axminster   01297 631314

Pepe Boatyard
Hayling Island   023 9246 1968

Performance Yachting & Chandlery
Plymouth   01752 565023

Peters PLC Chichester   01243 511033

Pinnell & Bax
Northampton   01604 592808

Piplers of Poole Poole 01202 673056

Pirate's Cave, The
Rochester   01634 295233

Powersail Island Chandlers Ltd
East Cowes Marina   01983 299800

Preston Marine Services Ltd
Preston   01772 733595

Price & Co Ltd, WF
Bristol   0117 929 2229

PSM Ltd Alderney   07781 106635

Purcell Marine
Clarenbridge   +353 87 279 3821

Purple Sails & Marine
Walsall   08456 435510

Quay West Marine
Poole   01202 732445

Quayside Marine
Salcombe   01548 844300

Racecourse Yacht Basin (Windsor) Ltd
Windsor   01753 851501

Rat Rigs Water Sports
Cardiff   029 2062 1309

Reliance Marine
Wirral   0151 625 5219

Rigmarine Padstow   01841 532657

Riversway Marine
Preston   0844 879 4901

RHP Marine Cowes   01983 290421

RNS Marine Northam   01237 474167

Sail Loft
Bideford   01271 860001

Sailaway
St Anthony   01326 231357

Salcombe Boatstore
Salcombe   01548 843708

Salterns Chandlery
Poole   01202 701556

Shipmate
Salcombe   01548 844555

Sandrock Marine
Rye   01797 222679

Schull Watersports Centre
Schull   +353 28 28554

Sea & Shore Ship Chandler
Dundee   01382 450666

Sea Cruisers of Rye Rye   01797 222070

Sea Span Edinburgh   0131 552 2224

Sea Teach Ltd Emsworth 01243 375774

Seafare Tobermory   01688 302277

Seahog Boats Preston   01772 633016

Seamark-Nunn & Co
Felixstowe   01394 451000

Seaquest Marine Ltd
St Peter Port   01481 721773

Seaware Ltd Penryn   01326 377948

Seaway Marine Macduff   01261 832877

Sharp & Enright Dover   01304 206295

Shearwater Engineering Services Ltd
Dunoon   01369 706666

Shipshape Marine
King's Lynn   01553 764058

Ship Shape Ramsgate   01843 597000

Shorewater Sports
Chichester   01243 672315

Simpson Marine Ltd
Newhaven   01273 612612

Simpson Marine Ltd, WA
Dundee   01382 566670

Sketrick Marine Centre
Killinchy   028 9754 1400

Smith AM (Marine) Ltd
London   020 8529 6988

Solent Marine Chandlery Ltd
Gosport   023 9258 4622

South Coast Marine
Christchurch   01202 482695

South Pier Shipyard
St Helier   01534 711000

Southampton Yacht Services Ltd
Southampton   023 803 35266

Sparkes Chandlery
Hayling Island   02392 463572

S Roberts Marine Ltd
Liverpool   0151 707 8300

SSL Marine
Eastbourne   01323 47900

Standard House Chandlery
Wells-next-the-Sea   01328 710593

Stornoway Fishermen's Co-op
Stornoway   01851 702563

Sunset Marine & Watersports
Sligo   +353 71 9162792

Sussex Marine
St Leonards on Sea   01424 425882

Sussex Yachts Lyd
Shoreham   01273 605482

Sussex Marine Centre
Shoreham   01273 454737

Sutton Marine (Dublin)
Sutton   +353 1 832 2312

SW Nets Newlyn   01736 360254

Tarbert Ltd, JSB Tarbert 01880 820180

TCS Chandlery
Essex Marina   01702 258094
TCS Chandlery Grays   01375 374702
TCS Chandlery
Southend   01702 444423

Thulecraft Ltd Lerwick 01595 693192

Torbay Boating Centre
Paignton   01803 558760

Torquay Chandlers
Torquay   01803 211854

Trafalgar Yacht Services
Fareham   01329 822445

Trident UK N Shields   0191 490 1736

Union Chandlery
Cork   +353 21 4554334

Uphill Boat Services
Weston-Super-Mare   01934 418617

Upper Deck Marine and Outriggers
Fowey   01726 832287

V Ships (Isle of Man)
Douglas   01624 688886

V F Marine Rhu   01436 820584

Viking Marine Ltd
Dun Laoghaire   +353 1 280 6654

Waterfront Marine
Bangor   01248 352513

Watersport and Leisure
Kings Lynn   01485 210236

Wayne Maddox Marine
Margate   01843 297157

Western Marine
Dalkey   +353 1280 0321

Whitstable Marine
Whitstable   01227 274168

Williams Ltd, TJ Cardiff 029 20 487676

Windjammer Marine
Milford Marina   01646 699070

Yacht & Boat Chandlery
Faversham   01795 531777

Yacht Chandlers Conwy   01492 572777

Yacht Equipment
Chelmsford   01245 223563

Yachtmail Ltd
Lymington   01590 672784

Yachtshop
Holyhead   01407 760031

You Boat Chandlery
Gosport   02392 522226

CHART AGENTS

Brown Son & Ferguson Ltd
Glasgow   0141 429 1234

Chattan Security Ltd
Edinburgh   0131 554 7527

Cooke & Son Ltd, B
Hull   01482 223454

Dubois Phillips & McCallum Ltd
Liverpool 0151 236 2776

Imray Laurie Norie and Wilson Ltd
Huntingdon 01480 462114

Kelvin Hughes
Southampton 023 8063 4911

Lilley & Gillie Ltd, John
North Shields 0191 257 2217

MARINE CHART SERVICES
Maritime House, 32 Denington Rd,
Wellingborough NN8 2QH
Tel: 01933 441629
Fax: 01933 442662
www.chartsales.co.uk
Access to many thousands of
Navigation Charts & publications in
different format.

Price & Co, WF
Bristol 0117 929 2229

Sea Chest Nautical Bookshop Plymouth
01752 222012

Seath Instruments (1992) Ltd
Lowestoft 01502 573811

Small Craft Deliveries
Woodbridge 01394 382655

Smith (Marine) Ltd, AM
London 020 8529 6988

South Bank Marine Charts Ltd Grimsby
01472 361137

Stanford Charts Bristol 0117 929 9966

Stanford Charts
London 020 7836 1321

Todd Chart Agency Ltd
County Down 028 9146 6640

UK Hydrographics Office
Taunton 01823 337900

Warsash Nautical Bookshop
Warsash 01489 572384

CLOTHING

Absolute
Gorleston on Sea 01493 442259

Aquatogs Cowes 01983 295071

Crew Clothing
London 020 8875 2300

Crewsaver
Gosport 01329 820000

Douglas Gill
Nottingham 0115 9460844

Fat Face fatface.com

Gul International Ltd
Bodmin 01208 262400

Guy Cotten UK Ltd
Liskeard 01579 347115

Harwoods Yarmouth 01983 760258

Helly Hansen
Nottingham 0115 979 5997

Henri Lloyd
Manchester 0161 799 1212

Joules 0845 6066871

Mad Cowes Clothing Co
Cowes 0845 456 5158

Matthews Ltd, D
Cork +353 214 277633

Mountain & Marine
Poynton 01625 859863

Musto Ltd Laindon 01268 491555

Ocean World Ltd
Cowes 01983 291744

Purple Sails & Marine
Walsall 0845 6435510

Quba Sails
Lymington 01590 689362

Quba Sails
Salcombe 01548 844599

Yacht Parts
Plymouth 01752 252489

CODE OF PRACTICE EXAMINERS

Booth Marine Surveys, Graham
Birchington-on-Sea 01843 843793

Cannell & Associates, David M
Wivenhoe 01206 823337

COMPUTERS & SOFTWARE

Dolphin Maritime Software
White Cross 01524 841946

Forum Software Ltd
Nr Haverfordwest 01646 636363

Kelvin Hughes Ltd
Southampton 023 8063 4911

Memory-Map
Aldermaston 0844 8110950

PC Maritime Plymouth 01752 254205

DECK EQUIPMENT

Aries Van Gear Spares
Penryn 01326 377467

Ronstan
Gosport 023 9252 5377

Harken UK Lymington 01590 689122

IMP Royston 01763 241300

Kearon Ltd George +353 402 32319

Pro-Boat Ltd
Burnham-on-Crouch 01621 785455

Ryland, Kenneth
Stanton 01386 584270

Smith, EC & Son Ltd
Luton 01582 729721

Timage & Co Ltd
Braintree 01376 343087

DIESEL MARINE/ FUEL ADDITIVES

Corralls Poole 01202 674551

Cotters Marine & General Supplies
Baltimore +353 28 20106

Expresslube Henfield 01444 254115

Gorey Marine Fuel Supplies
Gorey 07797 742384

Hammond Motorboats
Dover 01304 206809

Iron Wharf Boatyard
Faversham 01795 536296

Lallow, Clare Cowes 01983 760707

Marine Support & Towage
Cowes 01983 200716/07860 297633

Quayside Fuel
Weymouth 07747 182181

Rossiter Yachts
Christchurch 01202 483250

Sleeman & Hawken
Shaldon 01626 778266

DIVERS

Abco Divers Belfast 028 90610492

Andark Diving
Burseldon 01489 581755

Argonaut Marine
Aberdeen 01224 706526

Baltimore Diving and Watersports
Centre West Cork +353 28 20300

C & C Marine Services
Largs 01475 687180

Cardiff Commercial Boat Operators Ltd
Cardiff 029 2037 7872

Clyde Diving Centre
Inverkip 01475 521281

Divetech UK King's Lynn 01485 572323

Diving & Marine Engineering
Barry 01446 721553

Donnelly, R South Shields 07973 119455

DV Diving 028 9146 4671

Falmouth Divers Ltd
Penryn 01326 374736

Fathoms Ltd Wick 01955 605956

Felixarc Marine Ltd
Lowestoft 01502 509215

Grampian Diving Services
New Deer 01771 644206

Higgins, Noel +353 872027650

Hudson, Dave
Trearddur Bay 01407 860628

Hunt, Kevin
Tralee +353 6671 25979

Kaymac Diving Services
Swansea 08431 165523

Keller, Hilary
Buncrana +353 77 62146

Kilkee Diving Centre
Kilkee +353 6590 56707

Leask Marine Kirkwall 01856 874725

Looe Divers Hannafore 01503 262727

MacDonald, D Nairn 01667 455661

Medway Diving Contractors Ltd
Gillingham   01634 851902

MMC Diving Services
Lake, Isle of Wight   07966 579965

Mojo Maritime Penzance 01736 762771

Murray, Alex Stornoway 01851 704978

New Dawn Dive Centre
Lymington   01590 675656

Northern Divers (Engineering) Ltd Hull
01482 227276

Offshore Marine Services Ltd
Bembridge   01983 873125

Parkinson (Sinbad Marine Services), J
Killybegs   +353 73 31417

Port of London Authority
Gravesend   01474 560311

Purcell, D – Crouch Sailing School
Burnham   01621 784140/0585 33

Salvesen UK Ltd
Liverpool   0151 933 6038

Sea-Lift Diving Dover   01304 829956

Southern Cylinder Services
Fareham   01329 221125

Sub Aqua Services
North Ormesby   01642 230209

Teign Diving Centre
Teignmouth   01626 773965

Tuskar Rock Marine
Rosslare   +353 53 33376

Underwater Services
Dyffryn Arbwy   01341 247702

Wilson Alan c/o Portrush Yacht Club
Portrush   028 2076 2225

Woolford, William
Bridlington   01262 671710

ELECTRICAL AND ELECTRONIC ENGINEERS

AAS Marine
Aberystwyth   01970 631090

Allworth Riverside Services, Adrian
Chelsea Harbour Marina 07831 574774

Baker, Keith
Brentford   07792 937790

Belson Design Ltd, Nick
Southampton   077 6835 1330

Biggs, John Weymouth Marina,
Weymouth   01305 778445

BJ Marine Ltd Bangor   028 9127 1434

Boat Electrics Troon   01292 315355

Calibra Marine
Dartmouth   01803 833094

Campbell & McHardy Lossiemouth
Marina, Lossiemouth   01343 812137

CES Sandown Sparkes Marina,
Hayling Island   023 9246 6005

Colin Coady Marine
Malahide   +353 87 265 6496

Contact Electrical
Arbroath   01241 874528

DDZ Marine Ardossan   01294 607077

EC Leisure Craft
Essex Marina   01702 568482

Energy Solutions
Rochester   01634 290772

Enterprise Marine Electronic & Technical Services Ltd
Aberdeen   01224 593281

Eurotek Marine
Eastbourne   01323 479144

Evans, Lyndon
Brentford   07795 218704

Floetree Ltd (Loch Lomond Marina)
Balloch   01389 752069

Hamble Marine
Hamble   02380 001088

HNP Engineers (Lerwick) Ltd
Lerwick   01595 692493

Jackson Yacht Services
Jersey   01534 743819

Jedynak, A Salcombe   01548 843321

Kippford Slipway Ltd
Dalbeattie   01556 620249

Lynch Ltd, PA
Morpeth   01670 512291

Mackay Boatbuilders (Arbroath) Ltd
Aberdeen   01241 872879

Marine, AW
Gosport   023 9250 1207

Marine Electrical Repair Service
London   020 7228 1336

MB Marine Troon   01292 311944

MES Falmouth Marina,
Falmouth   01326 378497

Mount Batten Boathouse
Plymouth   01752 482666

New World Yacht Care
Rhu   01436 820586

Neyland Marine Services Ltd
Milford Haven   01646 600358

Powell, Martin Shamrock Quay,
Southampton   023 8033 2123

R & J Marine Electricians Suffolk Yacht
Harbour Ltd, Ipswich   01473 659737

Radio & Electronic Services Beaucette
Marina, Guernsey   01481 728837

Redcar Fish Company
Stockton-on-Tees   01642 633638

RHP Marine Cowes   01983 290421

Rothwell, Chris
Torquay Marina   01803 850960

Ruddy Marine
Galway   +353 87 742 7439

Rutherford, Jeff Largs   01475 568026

SM International
Plymouth   01752 662129

Sussex Fishing Services
Rye   01797 223895

Tony's Marine Service
Coleraine   028 7035 6422

Ultra Marine Systems
Mayflower International Marina,
Plymouth   07989 941020

Upham, Roger
Chichester   01243 528299

Volspec
Ipswich   01473 780144

Weyland Marine Services
Milford Haven   01646 600358

ELECTRONIC DEVICES AND EQUIPMENT

Anchorwatch UK
Edinburgh   0131 447 5057

Aquascan International Ltd
Newport   01633 841117

Atlantis Marine Power Ltd
Plymouth   01752 208810

Autosound Marine
Bradford   01274 688990

B&G Romsey   01794 518448

Brookes & Gatehouse
Romsey   01794 518448

Boat Electrics & Electronics Ltd
Troon   01292 315355

Cactus Navigation & Communication
London   020 7833 3435

CDL Aberdeen   01224 706655

Charity & Taylor Ltd
Lowestoft   01502 581529

Diverse Yacht Services
Hamble   023 8045 3399

Dyfed Electronics Ltd
Milford Haven   01646 694572

Echopilot Marine Electronics Ltd
Ringwood   01425 476211

Enterprise Marine
Aberdeen   01224 593281

Euronav Ltd
Portsmouth   023 9237 3855

Furuno UK
Fraserburgh   01346 518300

Furuno UK
Havant   023 9244 1000

Garmin (Europe) Ltd
Romsey   0870 850 1242

Golden Arrow Marine Ltd
Southampton   023 8071 0371

Greenham Regis Marine Electronics
Lymington   01590 671144

Greenham Regis Marine Electronics Poole	01202 676363
Greenham Regis Marine Electronics Southampton	023 8063 6555
ICS Electronics Arundel	01903 731101
JG Technologies Ltd Weymouth	0845 458 9616
KM Electronics Lowestoft	01502 569079
Kongsberg Simrad Ltd Aberdeen	01224 226500
Kongsberg Simrad Ltd Wick	01955 603606
Landau UK Ltd Hamble	02380 454040
Enterprise Marine Aberdeen	01224 593281
Marathon Leisure Hayling Island	023 9263 7711
Marine Instruments Falmouth	01326 375483
MB Marine Troon	01292 311944
Microcustom Ltd Ipswich	01473 215777
Nasa Marine Instruments Stevenage	01438 354033
Navionics UK Plymouth	01752 204735
Ocean Leisure Ltd London	020 7930 5050
Plymouth Marine Electronics Plymouth	01752 227711
Radio & Electronic Services Ltd St Peter Port	01481 728837
Raymarine Ltd Portsmouth	02392 714700
Redfish Car Company Stockton-on-Tees	01642 633638
Robertson, MK Oban	01631 563836
Satcom Distribution Ltd Salisbury	01722 410800
Seaquest Marine Ltd Guernsey	01481 721773
Seatronics Aberdeen	01224 853100
Selex Communications Aberdeen	01224 890316
Selex Communications Bristol	0117 931 3550
Selex Communications Brixham	01803 882716
Selex Communications Fraserburgh	01346 518187
Selex Communications Glasgow	0141 882 6909
Selex Communications Hull	01482 326144
Selex Communications Kilkeel	028 4176 9009
Selex Communications Liverpool	01268 823400

Selex Communications Lowestoft	01502 572365
Selex Communications Newcastle upon Tyne	0191 265 0374
Selex Communications Newlyn	01736 361320
Selex Communications Penryn	01326 378031
Selex Communications Plymouth	01752 222878
Selex Communications Rosyth	01383 419606
Selex Communications Southampton	023 8051 1868
Silva Ltd Livingston	01506 419555
SM International Plymouth	01752 662129
Sperry Marine Ltd Peterhead	01779 473475
Stenmar Ltd Aberdeen	01224 827288
Transas Nautic Portsmouth	023 9267 4016
Veripos Precise Navigation Fraserburgh	01346 511411
Wema (UK) Honiton	01404 881810
Wilson & Co Ltd, DB Glasgow	0141 647 0161
Woodsons of Aberdeen Ltd Aberdeen	01224 722884

ENGINES AND ACCESSORIES

Airylea Motors Aberdeen	01224 872891
Amble Boat Co Ltd Amble	01665 710267
Anchor Marine Products Benfleet	01268 566666
Aquafac Ltd Luton	01582 568700
Barrus Ltd, EP Bicester	01869 363636
British Polar Engines Ltd Glasgow	0141 445 2455
Bukh Diesel UK Ltd Poole	01202 668840
CJ Marine Mechanical Troon	01292 313400
Cleghorn Waring Ltd Letchworth	01462 480380
Cook's Diesel Service Ltd Faversham	01795 538553
Southern Shipwright (SSL) Brighton	01273 601779
Southern Shipwright (SSL) Eastbourne	01323 479000
Fender-Fix Maidstone	01622 751518
Fettes & Rankine Engineering Aberdeen	01224 573343
Fleetwood & Sons Ltd, Henry Lossiemouth	01343 813015

Gorleston Marine Ltd Great Yarmouth	01493 661883
Halyard Salisbury	01722 710922
Interseals (Guernsey) Ltd Guernsey	01481 246364
Kelpie Boats Pembroke Dock	01646 683661
Keypart Watford	01923 330570
Lancing Marine Brighton	01273 410025
Lencraft Boats Ltd Dungarvan	+353 58 68220
Lewmar Ltd Havant	023 9247 1841
Liverpool Power Boats Bootle	0151 944 1163
Lynch Ltd, PA Morpeth	01670 512291
MacDonald & Co Ltd, JN Glasgow	0141 810 3400
Mariners Weigh Shaldon	01626 873698
MMS Ardrossan	01294 604831
Mooring Mate Ltd Bournemouth	01202 421199
Newens Marine, Chas Putney	020 8788 4587
Ocean Safety Southampton	023 8072 0800
RK Marine Ltd Hamble	01489 583585
RK Marine Ltd Swanwick	01489 583572
Sillette Sonic Ltd Sutton	020 8337 7543
Smith & Son Ltd, EC Luton	01582 729721
Sowester Simpson-Lawrence Ltd Poole	01202 667700
Timage & Co Ltd Braintree	01376 343087
Vetus Den Ouden Ltd Totton	023 8045 4507
Western Marine Dublin	+353 1 280 0321
Whitstable Marine Whitstable	01227 262525
Yates Marine, Martin Galgate	01524 751750
Ynys Marine Cardigan	01239 613179

FOUL-WEATHER GEAR

Aquatogs Cowes	01983 295071
Crew Clothing London	020 8875 2300
Century Finchampstead	0118 9731616
Crewsaver Gosport	01329 820000
Douglas Gill Nottingham	0115 946 0844

FBI
Leeds 0113 270 7000

Gul International Ltd
Bodmin 01208 262400

Helly Hansen
Nottingham 0115 979 5997

Henri Lloyd
Manchester 0161 799 1212

Musto Ltd
Laindon 01268 491555

Pro Rainer
Windsor 07752 903882

GENERAL MARINE EQUIPMENT & SPARES

Ampair
Ringwood 01425 480780

Aries Vane Gear Spares
Penryn 01326 377467

Arthurs Chandlery, R
Gosport 023 9252 6522

Atlantis Marine Power Ltd
Plymouth 01752 208810

Barden UK Ltd Fareham 01489 570770

Calibra Marine International Ltd
Southampton 08702 400358

CH Marine (Cork)
Cork +353 21 4315700

Chris Hornsey (Chandlery) Ltd
Southsea 023 9273 4728

Compass Marine (Dartmouth) Dartmouth 01803 835915

Cox Yacht Charter Ltd, Nick
Lymington 01590 673489

CTC Marine & Leisure
Middlesbrough 01642 372600

Docksafe Ltd Bangor 028 9147 0453

Frederiksen Boat Fittings (UK) Ltd
Gosport 023 9252 5377

Furneaux Riddall & Co Ltd
Portsmouth 023 9266 8621

Hardware & Marine Supplies
Co Wexford +353 (53) 29791

Index Marine
Bournemouth 01202 470149

Kearon Ltd, George
Arklow +353 402 32319

Marathon Leisure
Hayling Island 023 9263 7711

Pro-Boat Ltd
Burnham-on-Crouch 01621 785455

Pump International Ltd
Cornwall 01209 831937

Quay West Marine
Poole 01202 732445

Rogers, Angie Bristol 0117 973 8276

Ryland, Kenneth
Stanton 01386 584270

Tiflex
Liskeard 01579 320808

Vetus Boating Equipment
Southampton 02380 454507

Whitstable Marine
Whitstable 01227 262525

Yacht Parts
Plymouth 01752 252489

HARBOUR MASTERS

Aberaeron	01545 571645
Aberdeen	01224 597000
Aberdovey	01654 767626
Aberystwyth	01970 611433
Alderney & Burhou	01481 822620
Amble	01665 710306
Anstruther	01333 310836
Appledore	01237 474569
Arbroath	01241 872166
Ardglass	028 4484 1291
Ardrossan Control Tower	01294 463972
Arinagour Piermaster	01879 230347
Arklow	+353 402 32466
Baltimore	+353 28 22145
Banff	01261 815544
Bantry Bay	+353 27 53277
Barmouth	01341 280671
Barry	01446 732665
Beaucette	01481 245000
Beaulieu River	01590 616200
Belfast Lough	028 90 553012
Belfast River Manager	028 90 328507
Bembridge	01983 872828
Berwick-upon-Tweed	01289 307404
Bideford	01237 346131
Blyth	01670 352678
Boston	01205 362328
Bridlington	01262 670148/9
Bridport	01308 423222
Brighton	01273 819919
Bristol	0117 926 4797
Brixham	01803 853321
Buckie	01542 831700
	07842 532360
Bude	01288 353111
Burghead	01343 835337
Burnham-on-Crouch	01621 783602
Burnham-on-Sea	01278 782180
Burtonport	+353 075 42155
Caernarfon	01286 672118
Caernarfon	07786 730865

Camber Berthing Offices – Portsmouth	
	023 92297395
Campbeltown	01586 552552
	07825 732862
Caledonian Canal Off. (Inverness)	01463 725500
Cardiff	029 20400500
Carnlough Harbour	07703 606763
Castletown Bay	01624 823549
Charlestown	01726 67526
Chichester Harbour	01243 512301
Clovelly	01273 431549
	07975 501380
Conwy	01492 596253
Cork	+353 21 4273125
Corpach Canal Sea Lock	
	01397 772249
Courtmacsherry	+353 8673 94299
	+353 23 46311/46600
Coverack	01326 380679
Cowes	01983 293952
Crail	01333 450820
Craobh Haven	01852 502222
Crinan Canal Office	01546 603210
Cromarty Firth	01381 600479
Cromarty Harbour	01381 600493
Crookhaven	+353 28 35319
Cullen	01542 831700
Dingle	+353 66 9151629
Douglas	01624 686628
Dover	01304 240400 Ext 4520
Dublin	+353 1 874871
Dun Laoghaire	
	+353 1 280 1130/8074
Dunbar	01368 863206
Dundee	01382 224121
Dunmore East	+353 51 383166
East Loch Tarbert	01859 502444
Eastbourne	01323 470099
Eigg Harbour	01687 482428
Elie	01333 330051
Estuary Control - Dumbarton	01389 726211
Exe	01392 274306
Eyemouth	01890 750223
	07885 742505
Falmouth	01326 312285
Felixstowe	07803 476621
Findochty	01542 831700
Fisherrow	0131 665 5900
Fishguard (Lower Hbr)	01348 874726

Fishguard	01348 404425	Lyness	01856 791387	Ramsgate	01843 572100
Fleetwood	01253 872323	Macduff	01261 832236	River Bann & Coleraine	
Flotta	01856 701411	Maryport	01900 814431		028 7034 2012
Folkestone	01303 715354	Menai Strait	01248 712312	River Blackwater	01621 856487
Fowey	01726 832471/2.	Methil	01333 462725	River Colne (Brightlingsea)	01206 302200
Fraserburgh	01346 515858	Mevagissey	01726 843305	River Dart	01803 832337
Galway Bay	+353 91 561874	Milford Haven	01646 696100	River Deben	01473 736257
Garlieston	01988 600274	Minehead (Mon-Fri)	01643 702566	River Exe Dockmaster	01392 274306
Glasson Dock	07910 315606	Montrose	01674 672302	River Humber	01482 327171
Gorey Port Control	01534 447788	Mousehole	01736 731511	River Medway	01795 596593
Gourdon	01569 762741	Mullion Cove	01326 240222	River Orwell	01473 231010
Great Yarmouth	01493 335501	Nairn Harbour Office	01667 452453	River Roach	01621 783602
Grimsby Dockmaster	01472 359181	Newhaven Harbour Admin		River Stour	01255 243000
Groomsport Bay	028 91 278040		01273 612872/612926	River Tyne/North Shields	0191 257 2080
Hamble River	01489 576387	Newlyn	01736 731897	River Yealm	01752 872533
Hayle	07500 993867	Newquay	07737 387217	Rivers Alde & Ore	07528 092635
Helford River	01326 250749	Newport Harbour Office	01983 525994	Rosslare Europort	+353 53 915 7921
Helmsdale	01431 821692	North Berwick	00776 467373	Rothesay	01700 503842
Holy Island	01289 389217	Oban	01631 562892		07799 724225
Holyhead	01407 763071	Padstow	01841 532239	Ryde	01983 613879
Hopeman	01343 835337	Peel	01624 842338	Salcombe	01548 843791
Howth	+353 1 832 2252	Penrhyn Bangor	01248 352525	Sark	01481 832323
Ilfracombe	01271 862108	Penzance	01736 366113	Scalloway	01595 880574
Inverness	01463 715715	Peterhead	01779 483630	Scarborough	01723 373530
Irvine	01294 487286	Pierowall	01857 677216	Scrabster	01847 892779
Johnshaven	01561 362262	Pittenweem	01333 312591	Seaham	07786 565205
Kettletoft Bay	01857 600227	Plockton	01599 534589	Sharpness, Gloucester Harbour Trustees	01453 811913
Killybegs	+353 73 31032	Polperro	01503 272809	Shoreham	01273 598100
Kilmore Quay	+353 53 912 9955	Poole	01202 440233	Silloth	016973 31358
Kinlochbervie	01971 521235	Port Isaac	01208 880321	Sligo	+353 91 53819
	07901 514350		07855 429422		+353 86 0870767
Kinsale	+353 21 4772503	Port St Mary	01624 833205	Southampton	023 8033 9733
Kirkcudbright	01557 331135	Porth Dinllaen	01758 720276	Southend-on-Sea	01702 611889
Kirkwall	01856 872292	Porthleven	01326 574207	Southwold	01502 724712
Langstone Harbour	023 9246 3419	Porthmadog	01766 512927	St Helier	01534 447788
Larne	02828 872100	Portknockie	01542 840833	St Ives	07793 515460
Lerwick	01595 692991	Portland	01305 824044	St Margaret's Hope	01856 831454
Littlehampton	01903 721215	Portpatrick	01776 810355	St Mary's	01720 422768
Liverpool	0151 949 6134/5	Portree	01478 612926	St Michael's Mount	07870 400282
Loch Gairloch	01445 712140	Portrush	028 70822307	St Monans (part-time)	07930 869538
Loch Inver	01571 844267	Portsmouth Harbour Commercial Docks	023 92297395	St Peter Port	01481 720229
	07958 734610	Portsmouth Harbour Control	023 92723694	Stonehaven	01569 762741
Looe	01503 262839			Stornoway	01851 702688
	07918 728955	Portsmouth Harbour	023 92723124	Strangford Lough	028 44 881637
Lossiemouth (Marina)	07969 213513	Preston	01772 726711	Stromness	07810 465825
	07969 213521	Pwllheli	01758 701219	Stronsay	01857 616317
Lough Foyle	028 7186 0555	Queenborough	01795 662051	Sullom Voe	01806 242551
Lowestoft	01502 572286	Queens Gareloch/Rhu	01436 674321		
Lyme Regis	01297 442137	Ramsey	01624 812245		
Lymington	01590 672014				

Sunderland	0191 567 2626
Swale	01795 561234
Swansea	01792 653787
Tayport Hbr Trust	01382 553799
Tees & Hartlepool Port Authority	01429 277205
Teignmouth	01626 773165
Tenby	01834 842717
Thames Estuary	01474 562200
Tobermory Moorings Officer	07917 832497
Torquay	01803 292429
Troon	01292 281687
Truro	01872 272130
Ullapool	01854 612091
Waldringfield	01394 276004
Walton-on-the-Naze	01255 851899
Watchet	07739 958441
Waterford	+353 51 874907
Wells-next-the-Sea	01328 711646
West Bay (Bridport)	01308 423222
	07870 240636
Wexford	+353 53 912 2039
Weymouth	01305 206423
Whitby	01947 602354
Whitehaven	01946 692435
Whitehills	01261 861291
Whitstable	01227 274086
Wick	01955 602030
Wicklow	+353 404 67455
Workington	01900 602301
Yarmouth	01983 760321
Youghal	+353 24 92626

HARBOURS

Bristol Harbour	0117 903 1484
Clyde Marina – Ardrossan	01294 607077
Jersey Harbours St Helier	01534 885588
Maryport Harbour and Marina Maryport	01900 818447/4431
Peterhead Bay Authority Peterhead	01779 474020
Sark Moorings – Channel Islands	01481 832260

INSURANCE/FINANCE

Admiral Marine Ltd Salisbury	01722 416106
Bishop Skinner Boat Insurance	
London	0800 7838057
Bluefin London	0800 074 5200
Castlemain Ltd St Peter Port	01481 721319
Clark Insurance, Graham Tyneside	0191 455 8089
Craven Hodgson Associates Leeds	0113 243 8443
Giles Insurance Brokers Irvine	01294 315481
GJW Direct Liverpool	0151 473 8000
Haven Knox-Johnston West Malling	01732 223600
Lombard Southampton	023 8024 2171
Mardon Insurance Shrewsbury	0800 515629
Marine & General Insurance Services Ltd Maidstone	01622 201106
Mercia Marine Malvern	01684 564457
Nautical Insurance Services Ltd Leigh-on-Sea	01702 470811
Navigators & General Brighton	01273 863400
Pantaenius UK Ltd Plymouth	01752 223656
Porthcawl Insurance Consultants Porthcawl	01656 784866
Saga Boat Insurance Folkestone	01303 771135
St Margarets Insurances London	020 8778 6161

LIFERAFTS & INFLATABLES

Adec Marine Ltd Croydon	020 8686 9717
Avon Inflatables Llanelli	01554 882000
Cosalt International Ltd Aberdeen	01224 826662
Glaslyn Marine Supplies Ltd Porthmadog	01766 513545
Hale Marine, Ron Portsmouth	023 9273 2985
Guernsey Yacht Club St Peter Port	01481 722838
IBS Boats South Woodham Ferrers	01245 323211/425551
KTS Seasafety Kilkeel	028 918 28405
Nationwide Marine Hire Warrington	01925 245788
Norwest Marine Ltd Liverpool	0151 207 2860
Ocean Safety Southampton	023 8072 0800
Polymarine Ltd Conwy	01492 583322
Premium Liferaft Services Burnham-on-Crouch	0800 243673
Ribeye Dartmouth	01803 832060
South Eastern Marine Services Ltd Basildon	01268 534427
Suffolk Marine Safety Ipswich	01473 833010
Whitstable Marine Whitstable	01227 262525

MARINAS

Aberystwyth Marina	01970 611422
Amble Marina	01665 712168
Arbroath Harbour	01241 872166
Ardfern Yacht Centre Ltd	01852 500247
Ardglass Marina	028 44842332
Arklow Marina	+353 402 39901
Ballycastle Marina	028 2076 8525
Banff Harbour Marina	01261 815544
Bangor Marina	028 91 453297
Beaucette Marina	01481 245000
Bembridge Harbour	01983 872828
Berthon Lymington Marina	01590 647405
Birdham Pool Marina	01243 512310
Blackwater Marina	01621 740264
Boston Marina	01205 364420
Bradwell Marina	01621 776235
Bray Marina	01628 623654
Brentford Dock Marina	020 8232 8941
Bridgemarsh Marine	01621 740414
Brighton Marina	01273 819919
Bristol Marina	0117 921 3198
Brixham Marina	01803 882929
Bucklers Hard Marina	01590 616200
Burnham Yacht Harbour Marina Ltd	01621 782150
Cahersiveen Marina	+353 66 947 2777
Caley Marina	01463 236539
Cardiff Marina	02920 396078
Carlingford Marina	+353 42 9373072
Carrickfergus Marina	028 9336 6666
Castlepark Marina	+353 21 477 4959
Chatham Maritime Marina	01634 899200
Chelsea Harbour Marina	07770 542783
Chichester Marina	01243 512731
Clyde Marina Ltd	01294 607077
Cobbs Quay Marina	01202 674299
Coleraine Harbour Marina	028 7034 2012
Coleraine Marina	028 703 44768
Conwy Marina	01492 593000

Cowes Yacht Haven	01983 299975
Craobh Marina	01852 500222
Crinan Boatyard	01546 830232
Crosshaven Boatyard Marina	+353 21 483 1161
Dart Marina Yacht Harbour	01803 837161
Darthaven Marina	01803 752242
Dartside Quay	01803 845445
Deganwy Quays Marina	01492 576888
Dingle Marina	+353 66 915 1629
Dover Marina	01304 241663
Dun Laoghaire Marina	+353 1 202 0040
Dunstaffnage Marina Ltd	01631 566555
East Cowes Marina	01983 293983
East Ferry Marina	+353 21 483 1342
Emsworth Yacht Harbour	01243 377727
Endeavour Quay	02392 584200
Essex Marina	01702 258531
Falmouth Marina	01326 316620
Falmouth Visitors Yacht Haven	01326 310991
Fambridge Yacht Haven	01621 740370
Fenit Harbour & Marina	+353 66 7136231
Fleetwood Haven Marina	**01253 879062**
Fox's Marina & Boatyard	01473 689111
Foyle Marina	02871 860313
Gallions Point Marina	0207 476 7054
Galway Harbour Marina	+353 91 561874
Gillingham Marina	01634 280022
Glasson Basin Marina	01524 751491
Gosport Marina	023 9252 4811
Hafan Pwllheli	01758 701219
Hamble Point Marina	02380 452464
Hamilton Dock	01502 580300
Harbour of Rye	01797 225225
Hartlepool Marina	01429 865744
Haslar Marina	023 9260 1201
Heybridge Basin	01621 853506
Holy Loch Marina	01369 701800
Holyhead Marina	01407 764242
Hoo Marina	01634 250311
Howth Marina	+353 1839 2777

Hull Marina	01482 609960
Hythe Marina Village	02380 207073
Inverness Marina	01463 220501
Ipswich Haven Marina	01473 236644
Island Harbour Marina	01983 539994
James Watt Dock Marina	01475 729838
Kemps Quay	023 8063 2323
Kilmore Quay Marina	+353 5391 29955
Kilrush Marina	+353 65 9052072
Kinsale Yacht Club Marina	+353 21 477 2196
Kip Marina	01475 521485
Kirkwall Marina	01856 871313
La Collette Yacht Basin	01534 885588
Lady Bee Marina	01273 593801
Lake Yard Marina	01202 674531
Largs Yacht Haven	01475 675333
Lawrence Cove Marina	+353 27 75044
Limehouse Marina	020 7308 9930
Littlehampton Marina	01903 713553
Liverpool Marina Bar & Grill	0151 707 6777
Lossiemouth Marina	01343 813066
Lowestoft Cruising Club	07913 391950
Lowestoft Haven Marina	01502 580300
Lymington Harbour Commission	01590 672014
Lymington Yacht Haven	01590 677071
Malahide Marina	+353 1 845 4129
Maryport Harbour and Marina	01900 814431
Mayflower International Marina	01752 556633
Melfort Pier & Harbour	01852 200333
Mercury Yacht Harbour	**023 8045 5994**
Meridian Quay Marina	01472 268424
Milford Marina	01646 696312
Millbay Marina Village	01752 226785
Multihull Centre	01752 823900
Mylor Yacht Harbour	01326 372121
Nairn Marina	01667 456008
Neptune Marina Ltd	01473 215204
Newhaven Marina	01273 513881
Neyland Yacht Haven	01646 601601
Northney Marina	02392 466321

Noss Marina	01803 839087
Oban Marina & Yacht Services Ltd	01631 565333
Ocean Village Marina	023 8022 9385
Padstow Harbour	01841 532239
Parkstone Bay Marina	
Parkstone Yacht Club Haven	01202 738824
Peel Marina	01624 842338
Penarth Quays Marina	02920 705021
Penton Hook	01932 568681
Peterhead Bay Marina	01779 483600
Plymouth Yacht Haven	01752 404231
Poole Quay Boat Haven	01202 649488
Poplar Dock Marina	
c/o Harbourmaster's Office	0207 308 9930
Port Edgar Marina & Sailing School	0131 331 3330
Port Ellen Marina	01496 302458
Port Hamble Marina	023 8045 2741
Port of Poole Marina	01202 649488
Port Pendennis Marina	01326 211211
Port Solent Marina	02392 210765
Portaferry Marina	07703 209780
Portavadie Marina	01700 811075
Portishead Quays Marina	01275 841941
Portland Marina	08454 30 2012
Preston Marina	01772 733595
Quay Marinas Rhu	01436 820238
Queen Anne's Battery	01752 671142
Ridge Wharf Yacht Centre	01929 552650
Royal Clarence Marina	02392 523523
Royal Cork Yacht Club Marina	+353 21 483 1023
Royal Harbour Marina, Ramsgate	01843 572100
Royal Harwich Yacht Club Marina	01473 780319
Royal Norfolk and Suffolk Yacht Club	01502 566726
Royal Northumberland Yacht Club	01670 353636
Royal Quays Marina	0191 272 8282
Ryde Leisure Harbour	01983 613879
Salterns Marina Ltd	01202 709971
Salve Engineering Marina	+353 21 483 1145

Sandpoint Marina (Dumbarton)		01389 762396
Saxon Wharf		023 8033 9490
Seaport Marina		01463 725500
Seaton's Marina		028 703 832086
Shamrock Quay		023 8022 9461
Sharpness Marine		01453 811476
Shepards Wharf Boatyard Ltd		01983 297821
Shotley Marina		01473 788982
South Dock Marina		020 7252 2244
South Ferriby Marina		01652 635620
Southdown Marina		01752 823084
Southsea Marina		02392 822719
Sovereign Harbour Marina		01323 470099
Sparkes Marina		023 92463572
St Helier Marina		01534 447708
St Katharine Marina Ltd		0207 264 5312
St Peter Port Marinas		01481 720229
St Peter's Marina		0191 265 4472
Stromness Marina		01856 871313
Suffolk Yacht Harbour Ltd		01473 659240
Sunderland Marina		0191 514 4721
Sunseeker International Marina		01202 381111
Sutton Harbour		01752 204702
Swansea Marina		01792 470310
Swanwick Marina		01489 884081
Tarbert Harbour		01880 820344
The Shipyard		01903 713327
Titchmarsh Marina		01255 672185
Tobermorey Harbour Association		01688 302876
Tollesbury Marina		01621 869202
Torpoint Yacht Harbour		01752 813658
Torquay Marina		01803 200210
Town Quay Marina		02380 234397
Troon Yacht Haven		01292 315553
Universal Marina		01489 574272
Victoria Dock Marina		01286 672346
Victoria Marina		01481 720229
Walton Yacht Basin		01255 675873
Waterford City Marina		+353 87 238 4944
Weymouth Harbour		01305 838423
Weymouth Marina		01305 767576
Whitby Marina		01947 602354

Whitehaven Marina	01946 692435
Whitehills Marina	01261 861291
Wick Marina	01955 602030
Windsor Marina	01753 853911
Wisbech Yacht Harbour	01945 588059
Woolverstone Marina	01473 780206
Yarmouth Harbour	01983 760321

MARINE ENGINEERS

AAS Marine Aberystwyth	01970 631090
Allerton Engineering Lowestoft	01502 537870
APAS Engineering Ltd Southampton	023 8063 2558
Ardmair Boat Centre Ullapool	01854 612054
Arisaig Marine Inverness-shire	01687 450224
Arun Craft Littlehampton	01903 723667
Atlantis Marine Power Ltd Plymouth	01752 208810
Attrill & Sons, H Bembridge	01983 872319
Auto & Marine Services Botley	07836 507000
Auto Marine Southsea	023 9282 5601
Baker, Keith Brentford	07792 937790
BJ Marine Ltd Bangor	028 9127 1434
Bristol Boat Ltd Bristol	01225 872032
Buzzard Marine Engineering Yarmouth	01983 760707
C & B Marine Ltd Chichester Marina	01243 511273
Caddy, Simon Falmouth Marina Falmouth	01326 372682
Caledonian Marine Rhu Marina	01436 821184
Caratek Hull	07957 922301
Cardigan Outboards Cardigan	01239 613966
Channel Islands Marine Ltd Guernsey	01481 716880
Channel Islands Marine Ltd Jersey	01534 767595
Cook's Diesel Service Ltd Faversham	01795 538553
Cragie Engineering Kirkwall	01856 874680

Wartsila Havant	023 9240 0121
Crinan Boatyard Ltd Crinan	01546 830232
Cutler Marine Engineering, John Emsworth	01243 375014
Dale Sailing Co Ltd Milford Haven	01646 603110
Davis Marine Services Ramsgate	01843 586172
Denney & Son, EL Redcar	01642 483507
DH Marine (Shetland) Ltd Shetland	01595 690618
Emark Marine Ltd Emsworth	01243 375383
Evans, Lyndon Brentford	07795 218704
Evans Marine Engineering, Tony Pwllheli	01758 703070
Felton Marine Engineering Brighton	01273 601779
Felton Marine Engineering Eastbourne	01323 470211
Ferrypoint Boat Co Youghal	+353 24 94232
Fettes & Rankine Engineering Aberdeen	01224 573343
Fleming Engineering, J Stornoway	01851 703488
Floetree Ltd (Loch Lomond Marina) Balloch	01389 752069
Fowey Harbour Marine Engineers Fowey	01726 832806
Fox Marine Services Ltd Jersey	01534 721312
Freeport Marine Jersey	01534 888100
French Marine Motors Ltd Colchester	01206 302133
French Marine Motors Ltd Titchmarsh Marina	01255 850303
GH Douglas Marine Services Fleetwood Harbour Village Marina, Fleetwood 01253 877200	
Golden Arrow Marine Southampton	023 8071 0371
Goodchild Marine Services Great Yarmouth	01493 782301
Goodwick Marine Fishguard	01348 873955
Gosport Marina Gosport	023 9252 4811
Griffins Garage Dingle Marina, Co Kerry	+353 66 91 51178

Hale Marine, Ron
Portsmouth   023 9273 2985

Hamnavoe Engineering
Stromness   01856 850576

Harbour Engineering
Itchenor   01243 513454

Hartlepool Marine Engineering
Hartlepool   01429 867883

Hayles, Harold
Yarmouth   01983 760373

Herm Seaway Marine Ltd
St Peter Port   01481 726829

HNP Engineers (Lerwick Ltd)
Lerwick   01595 692493

Home Marine Emsworth Yacht
Harbour, Emsworth   01243 374125

Hook Marine Ltd
Troon   01292 679500

Humphrey, Chris
Teignmouth   01626 772324

Instow Marine Services
Bideford   01271 861081

Jones (Boatbuilders), David
Chester   01244 390363

Keating Marine Engineering Ltd, Bill
Jersey   01534 733977

Kingston Marine Services
Cowes   01983 299385

Kippford Slipway Ltd
Dalbeattie   01556 620249

Lansdale Pannell Marine
Chichester   01243 512374

Lencraft Boats Ltd
Dungarvan   +353 58 68220

Llyn Marine Services
Pwllheli   01758 612606

Lynx Engineering
St Helens, Isle of Wight   01983 873711

M&G Marine Services
Mayflower International Marina,
Plymouth   01752 563345

MacDonald & Co Ltd, JN
Glasgow   0141 810 3400

Mackay Marine Services
Aberdeen   01224 575772

Mainbrayce Marine
Alderney   01481 722772

Malakoff and Moore
Lerwick   01595 695544

Mallaig Boat Building and Engineering
Mallaig   01687 462304

Marindus Engineering
Kilmore Quay   +353 53 29794

Marine Engineering Looe
Brixham   01803 844777

Marine Engineering Looe
Looe   01503 263009

Marine Engineering Services
Port Dinorwic   01248 671215

Marine General Engineers Beaucette
Marina, Guernsey   01481 245808

Marine Propulsion
Hayling Island   07836 737488

Marine & General Engineers
St. Sampsons Harbour, Guernsey
    01481 245808

Marine-Trak Engineering Mylor Yacht
Harbour, Falmouth   01326 376588

Marine Warehouse
Gosport   023 9258 0420

Marlec Marine
Ramsgate   01843 592176

Martin Outboards
Galgate   01524 751750

Meiher, Denis
Fenit   +353 87 958 4744

MES Marine Greenock   01475 744655

MMS Ardrossan   01294 604831

Mobile Marine Engineering Liverpool
Marina, Liverpool   01565 733553

Mount's Bay Engineering
Newlyn   01736 363095

MP Marine Maryport   01900 810299

New World Yacht Care
Helensburgh   01436 820586

North Western Automarine Engineers
Largs   01475 687139

Noss Marine Services
Dart Marina, Dartmouth   01803 833343

Owen Marine, Robert
Porthmadog   01766 513435

Pace, Andy Newhaven   01273 516010

**Penzance Dry Dock and Engineering
Co Ltd** Penzance   01736 363838

Pirie & Co, John S
Fraserburgh   01346 513314

Portavon Marine
Keynsham   0117 986 1626

Power Afloat, Elkins Boatyard
Christchurch   01202 489555

Powerplus Marine Cowes Yacht Haven,
Cowes   01983 290421

Pro-Marine Queen Anne's Battery
Marina, Plymouth   01752 267984

PT Marine Engineering
Hayling Island   023 9246 9332

R & M Marine
Portsmouth   023 9273 7555

R & S Engineering Dingle Marina,
Ireland   +353 66 915 1189

Reddish Marine
Salcombe   01548 844094

RHP Marine Cowes   01983 290421

River Tees Engineering & Welding Ltd
Middlesbrough   01642 226226

RK Marine Ltd Hamble   01489 583585

RK Marine Ltd
Swanwick   01489 583572

Rossiter Yachts Ltd
Christchurch   01202 483250

Ryan & Roberts Marine Services
Askeaton   +353 61 392198

Salve Marine Ltd
Crosshaven   +353 21 4831145

Seamark-Nunn & Co
Felixstowe   01394 275327

Seapower Ipswich   01473 780090

Seaward Engineering
Glasgow   0141 632 4910

Seaway Marine
Gosport   023 9260 2722

Shearwater Engineering Services Ltd
Dunoon   01369 706666

Silvers Marina Ltd
Helensburgh   01436 831222

Starey Marine
Salcombe   01548 843655

Tarbert Marine Arbroath 01241 872879

Tollesbury Marine Engineering
Tollesbury Marina,
Tollesbury   01621 869919

Tony's Marine Service
Coleraine   028 7035 6422

Vasey Marine Engineering, Gordon
Fareham   07798 638625

Volspec Ltd
Tollesbury   01621 869756

Wallis, Peter Torquay Marina,
Torquay   01803 844777

WB Marine Chichester   01243 512857

West Coast Marine
Troon   01292 318121

West Marine
Brighton   01273 626656

Weymouth Marina Mechanical Services
Weymouth   01305 779379

Whittington, G Lady Bee Marine,
Shoreham   01273 593801

Whitewater Marine
Malahide   +353 1 816 8473

Wigmore Wright Marine Services
Penarth Marina   029 2070 9983

Wright, M Manaccan   01326 231502

Wyko Industrial Services
Inverness   01463 224747

Ynys Marine
Cardigan   01239 613179

Youngboats
Faversham   01795 536176

1° West Marine Ltd
Portsmouth   023 9283 8335

MASTS, SPARS & RIGGING

JWS Marine Services
Portsmouth   02392 755155

A2 Rigging
Falmouth   01326 312209

Allspars Plymouth   01752 266766

Amble Boat Co Ltd
Morpeth   01665 710267

Arun Canvas & Rigging
Littlehampton   1903 732561

Buchanan, Keith
St Mary's   01720 422037

Bussell & Co, WL
Weymouth   01305 785633

Carbospars Ltd
Hamble   023 8045 6736

Cable & Rope Works
Bexhill-on-Sea   0101424 220112

Clarke Rigging, Niall
Coleraine   07916 083858

Coates Marine Ltd
Whitby   01947 604486

Dauntless Boatyard Ltd
Canvey Island   01268 793782

Davies Marine Services
Ramsgate   01843 586172

Eurospars Ltd
Plymouth   01752 550550

Exe Leisure
Exeter   01392 879055

Fox's Marine Ipswich Ltd
Ipswich   01473 689111

Freeland Yacht Spars Ltd
Dorchester on Thames   01865 341277

Gordon, AD Portland   01305 821569

Grimsby Rigging Services Ltd
Grimsby   01472 362758

Hamble Custom Rigging Centre
Hamble   023 8045 2000

Harris Rigging Totnes   01803 840160

Heyn Engineering
Belfast   028 9035 0022

Holman Rigging
Chichester   01243 514000

Irish Spars and Rigging
Malahide   +353 86 209 5996

JWS Marine Services
Portsmouth   02392 755155

Kildale Marine Hull   01482 227464

Lowestoft Yacht Services
Lowestoft   01502 585535

Laverty, Billy
Galway   +353 86 3892614

Leitch, WB
Tarbert, Loch Fyne   01880 820287

Lewis, Harry
Kinsale   +353 87 266 7127

Marine Resource Centre
Oban   01631 720291

Martin Leaning Masts & Rigging
Hayling   023 9237 1157

Mast & Rigging Services
Largs   01475 670110

Mast & Rigging Services
Inverkip   01475 522700

MP Marine Maryport   01900 810299

Ocean Rigging
Lymington   01590 676292

Owen Sails Oban   01631 720485

Pro Rig S Ireland   +353 87 298 3333

Ratsey, Stephen
Milford Haven   01646 601561

Riglt Ardrossan   07593 220213

Rig Magic Ipswich   01473 655089

Rig Shop Southampton   023 8033 8341

Roberts Marine Ltd, S
Liverpool   0151 707 8300

Ronstan
Gosport   023 9252 5377

Salcombe Boatstore
Salcombe   01548 843708

Seldén Mast Ltd
Gosport   01329 504000

Silvers Marina Ltd
Helensburgh   01436 831222

Silverwood Yacht Services Ltd
Portsmouth   023 9232 7067

Spencer Rigging
Cowes   01983 292022

Storrar Marine Store
Newcastle upon Tyne   0191 266 1037

Tedfords Rigging & Rafts
Belfast   028 9032 6763

TJ Rigging Conwy   07780 972411

TS Rigging Malden   01621 874861

Windjammer Marine
Milford Marina   01646 699070

Yacht Rigging Services
Plymouth   01752 226609

Yacht Shop, The
Fleetwood   01253 879238

Z Spars UK Hadleigh   01473 822130

NAVIGATION EQUIPMENT – GENERAL

Belson Design Ltd, Nick
Southampton   077 6835 1330

Brown Son & Ferguson Ltd
Glasgow   0141 429 1234

Cooke & Son Ltd, B
Hull   01482 223454

Diverse Yacht Services
Hamble   023 8045 3399

Dolphin Maritime Software Ltd
Lancaster   01524 841946

Dubois Phillips & McCallum Ltd
Liverpool   0151 236 2776

Garmin
Southampton   02380 524000

Geonav UK Ltd
Poole   0870 240 4575

Imray Laurie Norie and Wilson Ltd
St Ives, Cambs   01480 462114

Kelvin Hughes
Southampton   023 8063 4911

Lilley & Gillie Ltd, John
North Shields   0191 257 2217

Marine Chart Services
Wellingborough   01933 441629

Navico UK Romsey   01794 510010

PC Maritime
Plymouth   01752 254205

Price & Co, WF Bristol   0117 929 2229

Raymarine Ltd
Portsmouth   023 9269 3611

Royal Institute of Navigation
London   020 7591 3130

Sea Chest Nautical Bookshop
Plymouth — 01752 222012

Seath Instruments (1992) Ltd
Lowestoft — 01502 573811

Smith (Marine) Ltd, AM
London — 020 8529 6988

South Bank Marine Charts Ltd
Grimsby — 01472 361137

Southcoasting Navigators
Devon — 01626 335626

Stanford Charts
Bristol — 0117 929 9966
London — 020 7836 1321
Manchester — 0870 890 3730

Todd Chart Agency Ltd
County Down — 028 9146 6640

UK Hydrographic Office
Taunton — 01823 337900

Warsash Nautical Bookshop
Warsash — 01489 572384

Yachting Instruments Ltd
Sturminster Newton — 01258 817662

PAINT & OSMOSIS

Advanced Blast Cleaning Paint
Tavistock — 01822 617192/07970 407911

Herm Seaway Marine Ltd
St Peter Port — 01481 726829

Gillingham Marina — 01634 280022

Hempel Paints
Southampton — 02380 232000

International Coatings Ltd
Southampton — 023 8022 6722

Marineware Ltd
Southampton — 023 8033 0208

NLB Marine
Ardrossan — 01563 521509

Pro-Boat Ltd
Burnham on Crouch — 01621 785455

Rustbuster Ltd
Peterborough — 0870 9090093

Smith & Son Ltd, EC
Luton — 01582 729721

SP Systems I of Wight — 01983 828000

PROPELLERS & STERGEAR/REPAIRS

CJR Propulsion Ltd
Southampton — 023 8063 9366

Darglow Engineering Ltd
Wareham — 01929 556512

Propeller Revolutions
Poole — 01202 671226

Sillette – Sonic Ltd
Sutton — 020 8337 7543

Vetus Den Ouden Ltd
Southampton — 02380 454507

RADIO COURSES / SCHOOLS

Bisham Abbey Sailing & Navigation School Bisham — 01628 474960

East Coast Offshore Yachting – Les Rant Perry — 01480 861381

Hamble School of Yachting
Hamble — 023 8045 6687

Pembrokeshire Cruising
Neyland — 01646 602500

Plymouth Sailing School
Plymouth — 01752 493377

Southern Sailing
Swanwick — 01489 575511

Start Point Sailing
Kingsbridge — 01548 810917

REEFING SYSTEMS

Atlantic Spars Ltd
Brixham — 01803 843322

Calibra Marine International Ltd
Southampton — 08702 400358

Eurospars Ltd
Plymouth — 01752 550550

Holman Rigging
Chichester — 01243 514000

Navimo UK Ltd
Hedge End — 01489 778850

Sea Teach Ltd
Emsworth — 01243 375774

Southern Spar Services
Northam — 023 8033 1714

Wragg, Chris Lymington 01590 677052

Z Spars UK Hadleigh — 01473 822130

REPAIR MATERIALS & ACCESSORIES

Akeron Ltd
Southend on Sea — 01702 297101

Howells & Son, KJ
Poole — 01202 665724

JB Timber Ltd
North Ferriby — 01482 631765

Robbins Timber Bristol 0117 9633136

Sika Ltd
Welwyn Garden City — 01707 394444

Solent Composite Systems
East Cowes — 01983 292602

Technix Rubber & Plastics Ltd
Southampton — 01489 789944

Tiflex Liskeard — 01579 320808

Timage & Co Ltd
Braintree — 01376 343087

Trade Grade Products Ltd
Poole — 01202 820177

Wessex Resins & Adhesives Ltd
Romsey — 01794 521111

ROPE & WIRE

Cable & Rope Works
Bexhill-on-Sea — 01424 220112

Euro Rope Ltd
Scunthorpe — 01724 280480

Marlow Ropes Hailsham 01323 444444

Mr Splice Leicester — 0800 1697178

Spinlock Ltd Cowes — 01983 295555

TJ Rigging Conwy — 07780 972411

SAFETY EQUIPMENT

AB Marine Ltd
St Peter Port — 01481 722378

Adec Marine Ltd
Croydon — 020 8686 9717

Anchorwatch UK
Edinburgh — 0131 447 5057

Avon Inflatables
Llanelli — 01554 882000

Cosalt International Ltd
Aberdeen — 01224 588327

Crewsaver
Gosport — 01329 820000

Glaslyn Marine Supplies Ltd
Porthmadog — 01766 513545

Guardian Fire Protection
Manchester — 0800 358 7522

Hale Marine, Ron
Portsmouth — 023 9273 2985

Herm Seaway Marine Ltd
St Peter Port — 01481 722838

IBS Boats South Woodham Ferrers
— 01245 323211/425551

KTS Seasafety Kilkeel — 028 41762655

McMurdo Pains Wessex
Portsmouth — 023 9262 3900

Met Office Bracknell — 0845 300 0300

Nationwide Marine Hire
Warrington — 01925 245788

Norwest Marine Ltd
Liverpool — 0151 207 2860

Ocean Safety So'ton   023 8072 0800

Navimo UK Ltd
Romsey   01794 526800

Polymarine Ltd Conwy   01492 583322

Premium Liferaft Services
Burnham-on-Crouch   0800 243673

Ribeye Dartmouth   01803 832060

South Eastern Marine Services Ltd
Basildon   01268 534427

Suffolk Sailing
Ipswich   01473 604678

Whitstable Marine
Whitstable   01227 262525

Winters Marine Ltd
Salcombe   01548 843580

SAILMAKERS & REPAIRS

Allison-Gray Dundee   01382 505888

Alsop Sailmakers, John
Salcombe   01548 843702

AM Trimming
Windsor   01932 821090

Arun Canvas & Rigging
Littlehampton   01903 732561

Arun Sails Chichester   01243 573185

Bank Sails, Bruce
Southampton   01489 582444

Batt Sails Bosham   01243 575505

Bissett and Ross
Aberdeen   01224 580659

Boatshed, The
Felinheli, Bangor   01248 679939

Breaksea Sails Barry   01446 730785

Bristol Sails Bristol   0117 922 5080

Buchanan, Keith
St Mary's   01720 422037

C&J Marine Textiles
Chichester   01243 782629

Calibra Sails
Dartmouth   01803 833094

Clarke Rigging, Niall
Coleraine   07916 083858

Coastal Covers
Portsmouth   023 9252 0200

Covercare Fareham   01329 311878

Crawford, Margaret
Kirkwall   01856 875692

Crusader Sails Poole   01202 670580

Crystal Covers
Portsmouth   023 9238 0143

Cullen Sailmakers
Galway   +353 91 771991

Dolphin Sails Harwich   01255 243366

Doyle Sails
Southampton   023 8033 2622

Downer International Sails & Chandlery
Dun Laoghaire   +353 1 280 0231

Duthie Marine Safety, Arthur
Glasgow   0141 429 4553

Dynamic Sails
Emsworth   01243 374495

Flew Sailmakers
Portchester   01329 822676

Fylde Coast Sailmaking Co
Fleetwood   01253 873476

Freeman Sails
Padstow   07771 610053

Garland Sails Bristol   01275 393473

Goacher Sails
Cumbria   01539 488686

Gowen Ocean Sailmakers
West Mersea   01206 384412

Green Sailmakers, Paul
Plymouth   01752 660317

Henderson Sails & Covers
Southsea   023 9229 4700

Hood Sailmakers
Lymington   01590 675011

Hooper, A Plymouth   01752 830411

Hyde Sails
Southampton   0845 543 8945

Jackson Yacht Services
Jersey   01534 743819

Jeckells and Son Ltd (Wroxham)
Wroxham   01603 782223

Jessail Ardrossan   01294 467311

JKA Sailmakers
Pwllheli   01758 613266

Kemp Sails Ltd
Wareham   01929 554308/554378

Kildale Marine
Hull   01482 227464

Lawrence Sailmakers, J
Brightlingsea   01206 302863

Leitch, WB
Tarbert, Loch Fyne   01880 820287

Leith UK
Berwick on Tweed   01289 307264

Le Monier, Yannick
Galway   +353 87 628 9854

Lodey Sails Newlyn   01736 719359

Lossie Sails
Lossiemouth   07989 956698

Lucas Sails Portchester 023 9237 3699

Malakoff and Moore
Lerwick   01595 695544

McCready and Co Ltd, J
Belfast   028 90232842

McKillop Sails, John
Kingsbridge   01548 852343

McNamara Sails, Michael
Great Yarmouth   01692 584186

McWilliam Sailmaker (Crosshaven)
Crosshaven   +353 21 4831505

Sail Shape
Fowey   01726 833731

Montrose Rope and Sails
Montrose   01674 672657

Mountfield Sails
Hayling Island   023 9246 3720

Mouse Sails Holyhead   01407 763636

Nicholson Hughes Sails
Rosneath   01436 831356

North Sea Sails
Tollesbury   01621 869367

North West Sails
Keighley   01535 652949

Northrop Sails
Ramsgate   01843 851665

O'Mahony Sailmakers
Kinsale   +353 86 326 0018

O'Sullivans Marine Ltd
Tralee   +353 66 7124957

Owen Sails Benderloch   01631 720485

Parker & Kay Sailmakers –
East Ipswich   01473 659878

Parker & Kay Sailmakers –
South Hamble   023 8045 8213

Penrose Sailmakers
Falmouth   01326 312705

Pinnell & Bax
Northampton   01604 592808

Pollard Marine
Port St Mary   01624 835831

Quantum Sails
Ipswich Haven Marina   01473 659878

Quantum-Parker & Kay Sailmakers
Hamble   023 8045 8213

Quay Sails (Poole) Ltd
Poole   01202 681128

Ratsey & Lapthorn
Isle of Wight   01983 294051

Ratsey Sailmakers, Stephen
Milford Haven   01646 601561

Relling One Design
Portland   01305 826555

SO31 Bags
Southampton   023 8045 5106

Rig Shop, The
Southampton · 023 8033 8341

Rockall Sails
Chichester · 01243 573185

Sail Locker
Woolverstone Marina · 01473 780206

Sail Style Hayling Is · 023 9246 3720

Sails & Canvas Exeter · 01392 877527

Sail Register
Ulceby · 01469 589444

Saltern Sail Co
West Cowes · 01983 280014

Saltern Sail Company
Yarmouth · 01983 760120

Sanders Sails
Lymington · 01590 673981

Saturn Sails Largs · 01475 689933

Scott & Co, Graham
St Peter Port · 01481 259380

Shore Sailmakers
Swanwick · 01489 589450

SKB Sails Falmouth · 01326 372107

Sketrick Sailmakers Ltd
Killinchy · 028 9754 1400

Solo Sails
Penzance · 01736 366004

Storrar Marine Store
Newcastle upon Tyne · 0191 266 1037

Suffolk Sails
Woodbridge · 01394 386323

Sunset Sails Sligo · +353 71 62792

Torquay Marina Sails and Canvas
Exeter · 01392 877527

Trident UK
Gateshead · 0191 490 1736

UK McWilliam Cowes · 01983 281100

Underwood Sails Queen Anne's
Battery, Plymouth · 01752 229661

W Sails Leigh-on-Sea · 01702 714550

Warren Hall
Beaucette, Guernsey · 07781 444280

Watson Sails
Dublin 13 · +353 1 846 2206

WB Leitch and Son
Tarbert · 01880 820287

Westaway Sails
Plymouth Yacht Haven · 01752 892560

Wilkinson Sails
Burnham-on-Crouch · 01621 786770

Wilkinson Sails
Teynham · 01795 521503

Yacht Shop, The
Fleetwood · 01253 879238

SOLAR POWER

Ampair Ringwood · 01425 480780

Barden UK Ltd Fareham · 01489 570770

Marlec Engineering Co Ltd
Corby · 01536 201588

SPRAYHOODS & DODGERS

A & B Textiles
Gillingham · 01634 579686

Allison–Gray Dundee · 01382 505888

Arton, Charles
Milford-on-Sea · 01590 644682

Arun Canvas and Rigging Ltd
Littlehampton · 01903 732561

Boatshed, The
Felinheli, Bangor · 01248 679939

Buchanan, Keith
St Mary's · 01720 422037

C & J Marine Textiles
Chichester · 01243 785485

Covercare Fareham · 01329 311878

Covercraft Southampton · 023 8033 8286

Crystal Covers
Portsmouth · 023 9238 0143

Jeckells and Son Ltd
Wroxham · 01603 782223

Jessail Ardrossan · 01294 467311

Lomond Boat Covers
Alexandria · 01389 602734

Lucas Sails
Portchester · 023 9237 3699

Poole Canvas Co Ltd
Poole · 01202 677477

Sail Register
Ulceby · 01469 589444

Saundersfoot Auto Marine
Saundersfoot · 01834 812115

Trident UK
Gateshead · 0191 490 1736

SURVEYORS AND NAVAL ARCHITECTS

Amble Boat Company Ltd
Amble · 01665 710267

Ark Surveys East Anglia/South Coast
01621 857065/01794 521957

Atkin & Associates
Lymington · 01590 688633

Barbican Yacht Agency Ltd
Plymouth · 01752 228855

Battick, Lee St Helier · 01534 611143

Booth Marine Surveys, Graham
Birchington-on-Sea · 01843 843793

Byrde & Associates
Kimmeridge · 01929 480064

Bureau Maritime Ltd
Maldon · 01621 859181

Byrde & Associates
Kimmeridge · 01929 480064

Cannell & Associates, David M
Wivenhoe · 01206 823337

Cardiff Commercial Boat Operators Ltd
Cardiff · 029 2037 7872

Clarke Designs LLP, Owen
Dartmouth · 01803 770495

Cox, David Penryn · 01326 340808

Davies, Peter N
Wivenhoe · 01206 823289

Down Marine Co Ltd
Belfast · 028 90480247

Evans, Martin
Kirby le Soken · 07887 724055

Goodall, JL Whitby · 01947 604791

Green, James Plymouth · 01752 660516

Greening Naval Architect Ltd, David
Salcombe · 01548 842000

Hansing & Associates
North Wales/Midlands · 01248 671291

JP Services – Marine Safety & Training
Chichester · 01243 537552

MacGregor, WA
Felixstowe · 01394 676034

Mahoney & Co, KPO
Co Cork · +353 21 477 6150

Marinte Surveys UK
Emsworth · 07798 554535

Marintec Lymington · 01590 683414

Norwood Marine
Margate · 01843 835711

Quay Consultants Ltd
West Wittering · 01243 673056

Scott Marine Surveyors & Consultants
Conwy · 01492 573001

S Roberts Marine Ltd
Liverpool · 0151 707 8300

Staton-Bevan, Tony
Lymington 01590 645755/
07850 315744

Swanwick Yacht Surveyors
Southampton 01489 564822

Thomas, Stephen
Southampton 023 8048 6273

Towler, Perrin
Lymington 01590 718087

Victoria Yacht Surveys
Cornwall 0800 083 2113

Ward & McKenzie
Woodbridge 01394 383222

Ward & McKenzie (North East)
Pocklington 01759 304322

YDSA Yacht Designers & Surveyors Association
Bordon 0845 0900162

TAPE TECHNOLOGY

CC Marine Services (Rubbaweld) Ltd
London 020 7402 4009

Trade Grade Products Ltd
Poole 01202 820177

UK Epoxy Resins
Burscough 01704 892364

3M United Kingdom plc
Bracknell 01344 858315

TRANSPORT/YACHT DELIVERIES

Boat Shifters
07733 344018/01326 210548

Convoi Exceptionnel Ltd
Hamble 023 8045 3045

Debbage Yachting
Ipswich 01473 601169

East Coast Offshore Yachting
01480 861381

Forrest Marine Ltd
Exeter 08452 308335

Hainsworth's UK and Continental
Bingley 01274 565925

Houghton Boat Transport
Tewkesbury 07831 486710

MCL Transboat 08455 201900

Moonfleet Sailing
Poole 01202 682269

Performance Yachting
Plymouth 01752 565023

Peters & May Ltd
Southampton 023 8048 0480

Reeder School of Seamanship, Mike
Lymington 01590 674560

Seafix Boat Transfer
North Wales 01766 514507

Sealand Boat Deliveries Ltd
Liverpool 01254 705225

Shearwater Sailing
Southampton 01962 775213

Southcoasting Navigators
Devon 01626 335626

West Country Boat Transport
01566 785651

Wolff, David 07659 550131

TUITION/SAILING SCHOOLS

Association of Scottish Yacht Charterers Argyll 07787 363562
01852 200258

Bisham Abbey Sailing & Navigation School Bisham 01628 474960

Blue Baker Yachts
Ipswich 01473 780008

Britannia Sailing (East Coast)
Ipswich 01473 787019

British Offshore Sailing School
Hamble 023 8045 7733

Coastal Sea School
Weymouth 0870 321 3271

Conwy School of Yachting
Conwy 01492 572999

Tiller School of Navigation and Seamanship,
Banstead 0845 6123466

Dart Harbour Sea School
Dartmouth 01803 839339

Dartmouth Sailing
Dartmouth 01803 833399

Drake Sailing School
Plymouth 01635 253009

East Anglian Sea School
Ipswich 01473 659992

East Coast Offshore Yachting – Les Rant Perry 01480 861381

Gibraltar Sailing Centre
Gibraltar +350 78554

Glenans Irish Sailing School
Baltimore +353 28 20154

Hamble School of Yachting
Hamble 023 8045 6687

Haslar Sea School
Gosport 023 9252 0099

Hobo Yachting
Southampton 023 8033 4574

Hoylake Sailing School
Wirral 0151 632 4664

Ibiza Sailing School 07092 235 853

International Yachtmaster Academy
Southampton 0800 515439

Island Sea School
Port Dinorwic 01248 352330

JP Services – Marine Safety & Training
Chichester 01243 537552

Lymington Cruising School
Lymington 01590 677478

Marine Leisure Association (MLA)
Southampton 023 8029 3822

Menorca Cruising School
01995 679240

Moncur Sailing School, Bob
Newcastle upon Tyne 0191 265 4472

Moonfleet Sailing
Poole 01202 682269

National Marine Correspondence School Macclesfield 01625 262365

Northshore King's Lynn 01485 210236

On Deck Sailing
Southampton 023 8063 9997

Pembrokeshire Cruising
Neyland 01646 602500

Performance Yachting & Chandlery
Plymouth 01752 565023

Plain Sailing
Dartmouth 01803 853843

Plymouth Sailing School
Plymouth 01752 493377

Port Edgar Marina & Sailing School
Port Edgar 0131 331 3330

Portsmouth Outdoor Centre
Portsmouth 023 9266 3873

Portugal Sail & Power 01473 833001

Reeder School of Seamanship, Mike
Lymington 01590 674560

Safe Water Training Sea School Ltd
Wirral 0151 630 0466

Sail East
Felixstowe 01255 502887

Sail East
River Crouch 07860 271954

Sail East
River Medway 07932 157027

Sail East
Harwich 01473 689344

KINGFISHER MARINE

CHANDLERS • MARINE ENGINEERS • RIGGERS
BOAT BUILDING & REPAIRS • BOAT LIFTING

Kingfisher Marine is the one-stop marine store located in the heart of Weymouth on the quayside.

Come in and browse through our impressive range of Paints, boat maintenance products, safety equipment, ropes, deck hardware, Mercury outboards accessories and spares, Electrical and electronic equipment, rigid and inflatable boats, just about everything you could need from one company.

Talk to the experts in Marine engineering about our extensive workshop facilities for all your vessels maintenance and servicing needs. We are main dealers for Yanmar, Mercruiser and Mercury outboards.

Boat building, repairs and boat lifting complete the comprehensive range of services available

Whatever your boating requirements you're sure of a warm welcome

OPEN 7 DAYS A WEEK - ALL YEAR ROUND

10a Custom House Quay, Weymouth, DT4 8BG

Tel: 01305 766595

www.kingfishermarine.co.uk

Sally Water Training
East Cowes 01983 299033

Sea-N-Shore
Salcombe 01548 842276

Seafever
East Grinstead 01342 316293

Solaris Mediterranean Sea School
01925 642909

Solent School of Yachting
Southampton 023 8045 7733

Southcoasting Navigators
Devon 01626 335626

Southern Sailing
Southampton 01489 575511

Start Point Sailing
Dartmouth 01548 810917

Sunsail
Port Solent/Largs 0870 770 6314

Team Sailing
Gosport 023 9252 4370

Tiller School of Navigation
Banstead 01737 211466

Workman Marine School
Portishead 01275 845844

Wride School of Sailing, Bob
North Ferriby 01482 635623

WATERSIDE ACCOMMODATION & RESTAURANTS

Abbey, The
Penzance 01736 366906

Arun View Inn, The
Littlehampton 01903 722335

Baywatch on the Beach
Bembridge 01983 873259

Beaucette Marina Restaurant
Guernsey 01481 247066

Bella Napoli
Brighton Marina 01273 818577

Bembridge Coast Hotel
Bembridge 01983 873931

Budock Vean Hotel
Porth Navas Creek 01326 252100

Café Mozart Cowes 01983 293681

Caffé Uno Port Solent 023 9237 5227

Chandlers Bar & Bistro Queen Anne's
Battery Marina, Plymouth 01752 257772

Chiquito Port Solent 02392 205070

Cruzzo Malahide Marina, Co Dublin
+353 1 845 0599

Cullins Yard Bistro
Dover 01304 211666

Custom House, The
Poole 01202 676767

Dart Marina River Lounge
Dartmouth 01803 832580

Deer Leap, The
Exmouth 01395 265030

Doghouse Swanwick Marina,
Hamble 01489 571602

Dolphin Restaurant
Gorey 01534 853370

Doune Knoydart 01687 462667

El Puertos
Penarth Marina 029 2070 5551

**Falmouth Marina Marine Bar and
Restaurant** Falmouth 01326 313481

Ferry Boat Inn West Wick Marina,
Nr Chelmsford 01621 740208

Ferry Inn, The (restaurant)
Pembroke Dock 01646 682947

First and Last, The Braye,
Alderney 01481 823162

Fisherman's Wharf
Sandwich 01304 613636

Folly Inn Cowes 01983 297171

Gaffs Restaurant Fenit Harbour
Marina, County Kerry +353 66 71 36666

Godleys Hotel Fenit,
County Kerry +353 66 71 36108

Harbour Lights Restaurant
Walton on the Naze 01255 851887

Haven Bar and Bistro, The
Lymington Yacht Haven 01590 679971

Haven Hotel Poole 08453 371550

HMS Ganges Restaurant
Mylor Yacht Harbour 01326 374320

Jolly Sailor, The
Bursledon 023 8040 5557

Kames Hotel Argyll 01700 811489

Ketch Rigger, The Hamble Point
Marina Hamble 023 8045 5601

Kota Restaurant
Porthleven 01326 562407

La Cala Lady Bee Marina,
Shoreham 01273 597422

Le Nautique
St Peter Port 01481 721714

Lighter Inn, The
Topsham 01392 875439

Mariners Bistro Sparkes Marina,
Hayling Island 023 9246 9459

Mary Mouse II Haslar Marina,
Gosport 023 9252 5200

Martha's Vineyard
Milford Haven 01646 697083

Master Builder's House Hotel Buckler's
Hard 01590 616253

Millstream Hotel
Bosham 01243 573234

Montagu Arms Hotel
Beaulieu 01590 612324

Oyster Quay Mercury Yacht Harbour,
Hamble 023 8045 7220

Paris Hotel Coverack 01326 280258

Pebble Beach, The
Gosport 023 9251 0789

Petit Champ Sark 01481 832046

Philip Leisure Group
Dartmouth 01803 833351

Priory Bay Hotel
Seaview, Isle of Wight 01983 613146

Quayside Hotel Brixham 01803 855751

Queen's Hotel Kirkwall 01856 872200

Sails Dartmouth 01803 839281

Shell Bay Seafood Restaurant
Poole Harbour 01929 450363

Simply Italian Sovereign Harbour,
Eastbourne 01323 470911

Spinnaker, The
Chichester Marina 01243 511032

Spit Sand Fort
The Solent 01329 242077

Steamboat Inn Lossiemouth Marina,
Lossiemouth 01343 812066

Tayvallich Inn, The
Argyll 01546 870282

Villa Adriana Newhaven Marina
Newhaven 01273 513976

Warehouse Brasserie, The
Poole 01202 677238

36 on the Quay
Emsworth 01243 375592

WEATHER INFORMATION

Met Office Exeter 0870 900 0100

WOOD FITTINGS

Howells & Son, KJ
Poole 01202 665724

Onward Trading Co Ltd
Southampton 01489 885250

Robbins Timber
Bristol 0117 963 3136

Sheraton Marine Cabinet
Witney 01993 868275

YACHT BROKERS

ABC Powermarine
Beaumaris 01248 811413

**ABYA Association of Brokers & Yacht
Agents** Bordon 0845 0900162

Adur Boat Sales
Southwick 01273 596680

Ancasta International Boat Sales
Southampton 023 8045 0000

Anglia Yacht Brokerage
Bury St Edmunds 01359 271747

Ardmair Boat Centre
Ullapool 01854 612054

Barbican Yacht Agency, The
Plymouth 01752 228855

Bates Wharf Marine Sales Ltd
01932 571141

BJ Marine Bangor	028 9127 1434
Boatworks + Ltd St Peter Port	01481 726071
Caley Marina Inverness	01463 236539
Calibra Marine International Ltd Southampton	08702 400358
Camper & Nicholsons International London	020 7009 1950
Clarke & Carter Interyacht Ltd Ipswich/ Burnham on Crouch	01473 659681/01621 785600
Coastal Leisure Ltd Southampton	023 8033 2222
Dale Sailing Brokerage Neyland	01646 603105
Deacons Southampton	023 8040 2253
Exe Leisure Topsham	001392 879055
Ferrypoint Boat Co Youghal	+353 24 94232
Gweek Quay Boatyard Helston	01326 221657
International Barge & Yacht Brokers Southampton	023 8045 5205
Iron Wharf Boatyard Faversham	01795 537122
Jackson Yacht Services Jersey	01534 743819
Kings Yacht Agency Beaulieu	01590 616316
Kippford Slipway Ltd Dalbeattie	01556 620249
Lencraft Boats Ltd Dungarvan	+353 58 68220
Liberty Yachts Ltd Plymouth	01752 227911
Lucas Yachting, Mike Torquay	01803 212840
Network Yacht Brokers Dartmouth	01803 834864
Network Yacht Brokers Plymouth	01752 605377
New Horizon Yacht Agency Guernsey	01481 726335
Oyster Brokerage Ltd Ipswich	01473 602263
Pearn and Co, Norman (Looe Boatyard) Looe	01503 262244
Performance Boat Company Maidenhead	07768 464717
Peters Chandlery Chichester	01243 511033
Portavon Marina Keynsham	0117 986 1626
Prosser Marine Sales Ltd Glasgow	0141 552 2005

Retreat Boatyard Topsham	01392 874720
SD Marine Ltd Southampton	023 8045 7278
Sea & Shore Ship Chandler Dundee	01382 202666
South Pier Shipyard St Helier	01534 711000
South West Yacht Brokers Group Plymouth	01752 401421
Sunbird Marine Services Fareham	01329 842613
Trafalgar Yacht Services Fareham	01329 823577
Transworld Yachts Hamble	023 8045 7704
Walton Marine Sales Brighton	01273 670707
Portishead	01275 840132
Walton Marine Sales Wroxham	01603 781178
Watson Marine, Charles Hamble	023 8045 6505
Western Marine Dublin	+353 1280 0321
Woodrolfe Brokerage Maldon	01621 868494
Youngboats Faversham	01795 536176

YACHT CHARTERS & HOLIDAYS

Ardmair Boat Centre Ullapool	01854 612054
Association of Scottish Yacht Charterers Argyll	01880 820012
Blue Baker Yachts Ipswich	01473 780111/780008
Camper & Nicholsons International London	020 7009 1950
Coastal Leisure Ltd Southampton	023 8033 2222
Crusader Yachting Turkey	01732 867321
Dartmouth Sailing Dartmouth	01803 833399
Dartmouth Yacht Charters Kingswear	01803 752935
Doune Marine Mallaig	01687 462667
Four Seasons Yacht Charter Gosport	023 9251 1789
Golden Black Sailing Cornwall	01209 715757
Hamble Point Yacht Charters Hamble	023 8045 7110

Haslar Marina & Victory Yacht Charters Gosport	023 9252 0099
Indulgence Charters Wendover	01296 696006
Liberty Yachts West Country, Greece, Mallorca & Italy	01752 227911
Nautilus Yachting Mediterranean & Caribbean	01732 867445
On Deck Sailing Southampton	023 8063 9997
Patriot Charters & Sail School Milford Haven	01437 741202
West Country Yachts Plymouth	01752 606999
Falmouth	01326 212320
Puffin Yachts Port Solent	01483 420728
Sailing Holidays Ltd Mediterranean	020 8459 8787
Sailing Holidays in Ireland Kinsale	+353 21 477 2927
Setsail Holidays Greece, Turkey, Croatia, Majorca	01787 310445
Shannon Sailing Ltd Tipperary	+353 67 24499
Sleat Marine Services Isle of Skye	01471 844216
Smart Yachts Mediterranean	01425 614804
South West Marine Training Dartmouth	01803 853843
Sovereign Sailingl Kinsale	+353 87 6172555
Sunsail Worldwide	0870 770 0102
Templecraft Yacht Charters Lewes	01273 812333
TJ Sailing Gosport	07803 499691
Top Yacht Sailing Ltd Havant	02392 347655
Victory Yacht Charters Gosport	023 9252 0099
West Wales Yacht Charter Pwllheli	07748 634869
39 North (Mediterranean) Kingskerwell	07071 393939

YACHT CLUBS

Aberaeron YC Aberdovey	01545 570077
Aberdeen and Stonehaven SC Nr Inverurie	01569 764006
Aberdour BC	01383 860029
Abersoch Power BC Abersoch	01758 712027
Aberystwyth BC Aberystwyth	01970 624575

Aldeburgh YC	01728 452562
Alderney SC	01481 822959
Alexandra YC Southend-on-Sea	01702 340363
Arklow SC	+353 402 33100
Arun YC Littlehampton	01903 716016
Axe YC Axemouth	01297 20043
Ayr Yacht and CC	01292 476034
Ballyholme YC Bangor	028 91271467
Baltimore SC	+353 28 20426
Banff SC	01464 820308
Bantry Bay SC	+353 27 50081
Barry YC	01446 735511
Beaulieu River SC Brockenhurst	01590 616273
Bembridge SC Isle of Wight	01983 872237
Benfleet YC Canvey Island	01268 792278
Blackpool and Fleetwood YC	01253 884205
Blackwater SC Maldon	01621 853923
Blundellsands SC	0151 929 2101
Bosham SC Chichester	01243 572341
Brading Haven YC Isle of Wight	01983 872289
Bradwell CC	01621 892970
Bradwell Quay YC Wickford	01268 776539
Brancaster Staithe SC	01485 210249
Brandy Hole YC Hullbridge	01702 230320
Brightlingsea SC	01206 303275
Brighton Marina YC Peacehaven	01273 818711
Bristol Avon SC	01225 873472
Bristol Channel YC Swansea	01792 366000
Bristol Corinthian YC Axbridge	01934 732033
Brixham YC	01803 853332
Burnham Overy Staithe SC	01328 730961
Burnham-on-Crouch SC	01621 782812
Burnham-on-Sea SC Bridgwater	01278 792911
Burry Port YC	01554 833635
Cabot CC	01275 855207
Caernarfon SC (Menai Strait) Caernarfon	01286 672861

Campbeltown SC	01586 552488
Island YC Canvey Island	01702 510360
Cardiff YC	029 2046 3697
Cardiff Bay YC	029 20226575
Carlingford Lough YC Rostrevor	028 4173 8604
Carrickfergus SC Whitehead	028 93 351402
Castle Cove SC Weymouth	01305 783708
Castlegate Marine Club Stockton on Tees	01642 583299
Chanonry SC Fortrose	01463 221415
Chichester Cruiser and Racing Club	01483 770391
Chichester YC	01243 512918
Christchurch SC	01202 483150
Clyde CC Glasgow	0141 221 2774
Co Antrim YC Carrickfergus	028 9337 2322
Cobnor Activities Centre Trust	01243 572791
Coleraine YC	028 703 44503
Colne YC Brightlingsea	01206 302594
Conwy YC Deganwy	01492 583690
Coquet YC	01665 710367
Corrib Rowing & YC Galway City	+353 91 564560
Cowes Combined Clubs	01983 295744
Cowes Corinthian YC Isle of Wight	01983 296333
Cowes Yachting	01983 280770
Cramond BC	0131 336 1356
Creeksea SC Burnham-on-Crouch	01245 320578
Crookhaven SC	087 2379997 mobile
Crouch YC Burnham-on-Crouch	01621 782252
Dale YC	01646 636362
Dartmouth YC	01803 832305
Deben YC Woodbridge	01394 384440
Dell Quay SC Chichester	01243 514639
Dingle SC	+353 66 51984
Douglas Bay YC	01624 673965
Dovey YC Aberdovey	01213 600008
Dun Laoghaire MYC	+353 1 288 938
Dunbar SC Cockburnspath	01368 86287
East Antrim BC	028 28 277204

East Belfast YC	028 9065 6283
East Cowes SC	01983 531687
East Dorset SC Poole	01202 706111
East Lothian YC	01620 892698
Eastney Cruising Association Portsmouth	023 92734103
Eling SC	023 80863987
Emsworth SC	01243 372850
Emsworth Slipper SC	01243 378881
Essex YC Southend	01702 478404
Exe SC (River Exe) Exmouth	01395 264607
Eyott SC Mayland	01245 320703
Fairlie YC	01294 213940
Falmouth Town SC	01326 373915
Falmouth Watersports Association Falmouth	01326 211223
Fareham Sailing & Motor BC Fareham	01329 280738
Felixstowe Ferry SC	01394 283785
Findhorn YC Findhorn	01309 690247
Fishguard Bay YC Lower Fishguard	01348 872866
Flushing SC Falmouth	01326 374043
Folkestone Yacht and Motor BC Folkestone	01303 251574
Forth Corinthian YC Haddington	0131 552 5939
Forth YCs Association Edinburgh	0131 552 3006
Fowey Gallants SC	01726 832335
Foynes YC Foynes	+353 69 91201
Galway Bay SC	+353 91 794527
Glasson SC Lancaster	01524 751089
Glenans Irish Sailing School	+353 1 6611481
Glenans Irish SC (Westport)	+353 98 26046
Gosport CC Gosport	02392 586838
Gravesend SC	07538 326623
Greenwich YC London	020 8858 7339
Grimsby and Cleethorpes YC Grimsby	01472 356678
Guernsey YC St Peter Port	01481 722838
Hamble River SC Southampton	023 80452070
Hampton Pier YC Herne Bay	01227 364749
Hardway SC Gosport	023 9258 1875
Hartlepool YC	01429 233423
Harwich Town SC	01255 503200

Hastings and St Leonards YC	
Hastings	01424 420656
Haven Ports YC	
Woodbridge	01473 659658
Hayling Ferry SC; Locks SC	
Hayling Island	023 80829833
Hayling Island SC	023 92463768
Helensburgh SC Rhu	01436 672778
Helensburgh	01436 821234
Helford River SC	
Helston	01326 231006
Herne Bay SC	01227 375650
Highcliffe SC	
Christchurch	01425 274874
Holyhead SC	01407 762526
Holywood YC	028 90423355
Hoo Ness YC Sidcup	01634 250052
Hornet SC Gosport	023 9258 0403
Howth YC	+353 1 832 2141
Hoylake SC Wirral	0151 632 2616
Hullbridge YC	01702 231797
Humber Yawl Club	01482 667224
Hundred of Hoo SC	01634 250102
Hurlingham YC London	020 8788 5547
Hurst Castle SC	01590 645589
Hythe SC Southampton	02380 846563
Hythe & Saltwood SC	01303 265178
Ilfracombe YC	01271 863969
Iniscealtra SC	
Limerick	+353 61 338347
Invergordon BC	01349 852265
Irish CC	+353 214870031
Island CC Salcombe	01548 531176
Island SC Isle of Wight	01983 296621
Island YC Canvey Island	01268 510360
Isle of Bute SC	
Rothesay	01700 502819
Isle of Man YC	
Port St Mary	01624 832088
Itchenor SC Chichester	01243 512400
Keyhaven YC	01590 642165
Killyleagh YC	028 4482 8250
Kircubbin SC	028 4273 8422
Kirkcudbright SC	01557 331727
Langstone SC Havant	023 9248 4577
Largs SC Largs	01475 670000
Larne Rowing & SC	028 2827 4573
Lawrenny YC	01646 651212
Leigh-on-Sea SC	01702 476788
Lerwick BC	01595 696954
Lilliput SC Poole	01202 740319

Littlehampton Yacht Club	
Littlehampton	01903 713990
Loch Ryan SC Stranraer	01776 706322
Lochaber YC Fort William	01397 772361
Locks SC Portsmouth	023 9282 9833
Looe SC	01503 262559
Lossiemouth CC	
Fochabers	01348 812121
Lough Swilly YC Fahn	+353 74 22377
Lowestoft CC	01502 574376
Lyme Regis Power BC	01297 443788
Lyme Regis SC	01297 442373
Lymington Town SC	0159 674514
Lympstone SC Exeter	01395 278792
Madoc YC Porthmadog	01766 512976
Malahide YC	+353 1 845 3372
Maldon Little Ship Club	
	01621 854139
Manx Sailing & CC	
Ramsey	01624 813494
Marchwood YC	023 80666141
Margate YC	01843 292602
Marina BC Pwllheli	01758 612271
Maryport YC	01228 560865
Mayflower SC Plymouth	01752 662526
Mayo SC (Rosmoney)	
Rosmoney	+353 98 27772
Medway YC Rochester	01634 718399
Menai Bridge BC	
Beaumaris	01248 810583
Mengham Rythe SC	
Hayling Island	023 92463337
Merioneth YC	
Barmouth	01341 280000
Monkstone Cruising and SC	
Swansea	01792 812229
Montrose SC Montrose	01674 672554
Mumbles YC Swansea	01792 369321
Mylor YC Falmouth	01326 374391
Nairn SC	01667 453897
National YC	
Dun Laoghaire	+353 1 280 5725
Netley SC Netley	023 80454272
New Quay YC	
Aberdovey	01545 560516
Newhaven & Seaford SC	
Seaford	01323 890077
Newport and Uskmouth SC	
Cardiff	01633 271417
Newtownards SC	028 9181 3426
Neyland YC	01646 600267

North Devon YC	
Bideford	01271 861390
North Fambridge Yacht Centre	
	01621 740370
North Haven YC Poole	01202 708830
North of England Yachting Association	
Kirkwall	01856 872331
North Sunderland Marine Club	
Sunderland	01665 721231
North Wales CC	
Conwy	01492 593481
North West Venturers YC (Beaumaris)	
Beaumaris	0161 2921943
Oban SC Ledaig by Oban	
	01631 563999
Orford SC Woodbridge	01394 450997
Orkney SC Kirkwall	01856 872331
Orwell YC Ipswich	01473 602288
Oulton Broad Yacht Station	
	01502 574946
Ouse Amateur SC	
Kings Lynn	01553 772239
Paignton SC Paignton	01803 525817
Parkstone YC Poole	01202 743610
Peel Sailing and CC	
Peel	01624 842390
Pembroke Haven YC	01646 684403
Pembrokeshire YC	
Milford Haven	01646 692799
Penarth YC	029 20708196
Pentland Firth YC	
Thurso	01847 891803
Penzance YC	01736 364989
Peterhead SC Ellon	01779 75527
Pin Mill SC Woodbridge	01394 780271
Plym YC Plymouth	01752 404991
Poolbeg YC	+353 1 660 4681
Poole YC	01202 672687
Porlock Weir SC	
Watchet	01643 862702
Port Edgar YC Penicuik	0131 657 2854
Port Navas YC	
Falmouth	01326 340065
Port of Falmouth Sailing Association	
Falmouth	01326 372927
Portchester SC	
Portchester	023 9237 6375
Porthcawl Harbour BC	
Swansea	01656 655935
Porthmadog SC	
Porthmadog	01766 513546
Portrush YC Portrush	028 7082 3932